RICHARD BEAN: PLAYS FOUR

Richard Bean

PLAYS FOUR

OBERON BOOKS
LONDON

WWW.OBERONBOOKS.COM

First published in this collection in 2013 by Oberon Books Ltd
521 Caledonian Road, London N7 9RH
Tel: +44 (0) 20 7607 3637 / Fax: +44 (0) 20 7607 3629
e-mail: info@oberonbooks.com
www.oberonbooks.com

A catalogue record for this book is available from the British Library.

PB ISBN: 978-1-84943-493-5
E ISBN: 978-1-84943-936-7

Cover image by Ansel Krut, *Giants of Modernism #2* (2009)

Visit www.oberonbooks.com to read more about all our books and to buy them. You will also find features, author interviews and news of any author events, and you can sign up for e-newsletters so that you're always first to hear about our new releases.

Contents

Introduction   6

England People Very Nice   11

The Big Fellah   123

The Heretic   219

Introduction

Although he has recently become the author of the most publicly popular and critically acclaimed new British play of the 21st century – *One Man, Two Guvnors* – Richard Bean has always been notable for an ability to annoy audiences and critics, or at least those sections of them identified with the liberal left. And two of the projects to which they most objected feature in this edition.

When *England People Very Nice* was first shown at the National Theatre in London, there were a number of reported walk-outs by preview ticket-buyers – apparently offended by either the concept or specifics of a farce about immigration – which, in turn, led the *Guardian* newspaper to send a delegation of columnists to assess the dramatist's treatment of the toxic issue. All disapproved, with one of the writers being so appalled that she walked out at the interval. A member of the group of British left-wing dramatists that emerged in Britain in the '70s subsequently told me that he had left *England People Very Nice* in horror.

Later, during a performance of *The Heretic* at the Royal Court, I went into the Gents during the interval to find a number of theatre-goers loudly complaining, while taking a pee, that Bean had been taking the piss, apparently furious at having encountered a play that questioned the scientific and liberal media orthodoxy over climate change. 'It's a pity he had to falsify science for dramatic purposes,' complained one urinator, although the doubts about global warming theories expressed by Bean's heroine reflect the genuine views of sceptics, rather than his own invention.

The conventional observation would be that Bean, as a writer, winds people up the wrong way but I prefer to see it (as interviews with the dramatist suggest he also does) as winding them up the right way: he has little time for the idea that people should or would go to the theatre only to be agreed with.

Because of this willingness to open up dramatically subjects that some consider closed – such as immigration and climate change – Richard Bean has been categorised, by both admirers and detractors, as a 'right-wing playwright.' Another reason for this, though, is that there has long been an active mission in parts of the media to locate such a creature.

Historically, as in other parts of the arts, most dramatists have tended to be on the Left, perhaps because the greatest creative energy comes from opposing consensus and conventions, which, in British and American culture, have tended to be centre (or further) Right. Only Tom Stoppard in the 1980s (when Margaret Thatcher spoke warmly of his work) and David Mamet in recent years have seemed to fit the Identikit of a rightist playwright, although, in both cases, their alleged reactionary tendencies came at least partly from an intellectual fastidiousness that led them to resist pack thinking.

During his early years as artistic director of the National Theatre, Nicholas Hytner was frequently pressured by Conservative-leaning publications, in interviews and at press conferences, to explain the absence of Tory-ish authors, although there was little evidence of box office demand for such political balance. Empirical data that the National Theatre audience tends towards the liberal perspective can be found in the fact that, during performances of David Hare's *Stuff Happens*, which dramatised the build-up to the Iraq War, the actor playing a journalist who makes a speech justifying the conflict was listened to in frozen silence with occasional hissing.

In this context, it was perhaps inevitable that, when Bean and Hytner collaborated on *England People Very Nice*, its refusal of liberal taboos about humour based on racial characteristics led some to conclude (cheerfully or bleakly, from their different perspectives) that Hytner had finally captured his wild rightist and brought him home. This perception was further encouraged when Bean's *The Heretic* opened at the Royal Court (traditionally a left-wing theatre) in the same season as the National Theatre's climate change drama *Greenland*, which adopted, complete with symbolic Polar Bear, the majority academic and media opinion that the world was burning and the ice melting and that only scientists could save us.

For me, though, Bean (in common with Stoppard and Mamet in the above examples) is not a writer of the right but an natural contrarian who is instinctively uneasy with a generally accepted definition of what is right. During the Irish Troubles, the Unionist leader, Reverend Ian Paisley, was often described as the 'Abominable No-Man' because he was so unlikely to say yes to any change or concession. Paisley was always saying no to the same thing, but there is a strain in Bean's writing (also found in the theatrical work of George Bernard Shaw) that wants to say 'No' towards any opinion that is collecting a large 'Yes' petition. Or, rather, to say 'Yes?' or 'No?' because, as all the best writers for theatre understand, the stage is an arena built for contradiction, the dialogue form always inviting a response or rebuttal.

However, unlike the Rev Paisley – although more like Shaw – Bean always couches his counter-arguments in humour. The writer was, in one accidental sense, born to comedy – the announcement, 'Mr Bean is in reception' tends to cause a frisson when he reports to buildings such as the BBC – and honed his gag skills professionally when he became a stand-up comedian.

Revealingly, *The Big Fellah*, chronologically the second of the works collected here, contains a fireman who is a would-be comedian and is book-ended by after-dinner speeches, a form of stand-up comedy, delivered at St Patrick's Day suppers in New York by Costello, local fund-raiser and gun-runner for the IRA. This play shares some territory with the work of the Irish dramatist Martin McDonagh and in particular his *The Lieutenant of Inishmore*, which is also a black comedy about Republican terrorists.

However, whereas McDonagh's perspective is always Irish – his plays acknowledge the power of Irish romanticism even as they mock it – Bean, usefully for his reflex dissent on any issue, comes to the subject at a double distance: as an English Yorkshireman and because his central characters are all American supporters of the cause. These two geographical removes allow moments of typically Bean-ish provocation of conventional wisdom, as when Costello declares that Gordon Wilson, a Protestant who campaigned for peace after his daughter was killed by the IRA, is 'as good and true an Irishman as any that ever pulled on boots.' Equally fearless of received opinion is the scene in which Tom Billy, the wise-cracking fireman and IRA sympathiser, attacks Al-Quaeda for letting the cause of terrorism down by their indiscriminate savagery.

That speech seems to me a classic Bean moment because it leaves a liberal theatre-goer unsure whether to be offended on behalf of one side or the other or both. This extends the tactic of *England People Very Nice,* which, crucially, has racism not as its motive but its subject-matter. Across three hundred years, successive waves of immigration (French Huguenot, Irish, Jewish, Bangladeshi) arrive in East London, each national identity suspicious of and suspected by those already present.

Rarely have I known a piece of writing so unfairly traduced by its accusers; the suggestion from some that Bean is being racist completely misunderstands the drama. The Shakesperean canon offers two useful comparisons. *The Merchant of Venice* is potentially a racist play – which is why Jewish writers from Arnold Wesker to Howard Jacobson have written corrective fictional responses – but *Othello* is a play about racism. *England People Very Nice* is emphatically the latter.

But despite the play's use of a distancing device in which the history of immigration is being presented at a centre for asylum seekers – with a clear implication of prejudice in some of the portrayals – some critics and audiences persisted in a conviction that the playwright was editorially endorsing everything that was said, or, more often, anything that was said about the ethnic identity to which they belonged. A National Theatre source told me that, in correspondence from annoyed members of the audience, the complainants invariably objected only to the portrayal of their own tribe and would often commend the rest of the portrayals. In doing so, they were giving an illustration of racial selfishness that is also one of the points of the play.

In the same way, *The Heretic,* which those who disliked it chose to parody as an attack on the theory of climate change, is surely an attack on the closing down of debate and suppression of scepticism that has seemed to be the aim of some of the more evangelical scientists involved in the research. And evangelism is the apt comparison: Bean has great fun with the paradox of generally atheist or agonostic climate experts turning temperature charts into the sacred texts of a new fundamentalist creed.

An imperfect typist attempting to write *Plays 4* soon discovers the risk of the title coming out as *Plays $*. But, in the case of Richard Bean, the misprint doubles as a premonition. *The Heretic*, which closes this volume, opened in February 2011 and was followed in May of that year by the National Theatre premiere of *One Man, Two Guvnors*, Bean's contemporary transformation of Carlo Goldoni's 1743 farce *The Servant of Two Masters*, which has become one of the most profitable new plays in modern theatre history, still running in London (as a West End transfer) and around the world at the time of writing, almost two and a half years after it was first staged.

Detailed consideration of *One Man, Two Guvnors* must await *Plays 5* (or Plays %, as it is rendered in its still fitting slip-fingered version), alongside a couple of the next plays that Bean fans impatiently await. The Goldoni adaptation is in one sense atypical of Bean's work, being less ideologically confrontational than most of his original plays; and it would also be wrong to re-categorise the earlier plays as any sort of apprenticeship. However, with the benefit of the retrospect we now have, readers of this collection can see the writer moving towards the gag-writing power, ability to re-invigorate comic stereotypes and mastery of stage-craft and farce on a large stage that would bring him, in *One Man, Two Guvnors*, the vast and helplessly hysterical audience that his talent had always deserved.

Mark Lawson, October 2013

* *Mark Lawson presents Front Row on BBC Radio 4, Mark Lawson Talks To...... on BBC4, writes for The Guardian and is theatre critic of The Tablet.*

ENGLAND PEOPLE VERY NICE

Freedom is the freedom to say that two plus two make four.
George Orwell *(1984)*

Characters

A large, ethnically mixed company of actors is needed.
Some characters are recurring.

RECURRING CHARACTERS

NORFOLK DANNY / CARLO / AARON / MUSHI, 20s
The boy lover

CAMILLE / MARY / RUTH / DEBORAH, 20s
The girl lover

IDA, Pub barmaid

LAURIE, Pub landlord

RENNIE, Pub regular, originally from Barbados

CORE CAST FOR PROLOGUE / EPILOGUE –
ALTHOUGH ALL PLAYERS ARE PRESENT

YAYAH, Male Nigerian

PHILIPPA, Female English

ELMAR, Male Azerbaydzhan

TAHER, Male Palestinian

SANYA, Female Kosovan

IQBAL, Male Yemen

OFFICER KELLY, Male Ulster

OFFICER PARKER, Male English

TATYANA, Female Serbian

GINNY, Female English, stage manager

Set / Staging

The play requires a large stage with the facility to fly in flats, or use still, or video projections, to establish locations as required. This process should be playful and non-naturalistic. The only constant location is the pub, which can be naturalistic.

England People Very Nice was first performed at the Olivier Theatre, National Theatre, on 4 February 2009, with the following cast:

Philip Arditti
Jamie Beamish
Paul Chequer
Olivia Colman
Rudi Dharmalingam
Sacha Dhawan
Hasina Haque
Tony Jayawardena
Trevor Laird
Elliot Levey
Siobhán McSweeney
Neet Mohan
Aaron Neil
Sophia Nomvete
Daniel Poyser
Claire Prempeh
Fred Ridgeway
Avin Shah
Sophie Stanton
Michelle Terry
David Verrey
Harvey Virdi

Director Nicholas Hytner
Designer Mark Thompson
Director of Animation Pete Bishop
Lighting Designer Neil Austin
Music Grant Olding
Choreographer Scarlett Mackmin
Sound Designer John Leonard

Prologue

A bare stage.

GINNY: *(Off.)* Full company to the stage please!

The company of actors breeze on. Other asylum seekers enter accompanied by Immigration Centre Officers. They are in costume, depicting the early history of Britain – Angles, Vikings, Saxons, Celts, etc.

PHILIPPA: NOTES! It's almost...quite good.

A mobile phone is heard. It's YAYAH's. He's dressed as a Roman centurion with short sword, skirt, etc. He gives the short sword to a fellow asylum seeker and answers his phone.

YAYAH: *(On phone.)* Of course it's me woman!... Listen! I am not in Lagos so you will have to beat the girl yourself! Goodbye, I am in a meeting!

PHILIPPA: Tatyana, no smoking please! Pocklington Immigration Centre is a place of work!

TATYANA: Where can I smoke?

PHILIPPA: Nowhere in England. Today we're going to do a dress rehearsal working with Elmar's animation, I've seen it, it's absolutely amazing!

ELMAR: Every year in Azerbaydzhan I win the Silver Dragon for animated short.

TAHER: Who wins gold?

ELMAR: In Azerbaydzhan silver is first prize, if you win gold, you've come second.

PHILIPPA: Unfortunately, for us, Doctor Kuti has been given leave to remain. So Taher will now give his St John, the sarcastic army-trained Hampstead liberal who gets mugged.

TAHER: If Doctor Kuti has had his envelope, all the envelopes must be here?

PHILIPPA: Mister Kelly!?

OFFICER KELLY: The strike is over, yeah, but I don't know anything about envelopes.

TAHER: Our cases were heard – [in October]

YAYAH: – Sit down man! You're pissing me off! We have a show to do!

ELMAR: In Azerbaydzhan we have a saying, 'eating fish will not improve your swimming'.

PHILIPPA: Today we have music, the Pocklington Immigration Centre Officers officers' band.

A roll on the drums. And messy contributions from the band. Applause from the players.

What else?

GINNY: *(Distort / Off.)* Nazeerah!

PHILIPPA: Thanks Ginny. Miss Gupta has 'Home Office' interviews so I will take over the demanding roles of Mrs O'Neill and Camilla.

TATYANA: Camilla, the idiot!?

PHILIPPA: Yes. OK notes! Sanya?! Problem. I can hear the swearing. Ida is white working class Bethnal Green. To her 'facking', is not swearing – it's punctuation.

SANYA: FUCKING frogs!

PHILIPPA: No! Pong 'Frogs'. Pong – theatrical term, emphasise Frogs.

SANYA: Fucking FROGS! Fucking MICKS! Fucking YIDS! Fucking PAKIS!

PHILIPPA: Perfect!

TAHER: Swearing is the truth, of course, when I worked in Israeli theatre I notice they swear all the time, but do Israelis care a shit about the truth –

PHILIPPA: – Taher! If you mention Israel today, you're back in your cell. Can I do that, Mister Kelly?

OFFICER KELLY: Do what you like love.

TAHER: Gitmo!

PHILIPPA: If you'd like to go to Guantanamo Bay it can be arranged. Yayah?! Your line 'turn your mobile phones off please', be more threatening, as if something really really terrible might happen to them.

YAYAH: More threatening. Easy peasey!

PHILIPPA: Iqbal. You've shaved your beard off. Your beard was the reason we cast you as the mad imam.

GINNY: *(Distort/Off.)* Props don't have any more false beards.

IQBAL: I kept the hair, and last night I sat up and made a beard wig.

He puts a false beard on.

YAYAH: Ey! It looks just like your old beard.

IQBAL: Of course it does, it is my old beard.

ELMAR: In Azerbaydzhan we have a saying, 'don't expect miracles from a beard, it's only facial hair'.

TAHER: England is a free country, you're allowed to have a beard.

TATYANA: Why don't you have a beard? You're Palestinian.

TAHER: I'm a Christian! The reason I am seeking asylum in this country is because Hamas want to kill me for not having a beard.

YAYAH: I know why Hamas want to kill you, it's because you talk too much!

TATYANA: Go to Scotland, you can wear a dress too!

PHILIPPA: Stop! You've spent six months devising this play. Six months learning how England became a liberal, tolerant, democratic society. It would be a shame to cancel the show, but I can, because the work was in the work.

IQBAL: You had a note for me Philippa.

PHILIPPA: Yes, er… *(Reading.)* when you first come on can you try and not look like a…oh yes I remember…it doesn't matter now.

IQBAL: Not look like a what?

PHILIPPA: You've shaved the beard off now so it doesn't matter.

TATYANA: Not look like a mad dog!

PHILIPPA: Tatyana! Please.

TAHER: My idea for the Saudi Imam when I wrote it –

YAYAH: – you did not write that bit, it is all devised, by us. Collectively.

TAHER: The group turned my imam into a stereotype – mad, blind, hooks for hands. The imam will be better without the beard and the beard wig.

TATYANA: It is not a stereotype, they've all got beards!

PHILIPPA: Quiet! Please!

SANYA: Philippa, I don't think my character would say 'vis à vis'? She's a barmaid.

PHILIPPA: We took a democratic vote, to close all discussion on the script.

TAHER: She is third generation French. 'Vis à vis' is French.

PHILIPPA: Taher, just try not to help OK? The Irish act. Where are the Houlihans?

HOULIHANS: Aye / Hallooo there! / What now then!? So…

PHILIPPA: Really, really, terrific accent work!

HOULIHAN 1: We've worked on our *Oirish* with Officer Kelly there, aye we have so…

OFFICER KELLY: I'm from the north meself Miss, but me family is from Knocknagree, I mean I know it's not Galway, but it's better than a kick in the clems. And Geoff, Officer Parker, he's been working on their cockney.

OFFICER PARKER: Awight! That kind of thing.

COCKNEYS: Awight! / Wotcha! / Fack off! *etc.*

PHILIPPA: What can I say, fantastic! Now Houlihans, I need to believe that it's normal for your family to have a pig in the house. What I'm getting at the moment is – *'hey hey! we're the Houlihans! Look! We're all mad, and we got a fecking pig in the house!'*

HOULIHANS: Aye! / Right you are there! / No problem so!

TAHER: I research Irish Famine on Wikipedia. Irish Famine 1840! The Gordon riots 1780. In this play the two things happen in the same afternoon. Sixty years wrong!

PHILIPPA: Shakespeare had a clock in *Julius Caesar.* One thousand years wrong! Now, we might have an audience today, my husband, if you hear laughing, or crying, he cries easily, it's him.

TATYANA: Maybe he will snore all the way through.

PHILIPPA: There is no chance of that.

ELMAR: What's his name?

PHILIPPA: St John.

TAHER: Does he understand theatre?

PHILIPPA: No, he works for Vodafone. OK! Set for a run!

GINNY: *(Distort/Off.)* The wagon joke!

PHILIPPA: Yes, the wagon joke is back in.

TAHER: We are putting a joke back in which is not funny?

PHILIPPA: Taher, if we let you stay in this country, and after thirty years working as a driving instructor in Kettering you develop a drink problem – a*)* you'll understand the joke, and b*)* you'll find it funny!

GINNY: *(Distort/Off.)* Can we run the wagon joke lines. 'Oi mate'.

ADRIANA: Oi mate! Do you want a drink?

YAYAH: No, ta. I can't. I'm on the wagon.

TAHER: It is not funny!

PHILIPPA: Check your props! Alright in the box!?

They exit the stage and prepare their props etc.

Song: 'A True Born Londoner'
(After Defoe's 'The True Born Englishman')

> This stage depicts an age bygone
> The Thames before Londinium
> A leaky shack to call our home
> No cars no bars no mobile phone

YAYAH: Turn your mobiles off please. *(Beat.)* Or else.

	There is no Christ, nor even God
(Chalk giants.)	But pagan giants Gog and Magog
(Enter iron age man.)	This beast exemplar is the height
(And wife.)	And this, his cousin, is his wife

> With a ro do a derry diddle diddle do
> A ro do derry diddle di

(Enter Roman.)	First came the Roman with his rule
(Stabs man.)	And steeled the cockney with his tool
(Rapes woman.)	This seminal act improved the tribe
(Literate man/wife.)	And issued forth a learned scribe
(Men killed…)	The Saxons came, and came again
(Same woman raped.)	Were followed by the lusty Dane
(Men killed.)	They fought and fought eternal wars
(Woman raped again.)	The ladies loved the conquerors

> With a ro do a derry diddle diddle do
> A ro do derry diddle di
> With a ro do a derry diddle diddle do
> A ro do derry diddle di

(And so on…)	The western Angles beat the lot
	With the exception of the Scot
	The warlike Celt under foot was
	squelched
	And fleeing West became the Welsh
	With a ro do a derry diddle diddle do
	A ro do derry diddle di

With a ro do a derry diddle diddle do
A ro do derry diddle di

*Enter NORFOLK DANNY in his 17th century incarnation as a
Journeyman weaver in Spitalfields.*

This God resulting is our play
Four hundred years we'll roll away
A weaver, not poor, but not well heeled
A Norfolk man in Spitalfields

Act One

17th century Spitalfields. Fields and trees for the outskirts. The Tower of London dominates the skyline. Street life. The STREET VENDORS sing their cries. The TOWN CRIER ringing a bell.

SEA COALS: Sea coals! Come on mother, sort it out!

BEGGAR: Any spare farthings sir?

CRIER: Get a craft you lazy bastard! Oyez! Oyez! Oyez!

ALL: *(Joining in after the second.)* Oyez! Oyez!

CRIER: Following the Revocation of the Edict of Nantes by Louis the Fourteenth of France –

SEA COALS: – France!?

SAUSAGES: What's this got to do with us?

CRIER: – the Protestant Reformed Religion has been prohibited in that land. London is forewarned of a swarming.

CRIER starts to walk off.

SEA COALS: Swarming of what?!

CRIER: Frogs!

During the song the French arrive. Houses are built and they move in.

Frogs song (After traditional anti-French song of the time)

A plague of Frogs do come and live at ease
And fatter look than wretched refugees
Our English weavers all do curse their fates
The French will work for lower rates
Kindly protected from the stroke
Of Louis' Roman Cath'lic hawk
Them we so well will entertain
They will not choose go home again
And over time now the French rise high
As we sing our carping cry

And as they have all Merchant Masters made
And like the free born English, trade

In the pub.

IDA: Fucking frogs! My grandfather didn't die in the English Civil War so's half of France could come over here and live off the soup!

LAURIE: Your grandfather didn't die in the English Civil War. He was in here yesterday.

IDA: That's what I said. I said 'my grandfather *didn't die* in the English Civil War so's half of France could come here and live off the soup.'

RENNIE: I've got Frogs upstairs from me boy! All day long – farting, farting, farting!

LAURIE: This is a small island knowhatimean?!

RENNIE: They eat nothing but red meat and cabbage!

LAURIE: *(Re: pamphlet.)* That writer, Daniel Defoe, says here we shouldn't mind living cheek by jowl with fifty thousand foreigners.

IDA: Alright for him, he'll be glad of the company, he's spent the last twenty-eight years on a fucking desert island!

RENNIE: All them dissident writers! They don't have to live here boy!

IDA: By the time the bells go of a night, they're all back in Stoke Newington with all their lovely whatsanames –

LAURIE: – trees.

IDA: Fucking trees!

Enter DANNY .

LAURIE: Alright Norfolk?!

DANNY: Pint of Mad Dog please. What's new?

LAURIE: There is a great noise upon the land, the farting of a million Froglanders.

RENNIE: There'll be rivers of blood boy! War, across Europe!

DANNY: Religion you see.

LAURIE: I'll have none of your Reincarnation Society 'God is Dead' talk until you've coughed up the money for the room rental from last Tuesday.

DANNY gives LAURIE half a shilling. He takes it.

DANNY: God is Dead.

IDA and RENNIE laugh.

IDA: You'll never find yerself a nice girl, wiv all this Godlessness. You might as well go round shouting 'Plague!' And ringing a fucking whatsaname –

LAURIE: – bell.

RENNIE: All that red meat boy! Makes French girls hot. I mean hot, hot, hot!

IDA: What you need Danny, is a nice English girl who don't like sex. You'll be alright though son, you got your own loom now, ain'tcher!?

RENNIE: Life begins when you get your own loom boy!

LAURIE: What you on Norfolk? Silk?

DANNY: Yeah, narrow silk, with fancy trimming.

RENNIE: French men, they're worse! They eat that red meat raw!

LAURIE: Our girls ain't gonna be safe from Gallic overexcitement even in church.

SIDNEY DE GASCOIGNE meets with the BISHOP. He has his son with him. They've been eating.

BISHOP: Exactly how big will this big French church be?

DE GASCOIGNE: I would expect a congregation of two thousand.

DENHAM: Your grace, they have petitioned plans for a school.

DE GASCOIGNE: We want to teach our children French, so that they can recite the catechism – in French.

BISHOP: What makes you so sure that God speaks French? A child born in London is not French. He is irretrievably an Englishman, and 'gawd 'elp us all', a cockney. At least the moral health of Londoners will be protected if you have your own church. More beef?

DE GASCOIGNE: Not for me thank you. I can't speak for my son. Yves?

GASKIN: Non, merci.

BISHOP: Bit overcooked was it?

GASKIN: C'est bon.

BISHOP: You may cling to your Frenchness now, but I'll wager you die an Englishman.

DE GASCOIGNE: I don't gamble.

BISHOP: What's crossing the English channel in a barrel if not gambling?

DE GASCOIGNE: These barrel stories, are exaggerated. I paid passage from Dieppe.

DENHAM: How prosaic.

BISHOP: You have fled Catholic France and as Protestants we welcome you as brothers, but England has many surreptitious Catholics. Not all Catholics are violent Papists, BUT all violent Papists are Catholics. Our King is Catholic; however, he has a Protestant son-in-law, William of Orange –

DE GASCOIGNE: – Is this a prophesy or a plot?

BISHOP: If he were to become King, William will lead us in war against France. Will you cheer for England or cheer for France?

DE GASCOIGNE: That would be a test.

A huge church appears.

BLACKAMOOR: Turkish coffee boss?! Knock your block off coffee!

DANNY stands looking at the church. An Englishman walks past the church protecting his daughter from a group of young French men. CAMILLE, a French girl, makes eye contact with DANNY. The Lovers' musical theme plays.

CAMILLE: Hello!

DANNY: Bonjour! Comment ça va?

CAMILLE: You speak French sir?

DANNY: Un peu. Not really.

CAMILLE: Camille. Camille de Chaunay. My brother, André.

DANNY: Danny. They call me Norfolk Danny because I'm Norfolk bred and born.

CAMILLE: Au revoir, Norfolk Danny.

CAMILLE goes in to the church. DANNY stands at the back.

DE GASCOIGNE: *(Heavy French accent.)* Monsieurs dames, mes amis, bonjour, welcome, for the first time, to this house of God which we have so imaginatively called the French Church. I am the prologue to the sermon, I will be quick. Like you, I am here in Brick Lane, in England this foul smelling swamp, only because I want to worship my God free from the constraints of Papal instruction, and the threat of death. Like lovers in exile, we must maintain French culture. The English are drunks, incapable of intellectual discourse, they make a god of common sense, they hate their children, and would always rather be 'unting. We French, are superior in all things, watchmaking, textiles, armoury, and, of course, love.

There is uncontrolled sighing in the congregation.

Londoners fear our style, our sophistication, our romancing. They will not allow us through the gates into the city. So outside the walls, right here, let's build French homes, in streets with French names, and through extraordinary and relentless love making, let us populate these streets with French children and create a new Nîmes, a new Perpignan, a new Paris!

DANNY leaves. A gang of apprentices armed with knives and scissors arrive. CAMILLE watches.

HUGO: One on one, the Frogs, they're fucking nothing!

BENNY: Norfolk Danny! Have you paid your shilling?

DANNY: I've paid my two shilling Guild sub yeah.

DICK: Extra shilling now innit. Protection. Against the French.

DANNY: So this is a cutters' mob?

BENNY: They've started up with their own looms, paying fuck all wages.

DANNY: We can't have that can we...

DANNY pays his shilling. A Frenchman walks by holding a roll of cloth.

FRENCH MAN: Bonjour!

HUGO: Stand and fight you fucking cabbage eating farting Frog Papist!

DANNY: Papist? They're not Catholics!

HUGO: Frog lover now eh, Norfolk?

DANNY: They're Huguenots, Protestants, they follow John Calvin.

BENNY: Not Godless then, like you.

DANNY: Let's smash their looms, that's reasonable. But I'm not kicking a Protestant in the head for being Papist.

CAMILLE has seen this. She follows DANNY back to his cottage. Her brother ANDRÉ is in tow.

CAMILLE: You are a weaver?

DANNY: Yeah, I'm a Journeyman, got me own loom.

HUGO: Hang on to your pants Danny! Them French girls, knowhatimean!?

DANNY: You speak really good English.

CAMILLE: It was this facility that saved me. My mother is dead, and my father condemned to the galleys for a hundred years.

DANNY: Yeah? That's a lot of rowing.

HUGO goes off.

CAMILLE: Sir, do not mock me!

DANNY: I'm sorry, he was watching. He's Guild you see.

CAMILLE: What cloth do you weave?

DANNY: Narrow silk with fancy trimming.

CAMILLE: André, my brother, is apprenticed to the finest Master of Nîmes, making this cloth, Serge de Nîmes.

She gives DANNY a sample of denim.

CAMILLE: Two white vertical threads –

DANNY: – the warps. The warp goes to the top, the weft goes right to left.

DANNY uses his fingers to illustrate the warps. CAMILLE creates a weft with her own finger.

CAMILLE: A lone, weft, dyed blue completes the weave. De Nîmes.

DANNY: Denîmes? Coarse. Alright for work clothes. Can't see it ever catching on.

DANNY gives the denim back. ANDRÉ passes to CAMILLE another sample. She shows DANNY.

Silk?

CAMILLE: No! Bombasin. The warp is silk but the weft is wool.

DANNY: That's amazing.

CAMILLE: My brother can make this for you. And I could help your wife sir.

DANNY: Come to my house.

They go in.

The loom's atop, in the attic.

CAMILLE: Monte! Va vérifier le métier!

ANDRÉ climbs the stairs.

DANNY: I don't have a wife.

CAMILLE: Oh! I excel at all those labours that a woman of limited means might reasonably be expected to perform.

DANNY: You talk like a lady. I'm only a Journeyman.

CAMILLE: But you are not like the mob, I can tell, you have had an education –

DANNY: I was to be a priest. It's a narrow schooling and don't make me a gentleman.

CAMILLE: Your station does not interest me. I'm alive. My brother and I are the human jetsam of this conflict between my poor dead father, and the Pope.

DANNY: You said your father was on the galleys.

CAMILLE: He could never conform to the regime, and will surely now…be dead.

DANNY: And your mother?

CAMILLE: Beheaded.

DANNY: By religious men.

CAMILLE: Are you a Protestant sir?

DANNY: Neither Catholic nor Protestant. In the seminary I sought harder than any man, and with great confidence. And found nothing.

CAMILLE: But without God –

DANNY: – I'm lawless, wretched, and free. Have you ever taken all the fear and threats out of your heart, and using reason alone, have you questioned the existence of God?

CAMILLE: That would make me a heretic.

DANNY: That's me. That's what you're getting into. How did you escape France?

CAMILLE: In Marseille we stowed away on a ship bound for London but the jack o' tars found me, and ooh –

She collapses, and is caught by DANNY, enter ANDRÉ.

ANDRÉ: Le métier, c'est de la merde.

DANNY: What's he say?

CAMILLE: He says the loom is perfect.

ANDRÉ: Je vais me tirer pour tu fasses ton truc?

CAMILLE: Ne mets pas les pieds dans le pub. Allez!

ANDRÉ takes a penny from CAMILLE and then he leaves.

DANNY: I can offer you a roof and a meal. I can't pay André wages, the Guild –

CAMILLE: – Bon! I will sleep here. Where will you sleep?

DANNY: Are you promised?

CAMILLE: I can never return. I saw my mother's corpse dragged behind a little pony, the rope tight around her neck, the blood, the dust.

DANNY: When the sailors found you…on the ship?

CAMILLE: I traded my honour for my life.

DANNY: I'm sorry.

DANNY picks up a framed document on the wall.

This is the Guild ordinance. Rules for everything.

Reading 'No single man, shall take to his house a lecher'.

CAMILLE: Is that what I am to you? A French whore?

DANNY: You're a woman, and you're not my wife.

CAMILLE: No one can legislate for love!

DANNY: Love?!

CAMILLE: Yes, love! I will cook, and sew for you, our proximity will nurture feelings of lust, and we will fall in love. Do you not understand it is inevitable? Tomorrow you will swim the seven seas for one more kiss.

DANNY: I can't swim.

CAMILLE: Agh! It's true what they say about the English. You care nothing for love! We French are wasting our time here!

Bells sound.

DANNY: Curfew.

CAMILLE: Bed time?

DANNY: Yeah. Now, tell me the truth.

CAMILLE: I beg your pardon.

DANNY: One minute you say your mother was beheaded, the next minute she's getting dragged through the streets behind a pony with the rope round her neck, 'the blood', 'the dust'.

CAMILLE: Our fathers do get condemned to the galleys, and our mothers are beheaded, their bodies dragged through the streets!

DANNY: But not yours!

CAMILLE: I first exaggerated my father's plight, the galleys, with the sea captain. He had heard of that punishment for Protestants and was –

DANNY: – easily deceived.

CAMILLE: My inventions earned us a cabin.

DANNY: A cabin! So I'm just the last in a long line of mugs.

CAMILLE: All that matters is that I still breathe.

DANNY: Like a hawk sees a vole, deep in the roots of the corn, you saw my need for a woman.

Outside the cutters' MOB return, bloody, and drunk.

MOB: Rule, Britannia! Britannia rules the waves
Britain never never never will be slaves
Rule, Britannia! Britannia rule the waves
Britain never never never will be slaves!

They spot ANDRÉ hiding from them.

BEN: *(To ANDRÉ.)* Oi! Mate! You're not singing!?

DICK picks some threads off his coat.

ANDRÉ: Je ne parle pas Anglais.

HUGO: Look! He got threads on his coat!

BENNY: Whose loom are you working? Me, name, Benny. Your master? Name?

ANDRÉ: Danné.

HUGO: Norfolk Danny!?

BENNY: Won't be Norfolk. What type of cloth? Cloth!? *(Tugs his clothes.)*

ANDRÉ: Soie.

HUGO: Silk.

BENNY: What kind of soie? *(Mimes.)* Broad?

ANDRÉ: *(Mimes narrow.)* Non. Étroit.

BENNY: Narrow.

ANDRÉ: – avec… *(Mimes fancy trimming.)*

BENNY: Narrow silk with fancy trimming!

HUGO: Norfolk Danny! Let's kill the bastard!

In DANNY's.

CAMILLE: You have a need for a woman, I have a need for a man.

DANNY moves to kiss her but before he can BENNY and HUGO crash in.

DANNY: Did you want to talk to me Benny?

BENNY: Guild rules Norfolk, you can't have a whore indoors.

DANNY: I'm gonna make her my wife.

BENNY: And how you gonna provide for her after we've smashed your loom up?

HUGO: Let's have a feel darling!

HUGO grabs CAMILLE, DANNY rushes HUGO with his own shears, and stabs him.

HUGO: He done me!

BENNY: Jesus! You'll swing Norfolk, you'll swing mate.

HUGO: I want me muvver! Benny, mate, go get me muvver! Quick, please.

HUGO dies. DANNY picks up the bloody shears, and threatens the others.

DANNY: Who's next? Benny?! I will. They can only hang me once.

BENNY leaves.

Camille! Leave, go to Canterbury. I'll find you.

CAMILLE: Danny? I need to know. Do you love me?

DANNY: Stop talking about bloody love! Go! Run!

CAMILLE: I'll find you. If it takes a four hundred years, I'll find you.

CAMILLE runs off.

CRIER: Oyez! Oyez! Oyez! On this the twenty-third day of February in the year of our lord sixteen eighty-nine – James Stuart –

ALL: Papist / traitor! / dog! / Boo!

CRIER: – having fled his kingdom to take refuge in Catholic France –

ALL: Boo!

CRIER: – His daughter Mary and her husband, William of Orange, lead their subjects in military opposition to Catholic France.

SEA COALS: What's that in English?!

CRIER: We're at war with France!

ALL: War! / War with France!

The French congregation gather.

DE GASCOIGNE: Watcha! Turned out nice again! Cheer up love, it might never happen! Worse things happen at sea! Yes, I am speaking English! If you have difficulty understanding me I might ask you why. Some of you still have the fleurs de lis tattooed on your hearts. Your children, born here, cockaneeys, still speak French – why? France rejected you like a girl rejects a lover. A new page in history is writ today. England is at war with your sweetheart. I implore you not to give the English permission to question your loyalty! I am no longer Sidney de Gascoigne. From this day forth, I am brutal, short, pragmatic, Bert. Yes, Bert Gaskin, and my son Al-bert Gaskin. And I implore you all to similarly Anglicise your reputations.

Murmurs of disapproval.

I do this because she, France, broke my heart, but England, she offered me her bosoms!

MOB: A hanging! A hanging!

A cart with scaffold is pulled on. DANNY is running along behind the wagon, his hands are tied together and he is roped to the wagon. Travelling on the cart with them is the HANGMAN and a JUDGE / OFFICIAL. Some SOLDIERS to keep the peace.

SAUSAGES: Danny! Do you wanna drink!?

DANNY: Yeah!

They give DANNY a drink.

MOB / ALL: A drink! / Ale.

SEA COALS: *(To HANGMAN.)* Oi! Mate, do you want a drink?

HANGMAN: No, ta. I can't. I'm on the wagon.

DANNY is hauled up on to the wagon.

BEGGAR: Speech! Speech!

BENNY: You'll rot in hell Norfolk Danny!

DANNY: There is no hell! Nor heaven! This is the only paradise any of you will ever know.

IDA: What? Bethnal Green?

DANNY: Yes!

IDA: Where's your girl Danny?

DANNY: I don't know. I did not even kiss her, but I will not die, knowing nothing of love. I will be born again to find her.

IDA: Here's a penny! Sing him a song! No fucking whatsaname!

LAURIE: Religiosity.

IDA: He's Norfolk. Let's have a song of the country!

The HANGMAN puts a sack over his head, and slings the noose round his neck.

'Pleasant and Delightful' – traditional

STREET SINGER: It was pleasant and delightful one midsummer's morn
To see the green fields all covered with corn
And the blackbirds and thrushes sang on every green spray
And the larks they sang melodious at the dawning of the day

ALL: And the larks they sang melodious
And the larks they sang melodious
And the larks they sang melodious at the dawning of the day

OFFICIAL: Daniel James Ross born of Corpusty, near Saxthorpe, Norfolk.

DANNY is pushed off the cart, and the Tyburn jig commences. In silence.

END OF ACT.

Act Two

DANNY is still twitching on the rope. Enter MARY HOULIHAN (same actress as CAMILLE). She is nine months pregnant.

MARY: Agh feck! Me feet feel wore out, and looking like I done walked from Galway itself. And what a fecking pilgrimage! But the Houlihans are here, and we're all still breathing and dere's only da fecking fairies and Patrick hisself knows how we done it. Aye.

Silence, the crowd watch her.

HUGO: Excuse me miss. Are you Irish?

MARY: I am so. Is this London?

HUGO: Yes.

MARY: Have you seen me cousin Michael?

During the song the HOULIHAN family arrive consisting of MARY's brother PATRICK, his wife, a sow, and many children.

Song: Aaaargh Pat!

Mary: *(Singing.)* We had a farm in Galway
No bigger than a garden
But the taties got afflicted
So we walked the road to Dublin
I dream't to go to New York
But six pounds I could na raise
A shilling to London and sit on deck
And fecking freezing all the way.

Enter IRISH, singing. They all go into the one house which we see filling up with pigs, children, etc.

Aaaargh! Pat!
Won't you come away!
Come, come away my butty!
To live this poor I can't endure
And death is drawing near.
To London!
Come! Come away my dear!

In the pub.

IDA: Fucking Micks! Why – if one Mick wants to say something to another Mick – why can't he just say it. Why do they have to get pissed, beat each other up, and then write a fucking song about it?

LAURIE: Because Irish is an oral culture.

RENNIE: You can't have two religions in one country boy!

IDA: Protestant and Catholic. They're like chalk and whatsaname –

LAURIE: Cheese.

Enter HUGO and BENNY.

BENNY: Mum, quick, Gaskin's filling nan's house wi' Micks!

IDA: No!

IDA, BENNY and HUGO leave.

RENNIE: I got Irish upstairs from me boy, they got a pig in the house!

LAURIE: Three in one your pig. Heating, entertainment, and telling the time.

IDA is banging on the door where the HOULIHANS have gone in. HUGO and BENNY watch.

HUGO: Hundreds of Micks in there Ida, just walked in the door!

IDA: Get outa there! This is French housing!

A pig comes to the window and looks out.

BENNY: Yeah, we built it mate.

HUGO: One on one, the Micks, they're fucking nothing!

ALBERT GASKIN arrives, dressed in a smart suit, a businessman.

IDA: Oi. Gaskin! These Micks have broken into me old muvver's house!

HUGO: They've got a pig in there Mr Gaskin!

GASKIN: Do you have a loom to go to Mister Bosanquet? *(Rent book in hand.)* Ida…your old 'muvver' –

IDA: – Veronica Popineau.

GASKIN: – died last week. Owing rent.

IDA: She died Sat'day wiv nofin owing, and a new week starts on a Sunday. So I'd say her timing 'vis à vis' the rent was perfect.

GASKIN: You buried her Thursday. She *occupied* the parlour for five days.

IDA: She was fucking dead!

GASKIN: Two shillings 'storage'.

IDA: You promised this house to my Benny, he's got a girl up the whatsaname.

GASKIN: Duff?

IDA: Na, up the Roman Road, they're getting wed.

GASKIN: These rooms have gone to the Houlihan families.

IDA: Rooms? That's an house.

GASKIN: Each family gets a room each.

IDA: You're nofin but an house farmer! Where are we supposed to live?

GASKIN: Florent and his family have gone to Redbridge.

IDA: Redbridge? Never heard of it.

IDA leaves and goes back to the pub.

BENNY: You're not giving them jobs are you Gaskin?

GASKIN: England is a free country.

HUGO: They ain't done their Guild apprenticeships.

GASKIN: The Irish are the finest weavers in Christendom.

BENNY: 'Cheapest' you mean.

In the pub. Enter IDA.

IDA: Gaskin's gone and given me mum's house to a family of Micks!

RENNIE: They're all French houses them!

IDA: Gaskin's great grandfather'll be turning in his grave. He didn't paddle across the Channel in a fucking apple barrel to build houses for the Irish?!

LAURIE: I reckon them barrel stories are a bit exaggerated.

RENNIE: The rivers of London will run with blood boy!

LAURIE: Ses here there's illegal mass houses all over London.

RENNIE: Going on right under our noses boy!

IDA: Foreign priests are filling the heads of these Irish with the madness of Papism!

Enter FATHER CARLO with a loaf of bread, and a Caravaggio painting. He is an Italian priest, but not wearing priestly clothes at this point. He is played by the boy lover.

RENNIE: Should be illegal!

LAURIE: Yet the King's pushing through his Relief Act to tolerate Catholicism.

RENNIE: Spain! France! Rome! This will be war!

CARLO: Buon giorno!

IDA: Ciao Carlo love!

CARLO: How are you this day Mister Laurie?

LAURIE: Cosi, cosi! Grazi, for asking. The usual?

LAURIE hands over the bottle of red. CARLO pays, and LAURIE gives him the keys.

CARLO: Grazi!

CARLO slinks off to the function room where he dresses as a priest.

RENNIE: He's a Catholic priest! You got communion going on up them stairs!

IDA: Carlo? He runs an art appreciation class.

RENNIE: With a loaf of bread and a bottle of red wine!

LAURIE: Today'll be the still life. Table, bread, bottle of red.

IDA: You see a lot of shit like that.

RENNIE: The wine is the blood of Christ, bread is the body of Christ!

LAURIE: O'course! That's how them paintings work on a metaphorical level.

RENNIE: He's ramming Papism down the throats of the Irish under your roof boy!

LAURIE: You're wrong about these country Irish. They're not Catholic. I'll bet you a shilling none of them even heard of the Pope.

RENNIE: The Irish not Catholic?! Two shillings! You're on boy!

LAURIE: Right, let's go find an Irishman.

RENNIE and LAURIE leave the pub. Enter to the street, JOHN and ANNE O'NEILL. A boy with a barrow carries their substantial chests/cases. As they arrive two of the HOULIHAN brothers tumble into the street fighting. MARY follows them out.

HOULIHAN 1: Feck off, that's my stick!

HOULIHAN 2: No, it's my stick, so it is.

MARY: Fight in the street, will yer now! I'm trying to fecking give birth in there!

ANNE: The Irish that give the Irish a bad name are here, before us John.

JOHN: Aye, we'll have to grin and bear it as usual.

ANNE: Did you see that girl, no more than a child and already the devil's had her.

JOHN: There is no devil.

ANNE: You know what I mean, drink, lust, and ignorance.

BARROW BOY: Him there, that's Mr Gaskin.

JOHN: John O'Neill, my wife Anne. You got my letters?

GASKIN: Mr O'Neill, a pleasure. Madame, enchanté. A good journey?

ANNE: It was thrilling, sailing up the Thames, so exciting!

GASKIN: Your room is this way. Far from the common Irish. Where's your pig?

JOHN: I'm a publisher of Philosophical pamphlets.

GASKIN: Forgive me. I thought it was a cultural thing, most of the Irish –

ANNE: – Sir! We don't have a pig.

The O'NEILLS go into their house. RENNIE and LAURIE stand outside the HOULIHANS.

LAURIE: Don't knock! I've heard knocking is rude in their culture.

RENNIE: How can knocking be rude?

LAURIE: The English soldiers used to knock on their doors just before they burned their houses down. 'Knocking' and 'burning down' became connected.

They enter without knocking. PATRICK is having sex with his wife, MARY is giving birth.

MARY: Did yer not think to knock?! We're busy? I'm giving birth and me brother Patrick here is forcing himself on his wife against her will.

LAURIE: We won't keep you. Patrick, have you ever heard of the Pope?

PATRICK: The Pope!? Aye, yes, yes, the Pope, aye, yes I have, aye.

RENNIE: Ha, ha! Two shillings please, Laurie my man!

LAURIE: What do you know about the Pope?

PATRICK: I've heard say, she's a fine powerful beast for a three year old.

LAURIE: Yes!

RENNIE: You think the Pope is a horse!?

PATRICK: Ain't she the filly what won on the sands there at Omey Island?

LAURIE: Two shillings Rennie, thank you. No rush.

LAURIE hands over two shillings to RENNIE. At that moment MARY gives birth with a wail. PATRICK climbs off his wife to take a look at the baby.

MARY: What the feck do you think you're looking at?

PATRICK: Looking at me babby! I am the father ain't I!

LAURIE: Congratulations. We'll be going!

PATRICK: Agh, feck!

CATHERINE: Be Jaysus!

LAURIE: Lord save us! The baby's only got the one eye!

MARY: Sure, the other one'll come through in a bit!

PATRICK: Ah, it's another fecking freak. Get rid of it will yer now!

RENNIE: See you later!

LAURIE and RENNIE leave passing CARLO in the doorway.

LAURIE: Alright Carlo?

CARLO: The Irish, they are all wonderful painters. *(To the HOULIHANS.)* Buon giorno!

MARY: Who are you? The feckin' King of England?

LOVERS' MUSICAL STING.

CARLO: Father Carlo. I can offer you Mass? You are Irish? You belong to Rome?

PATRICK: No! We're from Galway!

CARLO: Agh! The bambino has one eye, in the middle, like the devil!

MARY: You're a 'glass half empty' kinda fella then, Father Carlo!

CARLO: Who is the father?

MARY: Me brother, Patrick, there, him.

CARLO: Your brother is the father!? You must know that it is wrong to make-a sexual intercourse with your own brother.

MARY: Well, Carlo, on that one, we'll have to agree to disagree.

CARLO: Do all your family, make love with each other?

PATRICK: Oh aye, yes, me auld mother brought us up right and proper, aye.

MARY: 'Don't sleep with strangers, it's dirty!' she'd say.

KATHLEEN: 'Keep it in the family, least yer know they've been!' That's one of hers!

CARLO: Sta Migna! Sei pazzo! And you such a sweet little ragazza!

MARY: Ah feck off Carlo! You're a right one for the ladies eh?

CARLO: You must come to mass, the room over the Britannia pub there. I will try and save your soul. Ask for the art appreciation class.

CARLO leaves. In the street. LAURIE and RENNIE talk to HUGO and BENNY. LORD GEORGE GORDON and retinue arrive.

LORD GEORGE: Here! We'll create a Courtyard Theatre in the Shakespearean tradition!

BLACKAMOOR: Coffee! Knockyerblockoffcoffee!

EELS: Live eels! Get yer eels!

LAURIE: I'm telling you this Irish girl, she's given birth to a one eyed baby.

HUGO: Boy or girl?

RENNIE: It doesn't matter boy! It's a monster.

BENNY: Watch your backs!

LORD GEORGE: *(To the crowd.)* Monsieurs dames! Mes amis!

SEA COALS: Sea coals! Open your hatches! Sea coals!

LORD GEORGE: J'arrive aujourd'hui –

BENNY: – we speak English!

HUGO: – nutter!

LORD GEORGE: I have brought my petition to Bethnal Green –

SAUSAGES: – sizzling sausages!

LORD GEORGE: – home of the most industrious, the most creative citizens of England, the French, the survivors of the Saint Bartholomew's Day massacre –

LAURIE: – what do you do then?

LORD GEORGE: I am Lord George Gordon. I am a 'Member of Parliament'.

SEA COALS: So that's what they look like is it?!

LORD GEORGE: – today I exhort you to rise up against an act of evil which the King has designed to appease the Whore of Babylon, the Pope.

HUGO: I like your trousers!

LORD GEORGE: – the Catholic Relief Act will ease into the vulnerable body corporate of England the soul-deceiving and all-enslaving superstitions of the Witch of Rome. This will not be a door opening to Papism, it will be the walls collapsing, allowing the sewers of Rome to corrupt, disease, and violate, with violation 'pon violation the constitution of we free men. Twenty thousand Irish Catholic terrorists are organising in secret Mass Houses –

BENNY: – an Irish one eyed child has been born in this very street!

LORD GEORGE: Proof that the devil is at work under our noses!

HUGO: Let's kill the monster!

BENNY: Not yet, I wanna hear what he has to say.

LORD GEORGE: Preachers of Hate are twisting Irish minds against us, us! Their hosts! Today I ask you to do two things: sign my petition against the Catholic Relief Act; wear a blue cockade in your hats; and march with me –

BENNY: – that's three things!

LORD GEORGE: Let us march against the House of Commons! NO POPERY!

HUGO: No Irish?

LORD GEORGE: No Irish!

ALL: NO POPERY! NO IRISH! NO POPERY!

The MOB move off chanting. CARLO works his way back into the pub.

RENNIE: One eye! Smack bang in the middle of the forehead.

IDA: How many legs?

LAURIE: Two I think.

IDA: Cloven feet?

In the pub, enter JOHN and ANNE O'NEILL.

JOHN: A glass of beer please, and my wife would like a port.

IDA: Can't you bleedin' read!?

JOHN: Your 'No Blacks, No Irish, No Dogs' notice in the window?

ANNE: *(Pointing at RENNIE.)* What about him?

IDA: Rennie?

LAURIE: He's not Irish.

ANNE: Do you judge a nation by its worst ambassadors?

IDA: Course!

ANNE: If I were to run an inn I would ban individuals for their behaviour, their nationality would be irrelevant.

IDA: Get yourself a pub then lady, run it like a fucking brothel, see how long you last!

RENNIE: Are you Catholics?

ANNE: No. Not all the Irish are for Rome. Or drunk. Or poor.

JOHN: I'm a publisher. I publish pamphlets on the Enlightenment.

LAURIE: You doubt the resurrection of Christ don't you?

ANNE: We raise questions of Epistemology.

IDA: He pissed 'em all off, that's why they crucified him!

JOHN: What is the logic of not serving a gentleman whose money is as good as any Englishman's?

IDA: It's a free country! I'm allowed to be fucking illogical!

ANNE: What a shame.

JOHN: You see, I am a member of the Humanist Society. The secretary has asked me to find a room in the East End where we can hold regular meetings.

ANNE: Three hundred steady drinking atheists.

LAURIE: The room's free of a Wednesday, after art appreciation. Ida?

IDA: Pint and a port!?

MARY with baby runs into the pub.

MARY: Where is he? Please! Carlo!? Art appreciation?

IDA: Up them apples!

MARY runs upstairs with the baby.

ANNE: She's had the baby then?

LAURIE: Yeah, it's got one eye, it's a right proper Cyclops.

RENNIE: You're looking at the work of the devil!

ANNE: There is no devil sir. That child is the product of poverty and ignorance.

MARY bursts into the function room.

MARY: Carlo!

CARLO: Mary! You have come!

MARY: Patrick wants to kill me babby!

CARLO: You are safe here with me. Mary, can you feel a connection, a timeless bond with me? Do you feel it?

MARY: I've just given birth. I can't feel a fecking thing. You should try it!

CARLO: But did you hear the music when we first met?

MARY: Aye, I heard it. It'll be the fairies. They've had it in for me ever since I stood on one of the little fellahs. My punishment for that accident is bleeding, regular, every month, from a place you wouldn't believe.

CARLO: We know each other, somehow, the Lord has brought me to London, brought you to London, to meet, to fulfil some greater purpose.

MARY: Ah! What a helluva line of chat, you're a regular charmer eh!

He holds her tight and clumsy.

CARLO: Oh! To hold you, to feel you! I know now what my life is for!

He tries to kiss, but she stops him.

MARY: So this is mass is it!? You'll be cracking open a bottle next! Stop! We can't kiss.

CARLO: Why not?!

MARY: You're not even a friend of the family.

CARLO collapses to his knees holding MARY's legs. Enter LAURIE, JOHN and ANNE.

LAURIE: Don't mind us Carlo, just showing the room.

CARLO jumps up, adjusts his tackle, and picks up the picture. It is the Caravaggio.

CARLO: Appreciate the art, here, Thomas frowns as he sticks a finger in Christ's wounds. Appreciate how Carravaggio shows *doubt* as a contagion!

JOHN: What I appreciate is how Caravaggio presents doubt as a human obligation.

ANNE: The 'frown' is the mother of The Enlightenment.

MARY: You sound like Jackeens from Dublin!?

ANNE: We're Irish, yes, Bray town, and publishers.

JOHN: We have said 'no thank you' to the supernatural.

The baby cries.

ANNE: Oh, what a beautiful baby! She's got her mother's eye.

CARLO: It's a punishment from God for incest!

JOHN: God has no hand in this. A deformed child is a consequence of nature.

LAURIE: What if God's intelligence designed nature? The deformed baby is then simultaneously a consequence of nature, *and* a punishment from God. Publish that mate.

In the street, the MOB, inflamed, carrying torches. LAURIE goes to the window.

MOB: NO POPERY! NO IRISH! NO POPERY!

LAURIE: They're killing Catholics. They're burning your brother's house.

HUGO: Give us the one eyed devil child!

LAURIE: They want the baby.

LAURIE exits.

MOB: Kill, Kill, Kill! *(And under through the next section.)*

CARLO: They're coming this way. Hide the bambino!

MARY hides the baby in a draw/box/cupboard.

BENNY: Throw the monster out or we'll burn you down!

JOHN: If we had any kind of monster we'd give her up to you now!

MOB: Irish! In the pub! Burn the pub!

BENNY: Fuck off! That's a decent pub!

CARLO: They're coming in, swords drawn.

RENNIE enters, ushering in HUGO and BENNY both with swords drawn.

RENNIE: I'm telling you, him there, he's a priest, and these two are Irish.

JOHN: We're Irish yes, but we're not Catholic.

ANNE: We're intellectuals from Wicklow.

HUGO: Where's your one eyed baby?

MARY: I'll not tell you. You'll have to kill me first!

HUGO grabs CARLO and puts a sword to his heart. BENNY keeps the O'NEILLS at bay with his sword.

HUGO: Cough up love! Or I'll run him through.

BENNY: I know him. He will!

CARLO: Don't tell them Mary!

MARY: She's not a monster, she's my little babby so!

HUGO thrusts his sword into CARLO. CARLO collapses, dying.

CARLO: Mary, my sweet, I am dying, I will see you in paradise.

JOHN: Maybe it's not the time to disappoint you father, but reason alone tells us that there is no heaven, and there's no hell neither.

ANNE: This is the only paradise you will ever know.

CARLO: Bethnal Green?

JOHN: Aye. It's a sobering thought isn't it.

CARLO dies. The baby cries giving away the location. HUGO lifts the lid.

HUGO: I'm telling you mate, that is the anti-christ and no mistaking.

BENNY holds MARY back with his sword. HUGO picks the baby up and takes it to the window where he shows his trophy to the crowd.

Here you go! I got the Catholic devil child!

HUGO throws the child out of the window. The doll/baby lands on the stage. The audience should see it land and be shocked with the texture of its bounce. Enter SCHIMMEL and family. Jews from the Pale.

SCHIMMEL: Oy gevalt! Did you see that! And you think it's tough being Jewish!

END OF ACT.

Act Three

1888. Continue from the last scene, the mob turn and watch the Jewish refugees arrive.

STREET SINGER: Behold! what beasts come wailing through
    the lock?
    On cattle ships to Saint Katherine's dock
    A human invasion of an alien variation
    The children of the He-brew Nation
    The Eternal People, oppressed, ground down
    A Shtetl to make of our tenter ground
    This swarming is the most unwelcome news
    For the French, the Irish. And the
    English… Jews.

The docks. The sound of a ship's horn, deep and mournful. Enter the elite of Anglo Jewry: CHIEF RABBI, LORD ROTHSCHILD and MP HARRY SAMUELS.

RABBI: Look at all these Luftmensch!

HARRY: Don't they say Chief Rabbi, 'one gets the Jews one deserves'.

RABBI: Hell, I must have killed in my sleep!

ROTHSCHILD: I must build them a synagogue.

RABBI: And quickly please Lord Rothschild! Or they will come to mine!

ROTHSCHILD: They're hungry.

RABBI: Yes, but quiet! Feed them, they'll start arguing!

ROTHSCHILD: Harry? This is your constituency, would a temporary shelter be possible? Food, a doctor, clothing and –

RABBI: – a Klezmer band!

HARRY: If we make it too easy for them, more will come.

RABBI: 'Dear Uncle Heime, sell the cow, come to London, there is a free meal.' Starvation is our best weapon!

HARRY: And we should tell them about South Africa.

RABBI: Yes, how wonderful it is!

ROTHSCHILD: Is it wonderful?

HARRY: Who cares! It's somewhere else!

ROTHSCHILD: We have to help. These are our people. What would Moses do?

RABBI: Moses would not be here. He'd be in New York already!

ROTHSCHILD: They need housing, hospitals, schools. Our mission is to turn these Jews into English Jews.

KATZ arrives, and starts selling the paper.

KATZ: Spread *The Revolution*!

HARRY: Anarchists.

KATZ: Support the Jewish Anarchist League!

ROTHSCHILD: *Jewish* anarchists! Is that possible?

RABBI: Apparently, there are many terrorists on these ships. Army deserters.

ROTHSCHILD: Chief Rabbi? Have you been dining at the Russian Embassy again?

RABBI: I have to eat!

Enter BLACK RUTH. She rather ostentatiously kisses KATZ, then starts selling the paper.

RUTH: You may join the Jewish Anarchist League here! Fight the awful business of international capital.

ROTHSCHILD: Good Lord, I recognise her.

KATZ and RUTH kiss again.

RABBI: I've heard these anarchists will sleep with anybody.

ROTHSCHILD: Are they Libertarians?

RABBI: God knows what they eat!

RUTH: Wouldn't it be fun to destroy marriage, religion, and chastity!

ROTHSCHILD: My God! It's Ruth, Tufty's daughter. Excuse me gentlemen.

ROTHSCHILD approaches RUTH.

RUTH: Lord Rothschild?

ROTHSCHILD: Ruth?

RUTH: Black Ruth.

ROTHSCHILD: What are you doing here?

RUTH: I'm organising a revolution, kicking off with a terrific dock strike.

ROTHSCHILD: At your own father's docks?

RUTH: Indeedy! Next a tailors' strike. Imagine, the Jewish tailors and the Irish dockers, united! I've organised a walk.

KATZ: March.

RUTH: A *march* to Parliament. Oh fuckioli! It's father! Spread the Revolution!

Enter LORD BALLAST, he sees RUTH and steams. He is a bald headed man with tufty red eyebrows. He is wearing a Rolls Royce of a coat.

ROTHSCHILD: Tufty! Have you seen your daughter, Ruth.

TUFTY: Oh buggerello, is she here again!? Excuse me gentlemen!

TUFTY goes over to RUTH.

Ruth! What's this bloody rag you're selling?

RUTH: *The Revolution.* A shilling.

TUFTY: It says here a penny.

RUTH: It's a shilling to you.

He pays for a paper, and gives it a quick scan.

Father, how many workers died stitching that coat?

TUFTY: Four. The typesetting is ruddy awful. 'The Jewish Anarchist League meets on the *sixty sixth* of September.'

RUTH: Oh cock au vin!

TUFTY: If a thing's worth doing, it's worth doing well!

He turns his back on her, and walks back to ROTHSCHILD.

Children eh? I should've stuck to breeding horses. Gentlemen! Welcome to my big dock!

ROTHSCHILD: Lord Ballast, the Chief Rabbi, and you know the MP, Harry Samuel.

TUFTY: Always, nice, to add more Jewish friends to the collection! So, you can see, thousands of these aliens are coming in every week. Criminals, anarchists, terrorists, and the odd religious nutter! Ha!

He slaps the RABBI on the back.

HARRY: The most pressing –

TUFTY: – I've had an idea. What if you Jews had your own country!?

RABBI: A homeland for the Jews would be –

TUFTY: – Have you ever considered Palestine?! Palestine is a country without a people, and the Jews, are a people without a country.

HARRY: – there are many Arabs and –

TUFTY: – AND the good news is the Ottoman Empire is about to go tits up, and Johnny Turk'll sell his own mother in a closing down sale!

KATZ: Spread the Revolution!

TUFTY: Half of these yid…dish speaking refugees are intent on destroying our way of life. Do you want to talk to one? Hey, you! Come here!

AARON comes over.

ROTHSCHILD: Shalom aleichem!

AARON: Shalom!

HARRY: How do you expect to survive in this town young man?

AARON: I am a printer.

TUFTY: Typesetting?

AARON: I can typeset, yes. My brother is here, and he says there are many newspapers in New York?

ROTHSCHILD: This is London.

AARON: No! The captain said it was New York!

TUFTY: You're not the first. *(To the gents.)* Come on let's go and eat!

The committee move off. TUFTY turns and approaches AARON. He slips him some money.

Hey! My card. Come and see me tomorrow. If you're looking for employment, they need a typesetter.

TUFTY exits. AARON approaches RUTH.

RUTH: Comrade! Take a paper. It's yours.

AARON takes the paper and the LOVERS MUSICAL STING PLAYS. RUTH is affected by the music, almost swooning. AARON is unmoved.

AARON: This typesetting's awful. I can typeset.

In the pub.

IDA: Fucking Yids! Ain't they never heard of soap and wa'er!? Last time any of this lot had a bath was two thousand years ago in the River Jordan. In the whole wide world is there one other whatsaname –

LAURIE: – independent civilised nation state –

IDA: – what is willing to take the scrapings of Russia, Poland, no questions asked.

RENNIE: I got them upstairs from me, fish for breakfast, fish for lunch, fish for tea!

LAURIE: There's no smoke without salmon with this lot.

RENNIE: Britain got an open door boy!

IDA: Why is it so fucking difficult to ask the odd question? Like, 'have you got smallpox?' 'Have you got cholera?'

LAURIE: 'Did you assassinate Tsar Alexander the second?'

The revolutionaries' flat in Whitechapel. RUTH, KATZ, AARON. A bed, and a printing press.

AARON: Aaron Biro, St Petersburg.

KATZ: Martin Katz, Bellozersk.

RUTH: Black Ruth, Stow-on-the-Wold. I'm cooking a peasant style paella, and there's plenty of vin de table.

AARON: In Russia I was earning seven roubles a week for typesetting and layout.

KATZ: We don't pay wages.

RUTH: On principle. Wages, you see, are chains. But you can sleep with me – if you want. There are no rules, you don't have to.

KATZ: Marriage is the institutionalised oppression of women.

RUTH: We're libertarians. Martin, go next door and ask Mrs T if we can borrow that spare mattress of hers. For you.

KATZ leaves, sulky.

Aaron, did you hear the music, at the docks, when we met?

AARON: I didn't hear anything. I suffer from tinnitis. From the printing presses.

RUTH: I was powerless. I felt watched, as if Cupid was taking aim.

AARON: Why are you using the standard nine point Clarendon upright? The layout is aggressively homogeneous. Do you have a set of nine point Bulmer italic?

RUTH: What are you talking about?

AARON: Printing. I love all aspects of printing but fonts are my real passion.

RUTH: Oh dear. Really?

AARON: Yes, I have invented a portable pen.

AARON takes out what looks like a narrow steel tube. It is his prototype ball point pen.

It has a rotating ball in a steel coated socket.

RUTH: Mister Aaron Biro, you're a clever cloggs aren't you!

She takes his hand and their two hands write with the biro.

It's beautiful, and functional, like you. Have you got a name for it?

AARON: I call it the 'Stahlmantel-kugel-in-tinte-mit-muffe'.

RUTH: Holy fuckioli! That's a mouthful!

AARON: People shorten it to –

She kisses him.

RUTH: – I should find you dull, and cerebral, but I can't resist you.

Enter KATZ, carrying mattress. He stands and watches.

We were discussing the next issue of *The Revolution.* It must include our 'God, and the dinosaurs' polemic.

KATZ: Why, if God made dinosaurs are they not mentioned in the Bible?

AARON: You could say the same about a round earth, bacteria, the circulation of the blood – the list is endless.

RUTH: Martin, we have discovered a great mind! The essay must be rewritten! I will sit with Aaron as he typesets. You can sleep in the scullery.

MARTIN KATZ exits with the mattress. AARON is at the press, and RUTH snuggles in beside him.

RUTH: We can make love all night now.

She kisses him.

AARON: My plan is to join my brother in New York and develop the pen for the American market. I need paid work so that I can save for my fare.

RUTH: You can look for enslavement tomorrow, Mister Biro, tonight you're free.

AARON: What kind of work is available for a Jew in London?

Lights down on the flat and lights up on the sweatshop.

Song: 'Oy vey!'

> Hard and bitter as death is this life
> Oy vey! Oy vey!
> All my strength for a crust for my wife
> Oy vey! Oy vey!
> The Sweater here he is a Jew
> Oy vey! Oy Vey!
> Hoffman and Singer they were too!
> Oy vey! Oy vey! Oy vey! Oy vey!

Enter LAZARUS, the sweater, and AARON.

LAZARUS: I will train you and then you will be able to earn twenty shillings a week.

AARON: You will pay me twenty shillings a week?

LAZARUS: When I have trained you, you will be able to earn twenty shillings a week.

AARON: Somewhere else?

LAZARUS: I am training you for life. You should be paying me. Take it or leave it.

> We all wish for death every day!
> Oy vey! Oy vey!
> Heat and steam we can't get away
> Oy vey! Oy vey!
> The Factory Act's kept out of sight
> Oy vey! Oy vey!
> We stop for God on a Friday night
> Oy vey! Oy vey! Oy vey! Oy vey!

AARON looks at TUFTY's card and leaves. MRS GASKIN kicks out the Irish.

MRS GASKIN: Come on! Let's be having you! Chop! Chop!

IDA: Oi! Mrs Gaskin, what the fuck are you doing?! These is Irish houses.

MRS GASKIN: My great great great grandfather didn't paddle across the English Channel in an apple barrel because he wanted advice from the likes of you.

IDA: You promised number sixteen to my girl!

MRS GASKIN: No Christians need apply.

HUGO: The yids wanna be near the sweatshops innit.

Enter RABBI. He shakes hands with MRS GASKIN.

MRS GASKIN: Morning Rabbi, turned out nice again!

RABBI: Yes, yes, I've got the money.

HUGO: Oi Mrs Gaskin, what you selling him?

MRS GASKIN hands over a big church key.

BENNY: You can't sell the church!

HUGO: Gaskin's selling the French church!

The RABBI disposes of the cross on the outside of the church and puts up a star of David.

BENNY: We ain't gonna stand for a synagogue round here Mrs Gaskin.

MRS GASKIN: Move then. It's a free country.

IDA: Where are we Irish supposed to go then?

MRS GASKIN: I've heard Redbridge is very nice.

IDA: Redbridge? I wouldn't be seen fucking dead in Redbridge!

TUFTY sits at his office desk. A SECRETARY enters.

SECRETARY: The minutes of the red squirrel society sir. And there is an alien to see you. He produced your card.

TUFTY: Send him in.

Enter AARON.

Did you find accommodation?

AARON: The Flower and Dean Street rookery.

TUFTY: Neighbors with Jack the Ripper! My theory is that Jack is a kosher butcher.

AARON: He is as likely to be an English gentleman.

TUFTY: Employment?

AARON: I'm typesetting *The Revolution*, and looking for paid work.

TUFTY: What do you want from life Aaron Biro?

AARON: Until last night I had wanted my pen to change the world but –

TUFTY: – another bloody writer eh?

AARON: Inventor. This is my portable pen. The 'Stahlmantel-kugel-in-tinte-mit-muffe'. Everybody shortens it to 'mitmuffe'.

TUFTY: 'Mitmuffe'? As in 'would you like to borrow my mitmuffe'?

AARON: Yes.

TUFTY: I wouldn't buy one because I'm prejudiced against anything German or German sounding.

TUFTY gets out some money and puts it on the table.

Change the typesetting from 'spread The Revolution' to 'destroy The Revolution' and I will give you fifteen pounds. Your ticket to New York.

AARON: Why does that concern you so much?

TUFTY: They're organising the Irish, the dockers, to strike. I own the docks.

AARON: I cannot help. I have chosen to stay in England. I've met a girl.

TUFTY: This girl, is she a well bred aristocratic Englishwoman?

AARON: Yes.

TUFTY: *(Stands.)* Holy moly buggeroli! Thirty pounds! Fifteen for your fare and fifteen to get you started in America with your mitmuffe!

AARON: No. I adore her.

TUFTY: Mister Biro, I could have you arrested for rape. Ruthey is my only daughter, and will in time recover her station. She will not marry a hairy Jew with no prospects! Fifty pounds!

AARON: I cannot be bought.

AARON makes to leave.

TUFTY: The offer stands! Any time!

TUFTY sits head in hands, distraught. A graffiti artist paints ENGLAND FOR THE ENGLISH on the synagogue wall. A banner proclaims THE BRITISH BROTHERS LEAGUE.

MOB: England for the English!

England for the English!

England for the English!

HARRY SAMUEL: I, Harry Samuel, have never put my religion, my Jewishness, ahead of my duties as your MP. That is why today I welcome to the East End the British Brothers League and their inspiration, Major Evans-Gordon!

Cheers.

MAJOR EG: Roman, Viking, Saxon, French, and Irish – all have integrated successfully, and with God's genius, created the Englishman. But a Hebrew can only marry a Hebrew, the synagogue is separative!

WOMAN: My boy is the only Christian in his 'ole school!

MAJOR EG: And what do they bring with them?

BENNY: Jack the Ripper!

HUGO: Jacob the Ripper!

Laughter.

MAJOR EG: If we don't act now this is the end of England! Join the British Brothers League, and we will close the door on this foul ingress of humanity!

Cheers. The flat. RUTH is there, and TUFTY. He stands, exasperated at the squalor.

TUFTY: Living here! With a Jew! What could be worse?

RUTH: Two Jews?

TUFTY: Holy moly fuckioli! Come home please! The servants miss you terribly!

RUTH: I have vital work here in Bethnal Green.

TUFTY: I spent an hour last week begging the Duke of Bedford not to introduce the American grey squirrel into Woburn Park. The British squirrel will stand no chance against this voracious, sexually charged, immigrant! Why Ruthey!? Why this lust for Hebrew flesh?!

RUTH: Mother told me that as a deb she was very fond of a Sassoon or two.

TUFTY: I'll get them a country of their own if it's the last thing I do, and with a bit of luck they'll all go and live there. It will bring peace to the world.

TUFTY starts to leave as the Jewish Anarchist League members arrive for their meeting. AARON and others arrive. They all tuck in to the food. The feeling is not revolutionary but convivial.

MORRIE: I've got chola, still warm, gefilte fish, pickled –

AARON: – excellent Morrie!

Enter KATZ with HUGO. HUGO looks a bit sceptical, lost, embarrassed.

MORRIE: I read your essay Mister Katz. It's the most comprehensive anarcho-communist analysis of capitalism I've ever read in Yiddish.

RUTH kisses AARON. KATZ approaches RUTH and takes her to one side.

KATZ: I have found you an Irish docker.

RUTH: Oh goodo!

KATZ: A tailors' and dockers' strike would do two things. It would break the barriers of racial antipathy between Jews and Irish and –

RUTH: – and it'll give Parliament and daddy a well deserved bloody nose.

KATZ: I'm relying on you Ruth. You have to deliver. Sleep with him.

KATZ moves away. RUTH is left thoughtful.

AARON: Does Katz love you?

RUTH: He has made love to me.

AARON: Don't torture me! I was a printer, an inventor, living entirely in my head until last night.

RUTH: Love is the invention of the oppressed sprung from the well of economic misery.

KATZ brings HUGO over to RUTH. AARON defers and backs away, and watches.

KATZ: This is Hugo. Black Ruth. One of the girls I was telling you about.

HUGO: Awight! Your china's been telling me you're one of them Libertarians.

RUTH: Indeed I am. Are the dockers organised?

HUGO: No. Most of us are married.

MORRIE claps his hands to start the meeting.

MORRIE: Shalom Aleichem! Sit down, sit down! Comrades! Chaverim! Quiet! First the minutes of the Jewish Anarchist League for –

AARON: – We must change our name! How can one be a Jewish anarchist! An anarchist rejects all authority, all religion, and reaches out to any and every worker. A Jew defers to a higher authority.

MORRIE: 'Jewish' is only an adjective, it means 'friendly, clean, well organised'.

KATZ: I am a 'Jewish anarchist' and I like these meetings, they're…they're –

MORRIE: – heimische!

AARON: But to be a Jew is to be particular.

MORRIE: Particular about everything! Milk and meat, washing –

AARON: – the meeting should be open to Christians, Hindus, Mohammadans.

MORRIE: You can do the catering!

RUTH: Tchisikov, are you an anarchist or a Jewish anarchist?

TCHISIKOV: I love death.

LILLY: In the pogroms they massacre Jews, not workers. Jews must reach inside, into their traditions.

KATZ: So you are the Orthodox Jewish Anarchist League!

LILLY: Throw stones, that's easy! Why not take those stones and build a nation. Israel will be built on anarchist principles.

KATZ: Ah! The Jewish Zionist Anarchist League!

THOMAS: I'm with Aaron. Jews are our worst enemies. Bastard communists like Marx, Engels, Jew capitalists like Rothschild, Montagu –

KATZ: – the anti-semitic Jewish Anarchist League!

RUTH: Chaps! Please! Aaron is right! We should drop Jewish from the name. God is an authoritarian. If I ever meet him I will spit in his eye.

LILLY: You will go to hell.

RUTH: Oh what a lot of cock au vin! There is neither hell nor heaven. This is the only heaven we will ever know.

LILLY: What? Bethnal Green?

RUTH: You could always move darling.

MORRIE: My uncle, he's moved out to this little village. Very quiet. Hendon.

RUTH: We need to find a way of attacking both religion and capital.

MORRIE: On Yom Kippur, I have noticed, the rich gather in the synagogue in seats set aside from the luftmensch.

LILLY: We can do nothing on the Day of Atonement but fast –

AARON: – Instead of fasting we should feast! A bacon sandwich eating competition outside the synagogue!

RUTH: You're a genius Aaron Biro!

TCHISIKOV: *(Standing.)* I love death!

RUTH and TCHISIKOV kiss. Everyone watches. Silence.

HUGO: I can get you some knock off bacon.

MORRIE: Of course! But would it be kosher?!

RUTH: Next meeting, the synagogue on Yom Kippur!

The meeting disperses. TCHISIKOV approaches RUTH.

TCHISIKOV: I am ready. Tomorrow. Aldersgate underground station.

RUTH: Look Tchisy, you don't have to, it was only an idea. Katzie!

KATZ comes over.

Tchisikov says he's ready. Tomorrow. Aldersgate.

KATZ: Did you decide –

TCHISIKOV: – Only suicide can express my love of death!

KATZ hugs TCHISIKOV. TCHISIKOV moves off. KATZ takes RUTH roughly by the arm.

KATZ: *(Bullying.)* If Tchisikov can blow himself up on the underground the least you can do is sleep with a docker.

HUGO comes over with a bit of a swagger. RUTH puts on a brave face.

RUTH: Dockers and tailors marching together will be quite a spectacle.

HUGO: Won't be easy. They've taken our houses, our schools, yer can't move in the hospital for tripping over some Hebrew coughing his guts up.

They start to leave, together. AARON approaches.

RUTH: Come on! I've never seen the docks at night!

AARON: Ruth!

RUTH: I am not impressed by jealousy. Social progress must take priority over –

AARON: – over love!?

RUTH: Yes! You have a night of typesetting. I have my own work.

RUTH and HUGO leave. AARON is distraught.

AARON: Will she sleep with him?

KATZ: Yes. We should put the Yom Kippur polemic on the back page.

AARON: No! The back page banner 'Spread The Revolution' is iconic, and must never be changed.

In the pub. RENNIE, and LAURIE. Enter IDA, taking her coat off.

IDA: Kaw! You can't move out there for yids! I mean, England, ever since the whatsaname –

LAURIE: – disestablishment of the church under Henry the Eighth –

IDA: – has been a Christian country!

LAURIE: Yom Kippur innit. The Day of Atonement.

RENNIE: Your Jew looks to God for absolution from offence.

IDA: That would be a solution, a fence. A fucking big fence round the whole fucking country!

LAURIE is reading. RENNIE is there too.

LAURIE: Your prayers are answered Ida, the Aliens Act got through Parliament.

IDA: 'Bout time too!

RENNIE: England is full boy!

LAURIE: Hang on! Says here, they're still letting them in! Except 'the destitutes, the mad, and the idiots'.

RENNIE: How do they know which ones are the idiots!?

LAURIE: They ask 'em at the docks.

RENNIE: What did you do in Russia?

LAURIE: I was an idiot!

RENNIE: Fuck that! You're not coming in!

LAURIE: Next!

They laugh. The synagogue is packed with observant JEWS. The sound of praying/singing. A Klezmer band are there waiting. Tuning up.

KATZ: Spread The Revolution!

MORRIE: Bacon sandwiches! Get your bacon butties!

RUTH arrives.

RUTH: Where's Aaron? Katzie, tell me! Where is he?!

KATZ: I've not seen him today. Spread The Revolution!

RUTH: Morrie, when did you last see Aaron?

MORRIE: Lunch I had simmus, he had kreplach in chicken soup –

RUTH: – Where is he!?

MORRIE: *(Shrug of the shoulders.)* He had a suitcase.

RUTH: Tchisikov!? Have you seen Aaron?

TCHISIKOV: No.

RUTH: Wait! You were supposed to blow yourself up on the tube?!

TCHISIKOV: One can only really love death if one believes in paradise.

RUTH: So what did you do?

TCHISIKOV: I left the bomb on the train and ran away. Sixty injured, and one dead.

RUTH: What? Someone really died? They're actually dead?

TCHISIKOV: Yes. A capitalist. Spread The Revolution!

RUTH approaches the leader of the klezmer band.

RUTH: Play. What are you waiting for?

MUSICIAN: The bride.

RUTH: This isn't a wedding! Play, and eat these. Bacon sandwiches!

The band play. The RABBI comes out!

RABBI: Oy gevalt! You can't play here! Not today, it is Yom Kippur!

MORRIE: What'll you have Rabbi!? Smoked, streaky or back?

JEW 1: Stop it! You can't eat on Yom Kippur.

JEW 2: They're not just eating, they're eating bacon!

RABBI: Oy a klog! Please stop this, or there will be violence!

The band stop. RUTH stands on a soap box.

RUTH: On your Jewish day of Yom Kippur, I invite you to reject oppression, reject authority, reject God. Eat bacon, dance, and make love!

RABBI: Do not tempt the wrath of the Lord!

RUTH: Lord of the Heavens! I give you ten seconds to destroy me, one, two, three, four, five, six, seven, eight, nine and hello! ten!

The klezmer band break into an up tempo number, and a fight starts. RUTH wrestles free of the situation. A riotous laugh cracks the air. The RABBI holds a copy of The Revolution.

RABBI: Buy a paper, it's so funny! Destroy The Revolution. Look! Destroy The Revolution! The Lord has shown his hand! You are destroyed!

An observant JEW stands on the soap box handing out copies of the paper. Another joins on the second soap box, and then on the third. They are joyful, laughing.

JEW 1: Look! Destroy The Revolution!

JEW 2: Ha, ha! Destroy The Revolution!!

The JEWS drive out the anarchists. RUTH is left alone, distraught. She is crying, wailing, it's desperate, she's on her knees with a copy of the paper.

RUTH: Aaron! My love! Where are you! Have you seen Aaron!? I wanted to tell him. I'm sorry! Aaron! Nothing matters without you!

A Sylheti LASCAR runs on. He approaches RUTH with a bit of cardboard.

LASCAR: Address. Master Attar. Big man barriwallah!

PHILIPPA: Lights! Ginny! Please!

General wash of lights.

What are you doing!?

LASCAR: Have I got something wrong?

PHILIPPA: We're taking an interval before the Bangladeshi act! And we've cut your bit.

POLICEMAN: No one told me.

PHILIPPA: Everybody, well done, the cockney accents are so authentic.

GINNY: *(Off/distort.)* Thank you everybody! Fifteen minutes. It's all fantastic!

TATYANA: Can I smoke now?

PHILIPPA: Yes please do. And I hope your cigarettes do exactly what they say they do on the tin. *(To herself.)* Kill.

TATYANA walks away. The cast disperse, except TAHER. OFFICER KELLY enters.

OFFICER KELLY: Their envelopes have just arrived. They're here no?

PHILIPPA: Oh shit!

GINNY: *(Off/Distort.)* Shall I give them out?

PHILIPPA: Hell! No, not yet. What is it Taher?

TAHER: Is…

PHILIPPA: – stop! I've warned you, if you mention Israel, that's it!

TAHER: Is –

PHILIPPA: – I mean it!

TAHER: Is this a play about immigration or is it about love?

PHILIPPA: Your point?

TAHER: The play is like four Romeo and Juliets, but what does it matter? I worry, we may have made the play too light, everybody falls in love – in love, out of love, why is it so important?

PHILIPPA: We discussed this during the research. The truest measure of racial and cultural integration in any society is the rate of inter-marriage, and you yourself –

TAHER: – I am agreeing with you! Working on this play I have come to savour the music when the lovers meet. It is the music of hope, humanity.

PHILIPPA: I'm amazed. At last we agree.

TAHER: Yes. Only love can free humanity from the shackles of history. And that is exactly what those bastard Israelis will never understand!

PHILIPPA: Taher, would you, could you, please, just fuck off out of my sight. You're on your INTERVAL!

GINNY: *(Off.)* Fifteen minutes please. Fifteen minutes everybody!

SNAP TO BLACK.

INTERVAL.

Act Four (Prologue)

GINNY: *(Off.)* Act Two beginners to the stage please!

ELMAR is alone on stage. He is joined by TAHER.

TAHER: Our envelopes are in the sound box. They have to give them to us.

ELMAR: In Azerbaydzhan we have a saying, don't kick a sleeping dog, it might wake up and bite your arse.

TAHER: You might have got leave to remain. Or are you expecting bad news?

ELMAR: I told them the truth.

TAHER: Why did you have to leave Azerbaydzhan?

ELMAR: My films, scripted by Aram Magomedli, ridiculed the government's violent suppression of free speech. I felt safe, because there was never anyone in government intelligent enough to understand the metaphor. But last year, my script writer, my friend, Aram Magomedli –

TAHER: – they killed him?

ELMAR: No. He became Minister of Culture.

Enter PHILIPPA.

Your husband is enjoying it I think.

PHILIPPA: I've asked him to sit further back.

ELMAR: That is because you know that this next act includes a portrait of your marriage. St John and Camilla, St John and Philippa?

PHILIPPA: I never expected him to come.

ELMAR: Camilla is a liberal, and you make her an idiot? Are you an idiot? The English tradition is liberal, tolerant. What are you saying?

Enter all the others from outside, TATYANA still smoking.

PHILIPPA: This is a place of work and smoking is illegal! If you want to smoke go back to Serbia where I imagine smoking is still compulsory! I'm not doing notes –

TATYANA: – We have been talking about Deborah.

PHILIPPA: Yes what?

SANYA: She is sixteen years old in the Blitz, yes?

TATYANA: And she gives birth to twins just after 9/11. She is nearly eighty.

PHILIPPA: And the problem is?

SANYA: Physiological!

PHILIPPA: Our characters are children, and their playground is time. One advantage of theatre, over say telecomms, is that one is not bound by reality. Now –

TATYANA: – our envelopes are here.

YAYAH: I want my envelope please.

TATYANA: You don't have the fucking right to keep our envelopes from us. If I have got leave to remain, I can go now!

PHILIPPA: *(Sigh.)* OK. Officer Kelly give the envelopes out please.

ELMAR: No! We have devised this play together. We are a society. Do not destroy that society before we need to. Tatyana, give us one more hour of your life. Then you can have your envelope for ever more.

YAYAH: Good point! I don't want my envelope. I will forget my lines.

PHILIPPA: Thank you, now –

TAHER: – I think there is a problem with Laurie's big speech.

PHILIPPA: *(Dropping her head in resignation.)* Agggh!

TAHER: Laurie is talking about *Pride and Prejudice*, yes? I look on Wikipedia and Elizabeth Bennet loves Fitzwilliam D'Arcy, not Colin Firth.

LAURIE: I have learned my lines now, I am going to say Colin Firth and that is that!

TAHER: But Colin Firth makes no sense –

PHILIPPA: – because it's my English humour not your Gaza Strip humour! Stick with 'Colin Firth'. Thank you. Check your props! House lights! The Blitz! Please!

The lights adjust, and a second world war air raid siren sounds.

Act Four

Summer 1941. The Blitz. An air raid siren. A Bethnal Green street, the Britannia Pub as was. The street of Victorian workers' houses is now overlooked by the Rothschild Buildings. All buildings are blacked out for night and war. In a doorway, Mohammad Sona Rasul aka MISTER MUSHI, beside him a large cooking pot full of clothes, etc. MUSHI is the boy lover. Two wet Bangladeshis run on chased by a policeman, they go off. Enter two STRETCHER BEARERS. They discover a body in a doorway. They are joined by a POLICE CONSTABLE.

CONSTABLE: Indian Lascar. Merchant navy. Stoker? Donkey wallah? Who knows?

STRETCHER BEARER 1: Who cares? He's dead.

CONSTABLE: He'll have jumped ship at Tilbury. They swim the dock.

STRETCHER BEARER 2: Criminal then, ain't he.

CONSTABLE: As a citizen of British India, he has the legal right to come ashore. So come on lads, show some compassion, he's a human soul, and some mother's son.

STRETCHER BEARER 1: You alright officer?

CONSTABLE: I've been on a course.

MUSHI is loaded onto the stretcher. He sneezes/coughs.

STRETCHER 2: That's all we need.

STRETCHER 1: Oi Mush! Hop it!

MUSHI is tipped off the stretcher and the bearers move off to find a corpse.

MUSHI: *(Giving CONSTABLE a bit of cardboard.)* Uncle friend! Big man barriwallah!

CONSTABLE: *(Reading.)* This address is Aldgate.

MUSHI: England people very nice!

CONSTABLE: There's good and bad in all. Come on Mush! This way.

They walk off. In the pub. IDA, LAURIE, and RENNIE. BENNY and HUGO sat away from them.

IDA: Fucking Yanks! Where are they? I'll betcha they swagger up when it's nearly over, pick up all the dead men's hats, and make an 'ollywood film about how John Wayne won the fucking war on his whatsaname.

RENNIE: Horse?

IDA: Na!

LAURIE: Tod.

Enter HARVEY KLEINMAN in the uniform of a volunteer ARP warden. He is IDA's husband.

HARVEY: Ida, get your blackouts sorted will yer.

IDA: You might be my husband Harvey Kleinman, but I'm at work, you don't fucking tell me what to do, not in here, alright!

LAURIE: Ida, get your blackouts sorted will yer.

IDA complies. RENNIE laughs.

RENNIE: See Solomon's shop took a hit Harvey!?

HARVEY: Yeah, they're all dead, yeah, tragic.

HARVEY joins BENNY and HUGO.

D'yer get anyfin outa Solomon's place?

BENNY: Cutlery. Silver boxed sets. Hugo flogged 'em up West.

HUGO: Here you go Mr Kleinman…

HUGO empties his pockets of a bundle of notes. HARVEY takes the money and pockets it.

HARVEY: Now gimme the rest of the money, or that's the last you'll see of my daughter.

HUGO produces a five pound note, which HARVEY takes. In MASTER ATTAR's house. Night time. ATTAR is a middle-aged Bangladeshi, dressed like Noël Coward. ATTAR is writing in a big ledger.

MUSHI: Why do you want all the lascar names Sahib Master Attar?

ATTAR: Merchant navy captains do not know the names of our people. It's only port serangs in Calcutta, and me, know the names. Serangs are all bastards, so when a ship is torpedoed the Indian Embassy talk to me. I am the only man who can tell a father whether his son is alive or dead.

MUSHI: Abdul Quereshi, coala wallah; Ashraf Miah, agwallah; that's it. Except, young boy, Taz, don't know family name, sorry, sahib.

ATTAR: Don't call me sahib, I'm a socialist. SS Clan Macarthur. Thirty one lascars, and little Taz. *(He closes the book.)* Is your room to your liking?

MUSHI: Oh yes. Very nice. But you said I had to share the bed?

ATTAR: Don't worry, he's not English. Hasmat Miah, he works nights boiler room Savoy Hotel. I think you have attractive personality. I want you to run my chocolate raffle. Easy money for the right man.

MUSHI: Easier than renting beds?

ATTAR: That's it! Personality! The English love a joke! You buy a chocolate bar from me for a ha'penny –

MUSHI: – buy from you, the socialist!?

ATTAR: That's enough personality. Sell seven tickets at a penny each. Easy money. But first you must think of a new name. Clan Line give ten pounds for information about lascars who have swum the dock.

MUSHI: I come England one reason. Father say must find half Christian, half Jewish girl, make twins. This decreed by Allah. Boy twin I give mosque, he will bring whole world to God. Keep girl, but boy haram to me.

ATTAR: Bollocks! Your father had too many sons and no land to give you. He made up that shit so you would leave home feeling good.

MUSHI: My father would not lie! He is Pir, holy man, direct descendant Shah Jalal, he said girl have Jewish name. Seven letters, first letter D.

In the pub, it's evening and a piano player tinkles away. DEBORAH is still in overalls.

IDA: Oi Deborah!? You gonna give us a song tonight doll?!

DEBORAH: Giss a break Mum, I just done an eight hour shift ain't I!

Enter a small group of Indian LASCARS. Silence. IDA comes over.

IDA: Fucking…heroes! The Indian Lascars! The engine room of the British Merchant Navy! Standing shoulder to shoulder wiv us in the fight against whatsaname –

LAURIE: – Totalitarianism.

The pub stand and applaud the LASCARS. IDA leads the cheers. The LASCARS stand and bow.

IDA: For you boys, drinks are on the house!

SHAH ABDUL: Two teas please Miss.

EGG NOG: They're very religious miss. I'm not, I'll have a large Egg nog please no ice.

IDA: That's more like it son, you might fucking die tomorrow!

HARVEY, IDA, DEBORAH, BENNY and HUGO form a family group.

RENNIE: Amaaazin' woman, Ida, she's like Britannia herself boy!

LAURIE: Ida? She ain't English, she's Irish. Irish who married a Jew.

RENNIE: No! Harvey is never Jewish boy!

LAURIE: Harvey Kleinman not Jewish! He's as Jewish as 'the hole in the sheet'. That's the worst mix – Irish and Jewish. You end up with a family of pissed up burglars run by a clever accountant.

Enter MUSHI, with pinstripe suit, carnation, a trilby, and a pocket full of chocolate bars.

MUSHI: Chocolate raffle! Penny ticket, everyone got penny!

SOLDIER: One for me, one for the lady!

MUSHI: *(To the LADY, kissing her hand.)* Ahh, lovely eyes!

LADY: You're a fast worker ain't yer!

MUSHI: No time to waste! Hitler coming! Chocolate raffle! Penny ticket!

LAURIE: I'm the guvnor here. What's your name son?

MUSHI: Er… Mush.

LAURIE: Mister Mush, meet my barmaid, Ida, to you she's the Queen of England. You wanna work my pub mate, you give her a bar of chocolate first.

MUSHI: *(Gives chocolate.)* Queen Ida, salaam aleykum! A gift from East.

RENNIE: He's got some personality boy!

IDA: I like you Mister Mushi!

MUSHI moves over to EGG NOG and SHAH ABDUL.

MUSHI: Salaam aleykum!

EGG NOG / ABDUL: Aleykum salaam!

MUSHI: My post office Sandwip.

SHAH ABDUL: Unagon.

EGG NOG: Mirganjbazar –

MUSHI: – near Badeshwar?!

EGG NOG: Yes!

MUSHI: All Sylheti Brothers! Chocolate raffle! Penny ticket!

He approaches DEBORAH at the piano. LOVERS MUSICAL STING. She buys a ticket.

Lovely eyes.

DEBORAH: I bet you say that to all the girls.

MUSHI: Yes I do. But with you I am not lying.

DEBORAH: Number thirteen?!

MUSHI: Thirteen lucky with Mister Mushi.

HUGO: This better be proper chocolate – alright!

MUSHI: All man working clothes. What you do?

RENNIE: Go on Debs! Tell him what you do!

Chord on the piano. The Gracie Fields song. The whole pub joins in on the chorus.

Song: Thingummybob

The song ends.

IDA: It is an'all!

MUSHI: Queen Ida! Please! Make draw!

He offers the hat with all the tickets in to IDA to draw. Comic chord on the piano.

IDA: The winning ticket is…number thirteen!

DEBORAH: *(Screams.)* It's me!

She kisses MUSHI and takes the chocolate. MUSHI grabs her arm.

HUGO: Get your fucking black paws off her alright!

Chilled silence. HUGO approaches MUSHI and nuts him. MUSHI falls to the ground bleeding. An air raid siren. The pub empties, not in a panic, but with urgency. DEBORAH and MUSHI leave together.

DEBORAH: Air raid. Tube'll be rotten crowded. I know where we can be alone.

MUSHI: Oh fuck! Sorry I only got Merchant Navy English. Shit, bastard, fuck.

DEBORAH: I like you, Mister Mushi, you got personality.

MUSHI: How you spell Deborah?

DEBORAH: D. E. B. O. R. A. H.

MUSHI: Seven letters beginning with D.

DEBORAH: This is my Nan's shelter. She don't use it.

She links arms and pulls him into the Anderson shelter. The drone of the Luftwaffe begins

I love your skin. You're beautiful.

She kisses him, properly.

MUSHI: Are you maiden?

DEBORAH: Cheeky. Mind your own business. What
about you?

MUSHI: Many commercial ladies. Every port – jiggy jiggy!

DEBORAH: Know what you doing then, eh? I like the war. Got
me own money, wear what I like, do what I like. I don't
want babies, well I wouldn't mind a girl. Be frightened
Mushi. You gotta feel it.

MUSHI: I'm scared.

DEBORAH: They bomb the docks, and the docks are a little
spit away. Hold me.

MUSHI holds her. A kiss.

The trick is to do something to stop thinking about the
bombs.

She kisses him. A bomb falls, not that far off.

MUSHI: Agh!

DEBORAH: It missed us Mushi. It killed someone else.

MUSHI: Oh no, no, no!!

DEBORAH: Don't think about them, think about this.

She puts his hand on a breast.

Is that nice? Ha! I know that's nice, I can feel you.

MUSHI: Oh fuck!

DEBORAH: You're funny. Lie down.

*MUSHI lies down. She slips the rest of her overalls off and gets in
beside him. They make love during the bombing. Morning. MUSHI
and DEBORAH asleep in each other's arms. On the street, ARPs and
FIREMEN bring the dead out from Bethnal Green tube.*

MILKMAN: Morning! Bomb hit the tube then?

FIREMAN 1: Na. Panic stampede. Hundred and seventy dead.

MILKMAN: Would you Adam and Eve it eh!? That's Harvey Kleinman. I'll tell his missus shall I?

FIREMAN 2: Someone has to.

MILKMAN: Yeah, but it's not usually the fucking milkman is it! Ha, ha!

MILKMAN goes off with a chuckle and a whistle and knocks on the Kleinmans' door. At this point HUGO and BENNY enter carrying a stolen wireless each.

Oh yeah, the early bird catches the worm.

HUGO: You wanna watch it mate, awight?!

MILKMAN: Fuck off you little dick. Benny, get your muvver out here. I need a word.

IDA opens the door. BENNY and HUGO go in.

(Handing over the milk.) Morning Ida. Pint of steri, pint of gold top.

IDA: Ta. What?

MILKMAN: Er… I've got some bad… I've got access to a bit of Cheddar.

IDA: Alright.

Cheddar handed over.

What is it Ted?

MILKMAN: There's been a panic stampede. Down the tube.

IDA: Oh no. Harvey. My Harvey! Is he alright?

MILKMAN: No. He's brown bread.

IDA goes off to the tube, wailing. Leaving MILKMAN on his own.

That went quite well I think.

MILKMAN moves off with a whistle. IDA stands over HARVEY's body.

IDA: I fucking loved him! I give him the whole of my life! DEBORAH!!!

DEBORAH wakes up. IDA sets off to the Anderson shelter. IDA opens the door without knocking. MUSHI sleeps on.

(Breaking up.) I don't think I can go on without him.

DEBORAH: Dad? Oh no. You got Benny. You got me.

IDA: Yeah. Who the fuck is that?

DEBORAH: Mister Mushi.

IDA: The chocolate raffle fellah?

DEBORAH: Yeah.

IDA: We'll be alright for chocolate then. Is he gentle wiv yer?

DEBORAH: I'm not gonna talk about it mum.

IDA: *(Breaking up.)* Your dad made love to me like a fucking film star!

DEBORAH: Put the kettle on. I'll be there in a tick.

LAURIE and RENNIE by an open grave.

LAURIE: I respected Harvey. You knew where you were with Harvey Kleinman.

RENNIE: He was a thief boy!

BENNY, HUGO, enter carrying the coffin. IDA and others follow. They start to lower the coffin.

LAURIE: He was an old fashioned East End thief. He'd break into your house, rob you blind, but he cared. That's the kind of inexplicable juxtaposition that makes the East End totally incomprehensible to outsiders.

IDA: I was gonna read a poem, out loud, but I've changed me mind. Instead I'm gonna say a word about Adolf Hitler – *(Breaking up.)* the man who has taken the love of my life from me! That word is 'CUNT!'

ALL: *(Murmurs of approval / and 'yeah cunt's / 'Hitler, what a cunt' etc.)*

IDA: Do you know what your dad would want most now girl?

DEBORAH: For me to marry Hugo.

IDA: And have a little baby girl. We could call her Harvey, after your dad.

DEBORAH: I was fourteen when I got engaged mom. Hugo was my first kiss.

IDA: This war's ruined you, who do you think you are?

DEBORAH: I'm the girl that makes the thing that drills the hole that holds the spring that drives the rod that turns the knob that works the thingummybob, mum.

IDA: Marry Hugo, then we can trust him. It's important in our line of work. You ain't a suffragette no more, so stop behaving like one, or you might get knocked down by an 'orse. You spent last night with a wog! What's all that about?

DEBORAH: I was alive in the morning. That's what that was about.

Enter MUSHI.

MUSHI: Deborah?!

BENNY: Not now mate! Alright!?

MUSHI looks at DEBORAH, she turns away. HUGO and BENNY follow MUSHI outside.

HUGO: Oi! Chocolate! I'm her fiancé.

MUSHI: English not good.

BENNY: That's not English mate, that's French.

HUGO: I'm gonna marry her.

MUSHI: No, no, no! You don't understand. She's mine. God, four centuries ago

BENNY grabs him by the throat.

BENNY: – Shut it! You fucking curried monkey.

Enter ATTAR with SHAH ABDUL, and EGG NOG. ATTAR is carrying the book.

ATTAR: Please accept my commiserations on the death of your father.

BENNY: You knew him?

ATTAR: I was burgled once, I presume it was him.

BENNY lets go of MUSHI. BENNY and HUGO back off.

BENNY: The wedding's tomorrow. You're not invited.

HUGO: One on one, you're fucking nothing!

HUGO and BENNY leave.

MUSHI: Master Attar. I can't live without her.

ATTAR: You'll die then. But you still have to work. Egg Nog needs a rice cook for his stupid cafe.

MUSHI: But I only cook rice on deck of ship.

EGG NOG: Easy menu, dal, rice, tikka chicken.

ATTAR: Egg Nog has set up a halal butchery.

MUSHI: Where?

EGG NOG: In my bathroom.

They enter the curry house.

See, tables, chairs, very nice.

ATTAR: And totally empty.

EGG NOG: All Indian lascars will come. Then the English.

ATTAR: Englishmen will never eat curry, they don't have the arse for it.

Bell as customers enter. EGG NOG leaves. ATTAR gets out the letters.

MUSHI: Why have you got the ship book?

ATTAR: In a minute. First your letters. Your father says 'Thank you for the money. Send some more, quick. Your uncle wants you to marry his daughter, your cousin. Anjum.' Photograph. Ugh! Very dark.

ATTAR gives MUSHI the letter and the photo. Enter EGG NOG.

EGG NOG: An Englishman with his wife! He want chicken!

ATTAR: Not chicken tikka! It's too dry! Drown the whole thing in gravy.

EGG NOG: No! Just put some rice on there Mushi.

ATTAR: Ah, don't listen to me, only been in England thirty years!

MUSHI: I can't marry my cousin. I must make twins with Deborah and the boy twin will bring the whole world to God.

ATTAR: Mushi, I ran away to sea because they beat me until I learned the Koran.

MUSHI: You are hafiz?!

ATTAR: I can recite the Koran in Arabic, a language I do not speak. One day I read it in Bengali. Next day, I read the Bible, Old Testament. The day after that, the Bible, New Testament. By the end of the week I was knackered. None of those books mention dinosaurs. The Koran is the word of God and he forgot to mention dinosaurs!

MUSHI: No God for you then?

ATTAR: I'm a trade unionist, a socialist, and an atheist. That's the full box set.

MUSHI: You will go hell Master Attar. For me, paradise.

ATTAR: This is the only paradise you will ever know!

MUSHI: What? Bethnal Green?

ATTAR: Shattering isn't it?!

EGG NOG exits with the plate.

Mushi, my friend, I am going back home.

MUSHI: No! We need you here!?

ATTAR: The war at sea is over, so for Sylhet, that's the end of the killing. Six thousand lascars dead and I am the only man who knows their names. The book. I didn't know how to tell you, but SS Clan MacArthur –

MUSHI: – no, no, no!

ATTAR: Torpedoed east of Madagascar. Two weeks after you jumped ship.

MUSHI: Little Taz?!

ATTAR: All lascars dead. For Taz, I was thinking maybe, Tassaduq.

MUSHI: Yes, must be.

ATTAR: Our people need to know who died, and who lives. I will take the book from village to village. You will now be the top man in Bethnal Green.

MUSHI: Me?! Why not Egg Nog, why not Shah Abdul?

ATTAR: Personality.

MUSHI: Do I have to dress like Noël Coward?

ATTAR: No, that's a personal thing. Make Englishmen of these boys, that is the highest goal, and not easy, many English are not worthy of the title.

Enter EGG NOG carrying the chicken tikka, untouched.

EGG NOG: Too dry. He wants gravy. Masala up anything. Quick!

ATTAR: Tomato, spices, cream –

EGG NOG: Don't put cream in there! Tomato and cream, are you fucking mad!?

ATTAR: English like cream in everything!

EGG NOG: Stop it! Never seen such a bloody mess! What the hell do I call that!?

ATTAR: *(Laughing.)* Tikka disaster!

MUSHI: No. Chicken tikka masala.

ATTAR exits, with hugs leaving EGG NOG and MUSHI to carry on. In the street.

NEWS VENDOR: Hitler dead! Germany surrenders! West Ham fixtures!

A street party combined with wedding reception. Everyone.

IDA: We lost yer dad but we got fru!

Enter HUGO as groom, BENNY as best man. DEBORAH puts on a veil and takes HUGO's hand. Confetti. ATTAR and MUSHI watch as HUGO carries her across the threshold of IDA's house. A NEWSPAPER VENDOR comes on to the street. His cries and newspaper selling is accompanied by an animated history of the 1950s and 60s. On each line below the NEWS VENDOR sells one paper

NEWS VENDOR: Britain and France invade Suez!

Beatlemania sweeps Britain!

John Lennon marries!

Beatles bigger than Jesus!

West Ham win World Cup!

Paul marries!

John marries Yoko!

Beatles split!

1970 something. EGG NOG's curry house transforms into MUSHI's curry house defined by the grotesque mural style depictions of paradise, and a photo of the West Ham team. DEBORAH walks in wearing a skirt above the knee.

MUSHI: Deborah! I can see your knickers! In my country you would be stoned!

DEBORAH: I'm not in your country. You're in mine.

MUSHI: You have never eaten in my restaurant in thirty years.

DEBORAH: I thought this place was Egg Nog's.

MUSHI: Egg Nog is a gambler, the greyhounds. He'd put money on the hare if the odds were good. I paid off his debts in 1952. He gave me the lease. Nice, yes? How you say in English…subtle?

DEBORAH: Hugo won't come in here.

MUSHI: Does he know about us?

DEBORAH: Dunno. He's not stupid.

MUSHI: That was thirty years ago.

DEBORAH: The one thing he can do well is bear a grudge. I'm only here cos he's in the Scrubs. Unfortunately he's getting out next week.

She sits at a table. MUSHI gives her a menu. She looks at it.

MUSHI: Your legs, I remember, they go all the way up don't they?!

DEBORAH: Why ain't you married Mushi?

MUSHI: I am married. I just didn't want to tell you.

DEBORAH: Is she here?

MUSHI: I hope not. She's supposed to be in Chittagong. *(MUSHI shows a photo.)* That's her. Anjum. My cousin.

DEBORAH: Is that allowed in Bangladesh? Marrying your cousin.

MUSHI: Allowed?! It's nearly bloody compulsory. Three daughters. Rayhana, Anika, and little Labiba. I watch you. You don't have children.

DEBORAH: It ain't a proper marriage. I'm not home every night. I'm gonna go down the housing, get me own place. I woulda liked a little girl.

MUSHI: Life is not for fun! Not for women anyway! You've left it too late!

DEBORAH starts crying, and stands to leave.

DEBORAH: Yeah, alright, don't rub it in. I think I'd better go.

MUSHI: That night in the blitz is the single most beautiful thing that has ever happened to me.

He grabs her arm.

Sorry. Goodbye.

DEBORAH: You got hold of my arm Mushi.

He lets her go. She leaves. Enter SHAH ABDUL, and EGG NOG.

EGG NOG: Mushi, we need your advice. How do we bring wife over?

SHAH ABDUL: I don't like English Betty. All powder and paint. Must marry Muslim.

MUSHI: What will Indian country girl do here? Sit indoors all day, crying! You boys work hard, send money home, when you fifty, fuck off back Chittagong, marry Miss World, stay in bed all day like Georgie Best! Women and children will never come! Only if three things happen. One – big flooding in Sylhet –

NEWS VENDOR: – Cyclone devastates Northern India! No local people involved.

MUSHI: Two – Pakistan civil war.

NEWS VENDOR: Pakistan troops invade Bengal!

SHAH ABDUL: What three?

MUSHI: *(Looking over shoulder at NEWS VENDOR.)* Three – er… I dunno, British government threaten to bang door shut on Indians for good.

NEWS VENDOR: New Immigration Act! Next year! Read the details!

MUSHI: Better get the women over double quick!

During the song – the women and children arrive. The women wear saris with an Indian and Hindu influence. The RABBI shakes hands with SHAH ABDUL and hands over the keys. The Islamic crescent replaces the Star of David.

Song: Babi He Write Me Come!

ANJUM: Babi he write me come!

WOMEN: Rajrani London, Rajrani London

ANJUM: Babi he write me come!

WOMEN: London maya! London maya!

ANJUM: I tell him I got no English tongue

WOMEN: Cholit Basha Cholit Basha

ANJUM: Across the seven seas and thirteen rivers
               There is a paradise.

               Many people love me in Sylhet
               Everything you want is very cheap
               My father died in my arms
               What you sow is what you reap
               God helped me, I got away
               Across the seven seas and thirteen rivers

Goodbye to Shah Jalal, I'll swear on my
  Koran
I'll never see my mother again

ANJUM: Babi he write me come

WOMEN: Rajrani London, Rajrani London

ANJUM: Babi he write me come!

WOMEN: London maya! London maya!

ANJUM: I tell him I got no English tongue

WOMEN: Cholit Basha Cholit Basha

ANJUM: Across the seven seas and thirteen rivers
                     there is a paradise

The housing office. MUSHI is there with ANJUM, and his three daughters. MUSHI is wearing a West Ham scarf. They are talking to BARRY, the housing officer. Populating the waiting room are EGG NOG, SHAH ABDUL with wives. Enter IDA and DEBORAH. They take a ticket.

BARRY: Right there's your keys!

MUSHI: Three bed Rothschild Buildings!

BARRY: Deborah Gaskin!

IDA: *(Standing.)* Right girl! Leave the swearing to me!

IDA sits before BARRY, DEBORAH stands behind.

BARRY: I have your age down here as –

IDA: – Don't you get arsey wiv me sunshine!

DEBORAH: – Mum?!

BARRY: Are you what the sociology books call an East End matriarch?

IDA: No! I'm her fucking muvver!

BARRY: You muvvers don't run the East End any more. This is the Welfare State, and this interview is with 'the individual applicant' Deborah Gaskin.

IDA: She's not a fucking individual, she's my daughter, English, and Befnal Green for generations!

BARRY: Mrs Deborah Gaskin. Are you homeless at the moment?

IDA: Course she ain't homeless, they're in with me ain't they!

BARRY: *(Writing.)* Not homeless. No points. Children?

DEBORAH: No, I ain't.

IDA: Her father, the only man I ever loved, died fighting Hitler. Ain't that worth a point? How are these fucking Pakis getting their points?

BARRY: Can I ask you madam to moderate your language.

IDA: I apologise. How are these fucking Pakistanis getting their points?

She picks up a chair and, starts smashing it up.

Were they homeless in Pakistan? Course they weren't! I betcha if she had brown skin you'd give her an house just like that!

BARRY joins a National Front gathering, with HUGO and BENNY. HUGO sprays NF on the wall and PAKIS OUT. Others sell BRITISH BULLDOG.

SPEAKER: So, it's official GLC policy to exclude whites from Brick Lane?

BARRY: Offer Bengalis housing anywhere else, they won't take it, don't feel safe.

HUGO: They want a Paki ghetto!

An orator, the SPEAKER, takes the stand. DEBORAH, IDA, and MUSHI are there.

SPEAKER: The tragedy of my lifetime has been to see this great nation contaminated by inferior cultures, but who has the guts to talk about the problem?! Only the National Front dare speak the truth. BRITAIN IS FULL!

Cheering. Particularly HUGO, and BENNY.

IDA: My girl can't get an house!

SPEAKER: It is GLC policy to exclude whites from public housing in Brick Lane.

BENNY: They just throw their rubbish out the windows!

MUSHI: They are Indian country girls, they never heard of rubbish collection.

SPEAKER: The National Front has a policy to end this self-inflicted decline through repatriation of coloured immigrants with financial compensation!

MUSHI: Good morning, I been here thirty years. I fought Hitler! This is my current wife, full British passport. I invented Chicken Tikka Masala, now British staple diet! How much cash for me to bugger off!?

DEBORAH: He don't mean you Mushi!

HUGO: He fucking does!

SPEAKER: We will never allow this corner of England to become a Pakistani ghetto!

MUSHI: 'Bangladeshi' ghetto. We won independence in nineteen seventy-one!

HUGO: Do you want some!

SPEAKER: March with me! Assert the right of the Englishman to the housing he built –

MUSHI: My house, Rothschild Buildings, was built by Jews!

SPEAKER: – to the schools and hospitals our taxes pay for!

They march off. In the pub. At the bar, IDA, RENNIE, LAURIE. At a table, DEBORAH.

IDA: Fucking Pakis!

DEBORAH: Mum!?

IDA: They come here, but they don't wanna be English!

LAURIE: And what is it that defines the English Ida?

IDA: I believe in certain fings.

RENNIE: Yes, like what?!

IDA: Tolerance!

DEBORAH: You been slagging them all day!

IDA: O' course I slag 'em, that's free speech innit!

RENNIE: Integration boy! Integration!

LAURIE: How's a Muslim woman gonna integrate round here?

IDA: Get your arse tattooed, a crack habit and seven kids by seven dads!

They laugh. Enter MUSHI with West Ham scarf. It goes quiet.

MUSHI: Pint of mad dog please Ida. Quiet! What's the matter?

RENNIE: Gonna West Ham Mushi?

MUSHI: No! They're playing The Arsenal. I refuse to spend ten quid to watch an offside trap.

MUSHI joins DEBORAH at the table.

Did you get a house?

DEBORAH: You're joking ain't yer.

MUSHI: Please don't vote National Front. Not you.

DEBORAH: I can't hate you Mushi, you're lovely.

MUSHI: I have a flat, over the restaurant. It has a bathroom. Come.

They exit to the street, hiding from HUGO and BENNY who are talking to JANICE standing outside her terraced house with a FOR SALE/SOLD.

BENNY: What's occurring Janice?

JANICE: Bought me house off the council yesterday, sold it today, thirty grand profit. Gonna go Redbridge.

HUGO: Redbridge is shit!

JANICE: Yeah, I know. But it ain't Pakistan. Knowhatimean.

HUGO: I'm gonna kill myself a Paki tonight!

BENNY: One on one, they're fucking nothing!

MUSHI and DEBORAH are in the flat. It is a beautiful bedroom, with drapes, textiles, cushions. In the middle is the single bed from the Anderson shelter. Evening to night.

DEBORAH: That's my Nan's bed, from the shelter.

MUSHI: Yes. Our bed. That junk shop on Roman Road.

DEBORAH: Are you alright Mushi, or are you a bit weird?

MUSHI: I love you. That's all.

DEBORAH: I had a boyfriend couple of years ago, he had a mouth like yours. When I was with him I used to shut my eyes, and imagine he was you.

MUSHI: Kissing is very dangerous.

DEBORAH: Let's burn the house down.

They kiss. Dark falls. They spend the night together. On the street, BENNY and HUGO wait near the mosque. EGG NOG comes out, alone. They follow him, and walk either side of him.

HUGO: Poppadom, poppadom, poppadom…

BENNY: Got the right time, mate? I don't want Paki time. Ha!

EGG NOG: No watch, sorry boss.

HUGO: Just tell him the fucking time, you curried piece of shit!

EGG NOG: Going home, Bethnal Green Road.

They grab him. EGG NOG tries to remove HUGO's restraining hand.

BENNY: Don't you dare call Bethnal Green 'home'.

They both kick as EGG NOG offers no resistance. HUGO stabs him, killing him.

HUGO: See, I told yer, one on one they're fucking nothing!

BENNY: Chuck the knife.

HUGO chucks the knife off into the wings.

And get rid of that shirt.

HUGO: He's ruined it! I only nicked it yesterday. Your mum'll wash it for us.

HUGO and BENNY move off quickly. The sun comes up on the body of EGG NOG. CAMILLA opens her door to go to work. Sirens. ST JOHN follows her out into the street.

CAMILLA: What I love about Spitalfields, is the eclectic mix, all humanity is here.

ST JOHN: And the houses are cheaper than Hampstead.

CAMILLA: Hampstead? Yuk! All that sterile homogeneity! We're in the East End now St John, to live, to work, to make a difference.

ST JOHN: I think I've made a terrible mistake. I've married Sidney Poitier!

Sirens, a POLICEMAN attends the body. Bangladeshis gather round the corpse.

CAMILLA: A murder! Right on our doorstep. Oh, it's so visceral!

ST JOHN: Someone's been killed, and you sound pleased?

CAMILLA: I did my VSO in Cambodia. I need this edge or else I can't function.

She walks off to work.

ST JOHN: *(Shouted after her.)* You work in a library!

A couple of doors further along the street HUGO leaves, with a surreptitious glance to the dead body. IDA steps out after him.

IDA: Oi! What's with this washing then?

HUGO: Yeah. Industrial accident. Is that alright? Mum?

IDA: Yeah. Go on. Off you go.

In the mosque, the Bangladeshi men. Essentially in two factions, the older lascar types and the first generation, more militant, armed with sticks.

SHAH ABDUL: Let us not forget the teachings of Shah Jalal, must love fellow man.

NAZ: We gotta get ourselves some defence force.

SHAH ABDUL: My son, how dare you interrupt your father!

NAZ: Yeah, you're my father, and I respect you and all that, but if the police ain't gonna do nofing, we gotta do it for ourselves innit! Revenge!

SHAH ABDUL: Man kills man, son kill son, cousin kill cousin?! No! Everyone, go home, knock on neighbor door, say Salaam Aleykum. Peace be with you.

NAZ: I ain't gonna be knocking on no doors! We gotta defend our territory, we gotta arm ourselves, gotta fight back!

SHAH ABDUL: Quiet please! Let our community leader speak!

MUSHI: My first night in this country. Policeman, like Dixon of Dock Green, helped me find Master Attar house. 'England people very nice!' I say. He say 'Son, there's good and bad in all'. Such wisdom. One skinhead kill one of us doesn't mean all England people bad! We must behave like Englishmen, march to Parliament –

NAZ: – like good little Pakis!?

MUSHI: – I came this country to work, not to fight in the streets!

NAZ: That might be true for you old men, yeah, but I was born here! These streets is ours yeah, them skinheads ain't even got no right to come here!

Uproar. The young walk out. The crowd disperses. SHAH ABDUL approaches MUSHI.

SHAH ABDUL: You direct descendant Shah Jalal! Your father, direct descendant Shah Jalal! Your job – make twins! Give boy to mosque, then we have leader with blood Shah Jalal! But what did you do with sacred legacy Shah Jalal?! You opened curry house called it Shah Jalal Tandoori!

MUSHI: Yes, I have failed, all time in England, only interested in money, drinking. I blame Master Attar. He sent me to Natural History museum, learn about dinosaurs. And I lost my faith.

SHAH ABDUL: That big dinosaur, diplodocus, it's plastic.

MUSHI: No!? Is it?! But why didn't Allah tell the prophet about dinosaurs?

SHAH ABDUL: Do you shout your mouth off about your cock ups!?

MUSHI: Of course, Allah not want to look silly.

SHAH ABDUL: Go hajj, make pilgrimage to Mecca, remind Allah that you still fear him.

MUSHI: I'm too young for hajj, and anyway I don't like camping.

SHAH ABDUL: You one man! Our community, many people, you must make sacrifices!

MUSHI: OK, OK, I will lay with Deborah, try and make those twins.

SHAH ABDUL: Inshallah.

The BRICK LANE MASSIVE come out of the martial arts club. They're variously armed.

Song: Brick Lane Boys

>Gonna go Chicksand cut through Spellman
>hang out Hanif bottom of Redman
>Burn down Diss Street tear through Clare
> Street
>Black mocassins like wheels on my feet
>Gonna go Brick Lane
>Gonna go insane
>Sex and pills let loose in my brain
>Brick Lane BoyZ Brick Lane BoyZ
>Curtains hairstyles, cars like toys
>Brick Lane BoyZ Brick Lane BoyZ
>Get together and make some noise
>Faz is a pill boy, Raz is a crack head
>Nizam's gotta get a girl into bed
>All street fighters, and brown rap writers
>Red box igniters and rude girl delighters
>Gonna go Brick Lane
>Gonna go insane
>Sex and pills let loose in my brain

During the next a lone skinhead, is knocked down, then hands over a street sign. Then he gets up, is knocked down again and hands over another street, knocked down again etc.

> Warden, Nelson, Sugar Loaf, Wellington
> Fournier, Rhoda, Old Nichol Street
> Brady, Buxton, Russia, Hoxton,
> Hopetown, Hanbury, Jamaica Street
> Brick Lane BoyZ Brick Lane BoyZ
> Curtains hairstyles, cars like toys
> Brick Lane BoyZ Brick Lane BoyZ
> Get together and make some noise

ST JOHN enters. He has a laptop in a case on a shoulder strap. They surround him.

NAZ: What have you got for me today man?

ST JOHN: You don't want to mug me. I live round here.

NAZ: We ain't gonna jack you man? Don't wanna disrespek ya. We just want de laptop, and yo cash yeah? And dat nice watch innit. Alright. Easy?!

ST JOHN suddenly spins away and twirls his lap top round with the shoulder strap. They laugh.

ST JOHN: Come and get it! I'm army trained! Who wants to die first!?

One of them takes his legs from under him and then they kick him badly. They take his laptop. MUSHI comes on the scene.

MUSHI: Get off him! Naz, I know your father, religious man, and look at you!

NAZ: Go chew khat old man.

MUSHI: *(Helping ST JOHN.)* Here, can you stand? I apologise on behalf of Bangladesh. Our young boys don't respect their elders.

ST JOHN: That's something they've learned from us.

MUSHI: Ah! So you're a liberal!

ST JOHN: How can you tell?

MUSHI: Only a liberal blames himself when he gets mugged.

They shake hands and MUSHI leaves. In the flat. DEBORAH is there, enter ANJUM.

DEBORAH: Oh my God!

ANJUM: Don't scare! I am his current wife.

DEBORAH: Anjum? Nice to meet you.

ANJUM: He's a good lover isn't he? Very quick. He give me three lovely girls.

ANJUM shows her a framed photograph.

Labiba, good English, all poetry; Rayhana, she like children. Anika, she want go University, but very lucky, I find her husband. I don't mind you / him just afternoons. No-one know, OK?

Enter MUSHI.

Thumy dong dheksony, armi thumur fiet safkormu. Bashtar Kowari!

ANJUM leaves. During the next MUSHI starts to undress in preparation for love making.

DEBORAH: What did she say?

MUSHI: She's not that keen on cleaning this flat. Now! I have to make love to you, properly, not to pass the time but to make twins! The boy I give to the mosque, the girl you can keep.

DEBORAH: I'm married to Hugo.

MUSHI: Come on! I've got the whole community on my back!

DEBORAH: There'll be a girl? I can keep the girl?

MUSHI: Yes! I've got bloody three already. Get your kit off!

DEBORAH: If I get pregnant, there's gonna be a bump. Hugo –

MUSHI: – You divorce Hugo, marry me.

DEBORAH: What about your wife, Anjum?

MUSHI: What's it got to do with her?!

DEBORAH: Come on then sailor, make love to me.

They kiss. Pockets of people are watching TV. There is a collective gasp as the first plane hits the towers.

What was that?

MUSHI: It sounded like the whole world screaming.

DEBORAH: I love these moments, when there's only me and you.

The second plane hits the towers. A second collective gasp.

What the bloody hell is that?!

MUSHI: Something really very terrible is happening. Wait here!

MUSHI runs out into the street.

SHAH ABDUL: Mushi! Terrorists fly airliner into twin towers.

MUSHI: What?! Wembley!?

SHAH ABDUL: New York, World Trade Centre.

MUSHI: No! This is all my fault! Lord, forgive me, I am trying now, I am trying.

In the pub. The usual suspects.

LAURIE: Says here, terrorists go to paradise where there's seventy-two sex slaves each, as much booze as you can drink, and lots of beautiful fountains.

RENNIE: I bet there's a fuck of a queue for the fountains boy!

Enter BARRY.

LAURIE: Alright Barry!?

IDA: You're that bloke from the housing! I ain't serving you!

BARRY: I told you Mrs Kleinman, the only way you're gonna get a council house if you're white is tell your doctor you're suicidal – pills is points.

IDA: I went to my doctor, told him I was suicidal, he wunt give me no pills, he offered me fucking counselling!

LAURIE: What you doing in my manor then Barry?

BARRY: Giving houses away to refugees. This one's got three wives.

IDA: It's illegal innit, whatsaname.

LAURIE: Polygamy.

BARRY: He gets full social for the first wife, thirty quid each for the other two. That's how fucking illegal it is.

IDA: Laurie, I'm off down York Hall for me whatsaname.

LAURIE: Women-only naked steam.

IDA leaves.

RENNIE: Women-only naked steam eh?! Be like Muslim heaven boy!

LAURIE: Seventy-two?! That's an unnecessary amount of sex slaves innit. I'd be happy enough with thirty or forty.

BARRY: You not getting enough Laurie?!

LAURIE: The last time I had sex, not only was Gary Glitter a free man, he was in the charts.

In the street. NAZ and RAYHANA are whitewashing over a Spearmint Rhino poster. LABIBA is handing out Sharia law leaflets. Passers by take leaflets. LABIBA is in hijab, RAYHANA in niqab.

LABIBA: Take a leaflet bruvver, and you muvver, read and discover. We're celebrating the Shaheed today, the ones wot blew you away, Mohammad Attar, who is now a martyr, and the glorious 19, the mujahideen, living clean in the Deen. Yeah.

Enter IDA she addresses the next line to the painters.

IDA: Oi! You can't do that!

NAZ: Go home, get dressed, whore!

IDA: What you call me yer little twat?!

LABIBA: He call ya a whore lady. Yeah.

NAZ: You're gonna have to dress modest round here now! Showing your everything, what are you grandma, sixty, seventy!

IDA: I could fucking eat you and spit you out! Hang on, I know your father! Oi Mushi, you seen this!?

MUSHI: Naz, ah, good you got a job at last eh?

IDA: Yeah, you're Shah Abdul's lad. You're the drug dealer.

NAZ: I don't mess with that shit no more.

LABIBA: He fought his personal jihad against drugs, yeah, come out glorious and victorious. Yeah.

RAYHANA: Don't get involved Dad.

MUSHI: Don't call me Dad! I'm old enough to be your father!

RAYHANA: You are my father.

MUSHI: Agh! Labiba! And Rayhana! Why you both gone hijabi?!

LABIBA: We celebrating, Sheik Osama, 9/11, and the mujahadeen in heaven.

MUSHI: Celebrating 9/11, in the street?! You've gone mad!?

LABIBA: The ummah is strong, this is our year, we got no fear.

MUSHI: Stop bloody rhyming will you!

RAYHANA: We're gonna clean up this manor with the Sharia Dad.

MUSHI: Where's Anika? Has she gone hijabi?

LABIBA: Anika is lost to her sisters. We gonna declare her Takfir.

MUSHI: Takfir! Don't talk about your sister like that. Go home! Stop this. Later, I'll give you both the maximum bollocking. Naz!? I'm going to see your father now!

MUSHI goes to the Mosque to find SHAH ABDUL, who is coughing.

I have bad news for you my friend. Your son is mentally ill. He's celebrating 9/11 in the middle of Whitechapel Market.

SHAH ABDUL: I want to beat him, but I am weak.

MUSHI: Your lungs are like mine, full of Merchant Navy coal.

SHAH ABDUL: *(Coughs.)* He is a wild man now.

MUSHI: Drugs?

SHAH ABDUL: No thanks, I'll have a lie down later.

MUSHI: My daughters gone hijabi, and they bully my wife into niqab! One minute I'm living with four beautiful Indian women, next minute I've got a house full of bloody Arabs!

SHAH ABDUL stands, picks up some library books.

SHAH ABDUL: Come with me.

MUSHI: Where are we going?

SHAH ABDUL: I have a meeting with the top lady in Tower Hamlets. Naz has been reading books from the council library.

MUSHI: I was looking for heroin one day under Labiba's bed, and I find all jihadi books from the library, and even worse –

SHAH ABDUL: – *(Stopping in his tracks.)* Terrorism manuals?

MUSHI: – no, the books were all overdue.

SHAH ABDUL: Our community lacking leadership. Is she pregnant yet?

MUSHI: Don't put the pressure on.

SHAH ABDUL: Maybe you're firing blanks.

MUSHI: No! I've been tested. I had to give a sample. They didn't give me a DVD, magazine, nothing.

SHAH ABDUL: What did you do?

MUSHI: I had to close my eyes and think of Shilpa Shetty.

CAMILLA's office in the town hall. She has access to a computer. Enter SHAH ABDUL and MUSHI.

CAMILLA: Salaam Aleykum

SHAH ABDUL: Hi.

CAMILLA: How can I help?

SHAH ABDUL: In Bethnal Green, we are from Sylhet, our Islam you could call it Sufi, our path to Allah is meditation, music, devotional poetry –

MUSHI: – we don't fly aeroplanes into buildings!

SHAH ABDUL: This your library book, my son renewed it seven times. *Milestones* –

MUSHI: – How many copies do you have? Ask the computer!

CAMILLA types in a search on the laptop.

SHAH ABDUL: Sayyid Qutb, author, hates the West. Hates! Everything!

CAMILLA: Tower Hamlets libraries have eleven copies of *Milestones.*

MUSHI: Eleven!? Bloody hell!

SHAH ABDUL: Mushi's daughters have books by –

MUSHI: – and tapes. Bilal Philips. How many copies you have!?

CAMILLA types in a search.

SHAH ABDUL: This man preaches all Wahhabi. This is all crazy Saudi Islam as political ideology. Nothing to do with Sylhet! He is Jamaican convert!

CAMILLA: Bilal Philips – eighty books and tapes.

MUSHI: *(Standing.)* Eighty! You are using my taxes to teach my children to hate their own country!

CAMILLA: I am committed to delivering equivalent services regardless of race, religion, gender, disability or sexual orientation. And, I didn't become a professional librarian to ban books.

SHAH ABDUL: Me, two years German prisoner of war camp. If you stock one copy *Mein Kampf,* that free speech, you stock eighty copies, you Nazi yourself!

Beat. Then an explosion, they all stand, there is a second, louder, explosion, followed by a third explosion, then a fourth. In the pub. LAURIE, BARRY, IDA and RENNIE is dancing with joy.

RENNIE: – Rivers of blood! Ha, ha, ha! Enoch Powell was right boy! He only got one thing wrong! It's not us boy! It's not us! Ha, ha!

LAURIE: I'm not BNP Barry, but these tube bombings gotta be good for you eh?

BARRY: We're absolutely fucking flying mate. Little things help. Today Tower Hamlets banned Christmas decorations in the offices. Health and Safety.

RENNIE: Health and Safety my arse!

IDA: My women-only naked steam, that's gone, gotta dress modest now. That's my culture that is, since way back, before the whatsanames –

LAURIE: – Romans.

RENNIE: How do you dress modest in a women-only naked steam?

LAURIE: I would consider voting BNP, if you had some black candidates.

BARRY: It won't be long before my party does have a black candidate. After 9/11, and today, skin colour is irrelevant. Culture. That's where the battle is. Take Rennie, he's black, but he's as British as hot tea in a flask.

RENNIE: We came here to work!

BARRY: But to Islamists he's a kaffur.

RENNIE: What's that boy?

BARRY: Kaffur. It means nigger. You're a nigger again Rennie, how's that make you feel? The good news is, I'm a kaffur an'all. We're brothers.

BARRY exits. RENNIE is distressed, contemplative. LAURIE moves over to comfort him.

LAURIE: If you take a little plastic Santa Claus, file his head down to a point, then poke yourself in the eye with it repeatedly. You could hurt yourself.

RENNIE doesn't laugh. He looks at LAURIE and stands, and leaves the pub, passing MUSHI and DEBORAH as they enter. DEBORAH is crying. They find a table, away from LAURIE/RENNIE.

IDA: What's the matter doll?

MUSHI: Twins! We've had the scan down the London!

IDA: I'm gonna be a fucking grandmuvver!

DEBORAH: – Mum! This is not good news! I'm married to Hugo!

IDA: I can put Hugo in the Scrubs for good. He killed Egg Nog.

MUSHI: Hugo kill Egg Nog?!

IDA: He give me his shirt to wash. Covered in blood it was, brand new Ben Sherman. I never washed it. I didn't want to be a whatsaname –

LAURIE: – accessory to the crime.

IDA: I bought the exact same shirt, put it through the wash. I got the blood stained Ben Sherman in the freezer in the back room here.

MUSHI: Champion! Ida take the bag down to the police station. Hugo goes to prison for evermore, and we can all get married!

IDA: What? Deborah marry you and move in. What about your wife? What about your daughters?

MUSHI: My daughters? No worries! They're all good girls.

In MUSHI's. LABIBA and RAYHANA with a computer. RAYHANA is on the mouse. Enter ANIKA.

LABIBA: Just click download man!

RAYHANA: Snow White and the Seven Dwarfs?

LABIBA: Yeah, you teaching that shit at your nursery, yeah, and this scholar says it's a koof conspiracy, promoting promiscuity, in da Muslim community.

RAYHANA: Can't open it. It's a PDF file.

LABIBA: We ain't got Adobe Acrobat!? Where did dad pick up dis gay compu'er?

ANIKA: Comet.

LABIBA: Man! Comet is a washing machine shop.

ANIKA: OK sister, *you* explain how Snow White is an attack on Muslim marriage?

LABIBA: Innit obvious man?! You got one girl living wiv seven dwarves and there ain't one of them midgets big enough to marry her!

ANIKA: Dad bought us this computer to share, I've got Uni work I need to do.

RAYHANA: Facebook.

LABIBA: *(Laughing.)* Yeah, some kuffar poked you today innit. Gary!

RAYHANA: Gary wants to know can he come on your flashmob iftar if he ain't a Muslim.

ANIKA: How come you know my password?

RAYHANA / LABIBA: Sisters!

ANIKA: OK, I can see where you two been. Rule number one with this computer – don't dowload shit. There's three beheading videos filed in iTunes.

LABIBA: I can't watch them beheadings! I have to look at the floor man!

RAYHANA: You can't tell us wot to do when you're on Facebook all the time.

LABIBA: Grooming the kuffar!

RAYHANA: Have the mosque approved your 'flashmob iftar'?

ANIKA: We're giving charity, zakat, you remember zakat do you Rayhana?

RAYHANA: It ain't zakat what you're doing, giving food to alcoholics.

ANIKA: Zakat should be local. The hungry round here are in Museum Gardens.

LABIBA: Man! They're not 'the hungry', they're 'the pissed'.

RAYHANA: Them tramps in Museum Gardens ain't Muslims.

ANIKA: Where does it say that zakat is just for Muslims?

RAYHANA: Ain't that kinda obvious?

ANIKA: That might be your faith, but it ain't mine.

LABIBA: Don't talk about faith sister, you're takfir!

ANIKA: Hey, look who learned another Arab word today! If people see my flashmob iftar on telly, they might stop thinking that all British Muslims spend every evening sitting in the garage boiling down hair dye!

LABIBA: This is your public relations, you tryna make the nation, understand the situation, get less apprehensive, about the Muslim offensive.

ANIKA: Don't record your rhymes on this shared computer. We could end up in Paddington Green cos of that last rap or yours. Technically, it's criminal.

LABIBA: It ain't that bad, and it ain't a rap, it's resistance rhyme.

RAYHANA: Is it a new one?

LABIBA: 'Improperganda'.

RAYHANA: That's clever. I wanna hear it.

LABIBA: Sister, it ain't never too late look
to quit your kuffar Facebook,
paradise waitin'
stop procrastinatin'
hate the disbelievers
they tryna deceive us
they will never believe us
Sheik Osama lead us
Shakespeare was a gay boy
knowhatisayboy
he get in the way boy
promoting fornication
to the Muslim nation
is not a situation
get my participation

it's improperganda
I don't misunderstand ya
I'm gonna get clean
halal living in the deen
God Save the Queen
I won't standfa that hymn
I follow Mohammad
Peace be upon him!

RAYHANA: Woo!

ANIKA leaves the room with a slam of the door. In the pub. RENNIE sitting silent, uncommunicative. LAURIE is reading the paper. No IDA.

LAURIE: Alright Rennie?

RENNIE stares at his pint, doesn't reply.

Talk to me. You're my best mate, you cunt.

RENNIE: This young boy, spit at me in the Post Office.

LAURIE: No!

RENNIE: In the queue. All these veiled women, you should see the money they picking up boy! They must have enough children! You work, you pays your stamp! Every week a stamp!

LAURIE: That is the central concept of insurance, you got to pay in, to get out.

RENNIE: Five year old, six year old. He looked me in the eye and spat at me.

LAURIE: Let me get you a drink Rennie. Cockspur? A little taste of Barbados. A glass of sunshine.

LAURIE gets a bottle of Cockspur rum from behind the counter and two glasses. He rejoins RENNIE and pours out two glasses.

RENNIE: Yeah.

LAURIE: Cheers. I can't wait to tell Ida. Ha, ha! That'll get her going.

RENNIE: Where is she?

LAURIE: Down the London. Deborah's started. They reckon it's twins.

RENNIE: Twins! Come on boy! We'd better have another drink!

They drink again. IDA arrives, unseen by LAURIE, seen by RENNIE.

What about you and Ida? Have you ever tried it on?

LAURIE: The boat race ain't too bad. And, you don't look at the mantlepiece when you're poking the fire but there's one big problem with Ida.

RENNIE: She got one helluva temper boy!?

LAURIE: All that 'fucking this and fucking that' – that's all an act Rennie, deep down she's just a little girl who early on lost the love of her life, Harvey Kleinman. They was neighbours, in the Rothschild buildings. Hers was Irish Catholics, his was Jewish. But one day they got Ida in to rake the coals on the Sabbath, they can't work on the Sabbath can they, yeah, she was what they call the Shabbes Goy. And that's how she first met Harvey. It was love at first sight. He was six, she was five. They married as soon as they could, on her fourteenth birthday. What is the greatest love story ever told? Romeo and Juliet? Elizabeth Bennet and Colin Firth. No. Harvey Kleinman and Ida Houlihan. Why? Cos theirs was an impossible love, a forbidden love. They didn't even know it was wrong.

RENNIE: They got competition now – Deborah and Mushi.

LAURIE: Debs is only following in her mother's footsteps. Ida was the pioneer. The first. The Sherpa Tenzing of cross cultural romance. All these different faiths, why do they wanna live separate? They're scared. They fear the power of love, because love laughs at the manufactured made up madness of religion and culture. What Ida did was monumental, so even though Harvey's dead, he still fills her up.

(Cracks.) There'll never be room for me mate. Sorry, I've upset meself.

RENNIE: *(Standing.)* I gotta go boy.

RENNIE leaves. LAURIE turns aware that IDA is there.

LAURIE: Oh fuck! How long you been –

IDA: – long enough.

IDA: I'm a fucking grandma Laurie!

LAURIE: Where they all gonna live?

IDA: There's a flat empty on Mushi's landing, so they've gone down the housing today.

LAURIE: Good luck to 'em.

IDA: Harvey don't fill me up no more. I've got room for you Laurie.

LAURIE: Yeah? Well…what if er… I mean there's nothing to stop us, you know, you and me, we could be together properly, you know, in whatsaname.

IDA: – Holy matrimony?!

LAURIE: Yeah!

In the Steiner nursery. RAYHANA, is wearing a niqab. Enter CAMILLA and ST JOHN.

CAMILLA: This is Galaxy's father, St John. Rayhana is Mister Mushi's daughter.

ST JOHN: Hi.

ST JOHN offers his hand to be shaken, RAYHANA refuses to shake it.

CAMILLA: We love the Steiner method.

ST JOHN: We also love the Montessori method, but you're cheaper.

RAYHANA: Galaxy is a lovely girl and –

CAMILLA: – I think she's potentially extraordinary.

RAYHANA: Her use of the sensorial equipment is normal. Her reading –

CAMILLA: – She's dyslexic, isn't she!? I told you!

RAYHANA: – is normal. However, in creative activity she fails to use her imagination but simply regurgitates stories from Walt Disney.

CAMILLA: *(Devastated.)* Oh my God! Really?!

RAYHANA: If you ask her to draw a monster, she'll draw Shrek.

ST JOHN: Shrek is Dreamworks, not Disney.

RAYHANA: Does she watch a lot of American DVDs at home?

CAMILLA: We try to limit –

ST JOHN: – yes, she does. We're both very busy, self-obsessed, and normally, in the evenings, a bit pissed.

CAMILLA: St John's been mugged. He's changed. He's started reading the *Spectator.*

RAYHANA: It's not normal for a British child to take all her culture from America.

ST JOHN: I refuse to be lectured to about 'normality' by a woman wearing a two-man tent.

CAMILLA: St John!?

ST JOHN: The girls in this nursery wear headscarves. Is it normal for a British five-year-old never to feel the sun on the back of her neck? You refused to shake my hand. Is that 'normal' behaviour for a grown up?

CAMILLA: She can't shake your hand, you know that!

RAYHANA: I'm sorry you were mugged. Those boys in those gangs are not Muslims.

ST JOHN: And yet, in the street, they shout 'whore' at Camilla.

CAMILLA: I think that's meant as a compliment.

ST JOHN: What makes someone Muslim?

RAYHANA: I can only give ten minutes to each set of parents.

MUSHI and DEBORAH with the pram in the waiting room of the housing department. BARRY is there behind his screen. A family of Somalis are at the counter.

DEBORAH: If you think I'm gonna give my baby boy to Shah Abdul, you must be nuts!

MUSHI: The boy is haram to me! I have to give him to the mosque and will bring the whole world to God! What's the problem, you get to keep the bloody girl! We go straight to the mosque after we get this flat sorted.

DEBORAH: I am not giving a baby to Shah Abdul, an old man, dying of emphysema.

MUSHI: He can get baby milk delivered from Tesco.com.

The Somali family are given keys and leave.

Look, Somalis. He gave them keys. They don't even speak English.

DEBORAH: They're refugees Mushi, there's a war on in Somalia.

MUSHI: Yes, and who started it? They did!

BARRY: Mister Rasul!

MUSHI and DEBORAH and pram go forward to the counter.

DEBORAH: Hello Barry.

BARRY: I don't know you Deborah. I'm at work. Understood.

MUSHI: We are seven now in a three-bed, sixteen Rothschild House, but the flat across the landing is now empty, they've gone Redbridge, if you give us that flat, we'll all be together.

BARRY: Like a village? Eighteen Rothschild House…has just been allocated.

MUSHI: Look Barry, Rothschild House is long time all Bangladeshi block. Works very well, no skinheads, good sense of community. Are you telling me you've given that flat to Somalis? Are they British! British passport!?

BARRY: Most people find that it helps if you smash up that chair.

MUSHI: This one?

BARRY: Yeah.

MUSHI picks up the chair and during the next smashes it against the glass. Enter NAZ

MUSHI: You can't give our houses away to Africans! I love this country! What gives you the right to ruin my bloody country!

DEBORAH: Mushi!

NAZ: It's me dad innit. He's fing.

MUSHI: Fing?

NAZ: Yeah.

MUSHI: Oh no. Deborah, we have to go to the mosque now.

DEBORAH: I told you I ain't going.

NAZ: Is this him then? The direct descendant of Shah Jalal?

MUSHI: Yes, that is the holy man.

NAZ: The new imam says he wants him to speak at the next Friday prayers.

MUSHI: When's that?

NAZ: Friday.

DEBORAH: He can't speak. He's only a day old.

NAZ: Jesus Christ spoke straight away, in the cradle, that's true lady, believe, that is what the Koran say.

DEBORAH: You can have whatever grand expectations you bloody like of my baby, sunshine and I hope he disappoints you! Me? I'm his mother and I'll be happy if he gets into Tech College. *(To MUSHI.)* I'll be in the pub.

She leaves with the pram.

MUSHI: *(To NAZ.)* Don't worry Naz. She'll come round. Let's go to the mosque now, see your father.

In the pub. DEBORAH is there with the twins in the pram. LAURIE is wearing a wedding button hole, and IDA is a bit dressed up, but not overly. IDA staring into the pram.

IDA: Ain't she beautiful. And look at him! Look at his little whatsaname –

LAURIE: – Penis.

IDA: Face!

DEBORAH: Where you been mom?

IDA: Been down the registry office. How mad am I? I fucking married him.

DEBORAH: Congratulations. Did you think of inviting your own daughter?

IDA: Didn't want to make a fuss.

DEBORAH: Who was your witness? Rennie?

IDA: Supposed to be but he didn't turn up.

LAURIE: I'm worried about him.

DEBORAH: Not like him not to be sat there. Laughing.

IDA: Come on Debs! What is it? You can tell me, I'm your muvver!

DEBORAH: Mushi wants to give the boy to the mosque.

IDA: Why's that then?

DEBORAH: He's gonna save the world, or something.

IDA: I can beat that for a problem.

DEBORAH: Don't tell me. Hugo.

IDA: Our Benny went to see him today, in prison. They're letting him out next week. Good behaviour.

DEBORAH: That is all we need. Does he know about me and Mushi?

IDA: Yeah. He says he's gonna kick the shit outa you, and throw you out the house. For me, for grassing him up, he's gonna rip my head off and shit down me neck.

DEBORAH: What we gonna do mum?

In SHAH ABDUL's house. The body is laid out on the bed. NAZ is there, as is ANIKA, and the blind IMAM ie: IQBAL with false beard on, hooks for hands etc. MUSHI touches the corpse.

MUSHI: You crossed the seven seas and thirteen rivers looking for paradise. You got it now and no mistaking. You deserve it my friend.

LABIBA: Where's the boy dad?

MUSHI: Labiba!? Why aren't you in bloody school?

LABIBA: I bunked off innit, cos I wanna hear this new imam speak.

NAZ: He's gonna speak now, like a study circle. They won't let him in Brick Lane mosque.

MUSHI: Of course they won't, they're not stupid.

NAZ: We're getting a new mosque.

LABIBA: We're told, it's gonna be gold, gonna be fixed, for the Olympics.

MUSHI: What is he? Saudi?

NAZ: Yeah, all their oil yeah, is for the ummah, the caliphate.

LABIBA: Inshallah, mashallah!

The IMAM starts speaking.

IMAM: You Muslims living in the West, you care more about how often your bins are emptied, than how your women dress. If a farmer wants to judge a bull, he does not look at the bull, he has a look at what the cows are up to. And Allah will judge you! In *Jew York, (Laughs.)* my little joke, in *Jew York* the women there had no discipline. *(Laughs.)* And then they were disciplined! *(Laughs.)* A woman must suck the snot from your nostrils if you ask her to!

MUSHI stands in disgust, and makes to leave.

NAZ: You gotta bring the boy Mushi, tonight. He's ours.

LABIBA: The boy to you is haram, understan', we is halal, and you is dajal!

MUSHI leaves.

IMAM: A woman is like a piece of pure white silk. One stain on the white silk and that silk is shit forevermore.

(Laughs.) Ashahadu an la ilaha ill Allah wa ashahadu anna Muhammadar Rasullah.

The pub. IDA, LAURIE and DEBORAH with twins. They're still wearing button holes. Enter RENNIE. He has an overcoat on, and is carrying a suitcase.

IDA: Where you going love?

RENNIE: Home.

IDA: What d'yer mean home? Vallance Road's your home love.

RENNIE: Barbados.

LAURIE: No!?

RENNIE: Heathrow by two o'clock.

LAURIE: No liquids, no shaving foam, no jam. You can't take jam on a flight. How much jam have you got in there Rennie?

They look at the suitcase as if it might have a bomb in it.

RENNIE: Jam? I don't have no jam.

LAURIE: Terrorists, they've destroyed us, psychologically, since when have the English been terrified of marmalade?

IDA: You can't leave us Rennie. You got a good job. Fresh air, outdoors, nature.

RENNIE: I'm a postman.

DEBORAH: Bye Rennie.

RENNIE: Did you get a house?

DEBORAH: You're having a laugh ain'tcha. Wouldn't give us nothing.

RENNIE: Somalis?

DEBORAH: Yeah.

RENNIE: I got them living upstairs from me boy!

LAURIE: They're laughing at us.

DEBORAH hugs RENNIE.

IDA: Can we come wiv yer! We could claim whatsaname!

LAURIE: Political asylum.

RENNIE: Goodbye Ida.

RENNIE has gone.

LAURIE: I've known him years. I don't want no one else to sit in that chair!

Enter MUSHI.

DEBORAH: Mushi, I've decided, I'm not letting you give my boy away!

MUSHI: Those wannabe-Arabs are not getting our boy and that's final!

DEBORAH: Why have you changed your mind love?

MUSHI: They've all gone Wahabi!

DEBORAH: You're out of the frying pan and into the fire cos Hugo's getting out next.

MUSHI: Oh no!

IDA: He'll kill me, kill you, kill Deborah, and kill the twins.

MUSHI: Alright, let me think!?

DEBORAH: What are we gonna do Mushi? Where can we go?

MUSHI: I got it! Yes! I know where we can go, and be safe, and happy.

DEBORAH: Where?

MUSHI: Redbridge!

SNAP TO BLACK.

Act Four (Epilogue)

PHILIPPA: Terrific! I'm not going to give any notes, from now on, you're on your own. I just want to say thank you, and good luck tonight.

YAYAH: Can I say something please! Thank you! Iqbal wants to say something.

IQBAL: Many of us were sceptical about a play showing how England *welcomed* immigrants, mainly because we are here imprisoned.

Some laughter.

TAHER: Take the beard off!

YAYAH: Shut up man, he's making his speech!

IQBAL takes the beard off.

IQBAL: I left Yemen to seek asylum in England. I am not here to turn England into Yemen. If England ever does become Yemen, I will have to seek refuge in another country. Philippa, we wanted to buy you a present but the most expensive thing in the shop is a Snickers bar. Here it is, not just a chocolate bar but a metaphor for much love, and gratitude.

He gives the Snickers bar to PHILIPPA who is nearly in tears.

PHILIPPA: Thank you. Thank you. Oh God, I'm overcome, really. Thank you.

She starts to cry. Enter OFFICER KELLY. He's still in costume but wearing his Officer hat.

OFFICER KELLY: Right. Got some envelopes here. Tatyana, Elmar, Taher, Iqbal, Yayah.

SANYA: Do you have an envelope for me?

OFFICER KELLY: Sorry. The bus is here, we're behind already. Come on! Chop, chop.

OFFICER KELLY goes off as do all the asylum seekers who don't have envelopes. YAYAH walks off whilst at the same time tearing his envelope up and reading the letter. TATYANA, ELMAR and TAHER sit and open their envelopes. PHILIPPA recovers and stands looking at those seated opening their envelopes. ELMAR stands to leave.

ELMAR: Thank you Philippa. You are a very talented director.

PHILIPPA: Elmar, if I can help, a friend of mine is a film producer –

ELMAR: – No. Not necessary.

He turns his back and leaves. TATYANA having read her letter stands, brushes past PHILIPPA and leaves quite energised.

TAHER: I apologise. I am sorry I am like I am. I have always been like this.

TAHER leaves.

OFFICER KELLY: Come on! Let's be having you!

Everyone leaves, except OFFICER KELLY, who from upstage watches IQBAL read his letter. IQBAL folds the letter and sits. KELLY realises what is going on and gives him a moment or two.

You alright son?

IQBAL: Yes. Thank you.

IQBAL leaves and OFFICER KELLY turns the lights out.

SNAP TO BLACK.

THE BIG FELLAH

Out of Joint and the Lyric Hammersmith present *The Big Fellah* by Richard Bean. First performed on 2 September 2010 at the Corn Exchange, Newbury with the following cast:

DAVID COSTELLO	Finbar Lynch
RUAIRI O'DRISCEOIL	Rory Keenan
MICHAEL DOYLE	David Ricardo-Pearce
KARELMA	Stephanie Street
TOM BILLY COYLE	Youssef Kerkour
ELIZABETH RYAN	Claire Rafferty
FRANK MCARDLE	Fred Ridgeway

Director	Max Stafford-Clark
Designer	Tim Shortall
Lighting Designer	Jason Taylor
Sound Designer	Nick Manning
Costume Supervisor	Katie Moore
Associate Director	Blanche McIntyre
Fight Director	Terry King
Dialect Coach	Charmian Hoare

Production Manager	Gary Beestone
Company Stage Manager	Richard Llewelyn
Deputy Stage Manager	Helen Bowen
Assistant Stage Manager	Kitty Stafford-Clark
Re-lighter	Greg Gould

Set / Staging

Most of the action takes place in an apartment in the Woodlawn district of the Bronx.

Other locations are Costello's speeches at St. Patrick's Day dinners, and the art gallery settings for Ruairi's meetings with Karelma. Both these can be done without fixed staging.

The apartment is formed out of the first floor of an old brownstone. It's a man's place and generally cramped, lacking style, and scruffy. There is a kitchen/diner/reception type arrangement. Stage right and in the back wall are four doors, three to bedrooms, and one to a bathroom. The entrance to the apartment is stage left. A big sash window stage left looks out on to 237th street. On one of the walls an acoustic guitar hangs as a decoration. An old two seater sofa, an armchair, and coffee table, fill the space. Some sporting trophies – baseball and/or ice hockey, maybe a team photo with a young Michael. One or two posters of rock bands of the sixties and a big bad landscape, redolent of a romanticised Ireland.

Through the different time periods the apartment furniture might change with the fashions of the time, as well as predictable updates of the domestic technology.

Characters

DAVID COSTELLO
37 in 1972

MICHAEL DOYLE
20s in 1972

RUAIRI O'DRISCEOIL
20s in 1972

TOM BILLY COYLE
20s in 1972

KARELMA
20s in 1972

ELIZABETH RYAN
30s in 1981

FRANK MCARDLE
50s in 1987

Prologue

1972. DAVID COSTELLO is isolated in a spot. A surround soundscape of chatter, eating, cutlery/crockery clanging. The audience is the St. Patrick's day parade dinner crowd. COSTELLO is dressed in a full Brian Baru and Irish kilt. He lights a cigar. He's cool. He's done this before. He picks up a wine glass and taps it with a fork. This has no effect on the chatter which continues with only a few shushes thrown in. He tries again with the wine glass. No change. He looks stage left and mimes a blow on the pipes. There is an almighty and comic blast on the pipes, rather longer than COSTELLO wanted. It is followed by laughter and applause. He speaks in a New York accent.

COSTELLO: I won't keep you long. I understand that one of you's godda go to work in the morning.

(Laughter.)

I'd like to thank the chef, Jimmy Schultz, and all his staff for a real terrific meal – as ever!

(Applause.)

Hell! At five hundred dollars a plate – it's godda be good!

(Laughter.)

It woulda been a lot cheaper if we'd all been born Protestant!

(Laughter.)

THE FIRST EVER NEW YORK ST.PATRICK'S DAY PARADE WAS IN 1766!

(Small cheer.)

In nineteen seventy-two, two hundred and six years later, WE'RE STILL MARCHING!

(Many cheers.)

America has given each of us the opportunity to fulfil our true potential! God Bless America!

ALL: God Bless America!

COSTELLO: Some of us have prospered.

(Laughter. COSTELLO acknowledges that the laughter is directed at him.)

And America asks only one thing of us – that we become Americans.

I am an American… AND, I am Irish!

(Cheers. COSTELLO is in tears.)

This year, the parade, this dinner, it feels different. Just over a month ago, in Derry, thirteen unarmed Irishmen were murdered in cold blood by foreign soldiers!

(Grumbles of disgust.)

I fought one war for America. Korea. Many of you have sons in Vietnam. I killed men, men I did not know, men who would have killed me had I not killed them. And I'd do it again if my nation asked me to.

(He gets out a handkerchief and wipes his tear filled eyes.)

I really do not know if these wars in Asia are just wars – this guy…whatshisname… Chomsky thinks they're not, but I didn't see him over there –

(Laughter.)

War is hell! But more disgusting than war is tyranny. Our black American brothers in the Civil Rights movement have finally removed the stain of racial discrimination from this nation and yet today our Irish Catholic men and women exist only as targets in the cross hairs of the British rifles.

(Supportive grumbles.)

Kissinger and Nixon, I make no apologies for putting them in that order –

(Laughter.)

– they got one eye on the Soviet Union, one eye on Vietnam, and one eye on the moon!

(Laughter.)

If my math is correct – they got one good eye left!

(Laughter.)

Look to Ireland Mr. Kissinger! Look to your 'ancestral home' Mr. President!

(Laughter.)

There's forty million Irish Americans ready to back you for a second term if you do the right thing!

(Cheers.)

What is the right thing? I know what it ain't! It ain't détente. Was it détente when my father, and four hundred thousand of his American buddies died kicking the Nazis outa France!? No! Do the right thing!

(Applause.)

OK, OK, I'm not calling for a beach landing in Galway.

(Laughter.)

But take the reins off of our money!

(Yeah!)

Quit supplying arms to the Brits!

(Yeah!)

And Kissinger, stick your détente up your derrière, and get your German ass over to London with this message – 'No direct rule, Brits out!'.

(Cheering.)

Our struggle for freedom needs money. Earlier today, the police, the firemen, the longshoremen, the Irish workers who keep this great city alive filled the buckets on the parade with hard earned dollars and quarters. But from you guys – the blessed sons of Ireland in America – I don't want five dollar bills, I don't want ten dollar bills. I want cheques!

(Laughter.)

'For freedom comes from God's right hand
And needs a Godly train
And **WEALTHY** men must make our land

(Knowing laughter.)

A nation once again!'

(Huge cheering.)

To black.

.

Act One

Sunday March 19ᵗʰ 1972. It's mid morning. The Woodlawn apartment in the Bronx. Lots of buckets full of money, mainly dollars and silver, are piled up around the room. All are decorated with amateurishly painted shamrocks. RUAIRI is diallng a number on the phone. He is an Irishman of about 28. He is wearing only underpants, and a vest. He talks with a strong Cork accent.

RUAIRI: *(On the phone, talking secretively.)* It's me… ME! …that fireman's place. Yous can check out the apartment, and him, kill two birds with the one stone… I am not getting on the number 4 train in the Bronx wi' eighteen buckets full o' fucking money!… Mr Costello, Jesus! There's so much money I'VE GOT A FUCKING HARD ON! … Sh!

(A noise from the other bedroom as MICHAEL rolls out of bed yawning and groaning.)

…see…yer've woken him up now wi' yer shouting…

…Two forty-seven and Martha, …apartment 4, number 87, … it'll only tek yer five minutes. Big ugly fucking brownstone…see yous.

RUAIRI puts the phone down. He opens the curtains. MICHAEL comes out of his room. He is suffering from a hangover. He is a young, well built man of about 25. He wears pyjama bottoms and a singlet. He speaks in a blue collar New York accent without a hint of Irish.

RUAIRI: Yer look as sick as a small hospital.

MICHAEL: Yeah.

RUAIRI: I couldn't live in this bit of the Bronx.

MICHAEL: The blacks?

RUAIRI: The 'Oirish'. Woodlawn reminds me of the very worst bit of Tipperary. I bet if yer go in that church there they'll have a statue of the Virgin Mary weeping blood every Easter, and a priest tryna fuck the kids.

MICHAEL: What's the weather like?

RUAIRI: Soft.

(During the next MICHAEL makes coffee using a Bialetti.)

Yer not that Irish are yer Michael?

MICHAEL: No.

RUAIRI: A true born Irishman would know what I meant by 'soft'. Soft rain. But yer didn't know what the fuck I was talking about did yer?

MICHAEL: No.

RUAIRI: And yer awful laconic fer an Irishman with yer little 'No' here and a little 'No' there. Have yer got a sister called Mary?

MICHAEL: No.

RUAIRI: Yer not Irish then. But there's hope yet – yer've got a guitar. Do yer play?

MICHAEL: No.

RUAIRI: Good. I fucking hate Irish music. The worst song in the world is that Johnny O'Leary song – 'The Hair Fell Off Me Coconut'? Do you know it?

MICHAEL: No.

RUAIRI: *(Singing.) Oh the hair fell off me coconut*
The hair fell off me coconut
Oh the hair fell off me coconut
And how do you like it baldy?

I'm a Pink Floyd man meself.

(RUAIRI has his hands on the guitar and pulls at it but it's nailed to the wall.)

RUAIRI: – Yer've nailed a musical instrument to the wall so! Frank McArdle, he'd kill yer for less.

MICHAEL: Who's Frank McArdle?

RUAIRI: South Armagh alcoholic. I was in the Kesh with him. For this, Frank, he'd blindfold yer, drill yer kneecaps, beat yer till yer were lard, set fire to the lard, and then piss on yer to put yer out, so's he could beat yer, and light yer up, all over again. He's a big music lover yer see.

MICHAEL: It's my grandfather's. He was from Omey Island near Clifden.

RUAIRI: I've won good money on them sands on board some of Ireland's finest horses.

MICHAEL: You were a jockey?

RUAIRI: What the fuck else are yer gonna do with a little Irishman wi' no schoolin'?

MICHAEL: Tom Billy said your brother could sell me a plot of land in Ireland.

RUAIRI: I'll sell yer a bit of Omey Island itself. And it'll be a practical purchase. A little strip, three by six.

MICHAEL: How many acres is that?

RUAIRI: Three fucking *foot* that way, and six fucking *foot* that way. Yer get the six by three bit of Omey Island, a stone, and the coffin itself. Five hundred dollars deposit, and then when you can, another coupla grand.

MICHAEL: Two thousand bucks?!

RUAIRI: Yer get to fly Aer Lingus – first class.

MICHAEL: But what's the point, I'd be dead?

RUAIRI: You're not a believer then?

MICHAEL: No.

RUAIRI: Get dressed. The Big Fellah's on his way.

MICHAEL: Is he gonna tell you where they're sending you?

RUAIRI: Ah, there's no debate, it'll be Canada, and I fucking hate Canada. All that wild open space, and not been able to move fer fucking moose shit.

MICHAEL: I didn't know you'd been?

RUAIRI: I seen it on the telly. I'll be dead in a week, you watch. Eaten alive by beavers.

RUAIRI busies himself with the buckets. Enter KARELMA. She is an attractive Puerto Rican of about 25. She is wearing only a T shirt and knickers.

KARELMA: Hiya guys.

MICHAEL: Michael. It's my apartment.

KARELMA: Karelma. Good morning Ruairi.

RUAIRI: *(Sulking.)* Aye.

KARELMA checks out the buckets full of money.

KARELMA: So does this money go to the IRA?

RUAIRI: Hell no! What makes yer think I would be involved with them fucking thieving, murdering, bandits?

KARELMA: Cos last night, in the pub, you told me that you were an IRA freedom fighter on the run, busted outa some jail in Ireland by the IRA and had been hiding up in New York for six months waiting to get smuggled into Canada by the IRA.

RUAIRI: *(Laughing.)* Now, any man, after a few drinks, might make up a white lie like that if he thinks there might be a fuck in it. Michael, you're a fireman, I bet you exaggerate about how many cats yer've rescued, if yer chatting up a lovely looking cat lover.

MICHAEL: Ruairi saying that he's in the IRA is conclusive proof that he's not in the IRA.

RUAIRI: No true member of the IRA would be that stupid.

KARELMA: Pulling pints in an Irish bar on parade night is a weird take on 'lying low'.

RUAIRI: I was wearing a wig.

KARELMA: A green wig. Can I use your bathroom Michael?

MICHAEL: Sure. This one here.

(MICHAEL opens the door for her, she goes in.)

(Whispering.) She's really hot.

RUAIRI: Yeah, I coulda flahed the arse of her if she'd a let me. Must be a lesbian.

Intercom sounds. MICHAEL goes to it.

MICHAEL: Yeah?

TOM BILLY: *(Distort.)* Coyle!

MICHAEL buzzes to let him in.

MICHAEL: Coyle – with their buckets.

RUAIRI goes to look out the window.

MICHAEL: If it isn't Canada, you could stay here, ya know, three bedrooms is too big for me on my own. If Costello OKs it for the safe house, and pays a retainer, then you can have one of the rooms.

RUAIRI: I'm sick o' me brother's for sure.

Enter TOM BILLY. He is about 25. He's wearing full NYPD uniform. He is carrying a pile of buckets, which he hands over, and two NYPD flak jackets.

TOM BILLY: There's a couple of faggots out there on your sidewalk man, holding hands. Men. Holding hands. In America.

MICHAEL: Yeah?

TOM BILLY: Fucking spic and a fucking brick top white guy. Thank Christ there ain't a single fucking womb between them. Where d'yer want these buckets man?

MICHAEL: Here.

MICHAEL takes the buckets off TOM BILLY.

RUAIRI: What's that other lump o' stuff yer got there?

TOM BILLY: Flak jackets.

TOM BILLY gives them to RUAIRI.

RUAIRI: I see it's left to me to paint over the lettering is it?

TOM BILLY: Hey! The Big Fellah said they wan' a coupla flak jackets. I get two fucking flak jackets. All of a sudden I'm a fuck up!

RUAIRI: Turn yer amplifier down yer big noisy langer!

MICHAEL: We got company.

RUAIRI heads off down the corridor and slings the flak jackets into a room.

TOM BILLY: I godda gig tonight? Comedy Kitchen, West Third and Bleeker. Open mike, ten minutes.

MICHAEL: Sorry man, I got a shift.

TOM BILLY: Bullshit!

TOM BILLY grabs him round the neck and playfully squeezes him.

MICHAEL: Agh! Easy man!

RUAIRI: Yer've not got a funny bone in yer body, and I say that as a good friend.

TOM BILLY: Fuck you!

MICHAEL: Don't do the nigger material man.

TOM BILLY: Why not?

KARELMA enters from the bathroom.

KARELMA: *(To COYLE.)* Hi?

MICHAEL: Karelma, this is Officer Coyle.

KARELMA: Coyle, Doyle, cop, fireman. You've got pretty broad horizons Michael?

TOM BILLY: Are you taking the piss!? If you're not legal I'm gonna run your pretty ass outa town.

KARELMA: *(Indicating RUAIRI.)* He's the IRA killer man, you're the New York cop. Why don't you run him outa town?

TOM BILLY: Excuse me lady, are you slandering the character of this gentleman?

MICHAEL: Cut her some slack Tom Billy!

TOM BILLY moves towards the door.

TOM BILLY: You don't exist lady! I'm outa here. Comedy Kitchen, West –

RUAIRI: – Fuck off!

RUAIRI slams the door on him.

MICHAEL: Are you illegal?

KARELMA: I'm as American as you man.

(KARELMA rolls a joint. During the next she lights it, smokes it and passes it on to MICHAEL.)

Your 'nation' is your head, yeah. I believe in freedom. So I'm here. In America. You're Irish, Rory, what do the Irish nation believe in?

RUAIRI: Drinking, singing, and some of them do a bit of cow farming.

KARELMA: Puerto Ricans wanna be Americans.

RUAIRI: They invaded yer fucking country! I'm glad yer wouldn't let me fuck yer last night. Why would I want to fuck an idiot!

KARELMA: Manhattan Island was stolen from the Wappinger Indian nation.

RUAIRI: They sat down with that Dutch fellah and agreed a price!

KARELMA: Sixty motherfucking guilders worth of trinkets. For the whole of Manhattan Island.

RUAIRI: They didn't live here all the time.

KARELMA: I'm sooo glad I didn't fuck you last night. Why would I want to fuck an idiot?

MICHAEL starts sorting money, not counting it. ie: putting notes of equal denominations in piles.

RUAIRI: Yer like him don't yer.

The doorbell rings.

COSTELLO: *(Distort.)* Ruairi?

RUAIRI: The Big Fellah. Make yersen decent Michael. How do you work this?

MICHAEL goes to his room. RUAIRI eventually works it out, and buzzes COSTELLO in.

KARELMA: Who is this guy?

RUAIRI: You'll have to be on your way down the road now lover. And don't you go worrying about hurting me feelings last night. I been punched every day of me fucking life.

Enter COSTELLO carrying a briefcase.

COSTELLO: Is this it?

RUAIRI: Aye.

COSTELLO takes a walk around the flat getting a feel of the dimensions. He opens the bathroom door, looks in. He stops, as if shocked, under the guitar on the wall.

RUAIRI: I know.

Enter MICHAEL, dressed.

COSTELLO: Michael?

MICHAEL: Yes sir.

COSTELLO: OK.

(To KARELMA.) Goodbye honey.

KARELMA: Heeeey, man –

MICHAEL: Karelma it looks like –

KARELMA: – no way man. I'm your guest. Stand up to them Doyle.

MICHAEL: This has been a long standing arrangement. That we would bring the buckets back here, and Mr. Costello would collect them.

KARELMA: OK. Collect the motherfucking buckets.

MICHAEL: I'm sorry. It's been nice to meet you.

KARELMA: I'm not leaving. You'll have to get these IRA boys to shoot me.

MR. COSTELLO looks at RUAIRI.

KARELMA: I'm staying man.

MR. COSTELLO sits and opens his briefcase on the coffee table. He takes out a revolver and places it on the top of the case. Karelma stands, quickly, and then exits to the spare room. MICHAEL follows her there.

KARELMA: *(Off.)* Get out!

MICHAEL is pushed out of the room.

MICHAEL: Karelma –

KARELMA: – fuck you Doyle.

KARELMA walks straight past MICHAEL and out. MICHAEL follows her into the lobby area.

MICHAEL: – wait!

COSTELLO stands by the door, and inspects the lock casually. He then closes the door, effectively locking MICHAEL out.

RUAIRI: Work quite well, eh, as a little safe house I mean.

COSTELLO: Yeah.

RUAIRI: He's got the three rooms back there, so one for himself, that's two for us. Is it to be Canada? For me? Do you know yet?

COSTELLO: I wanna talk to you about that.

Enter MICHAEL.

MICHAEL: Sorry sir, she –

COSTELLO: – Michael, would you mind, I need to have a word with Ruairi in private. I like the apartment. It's kinda …perfect.

MICHAEL: OK sir, I'll er… OK.

MICHAEL goes into his room.

RUAIRI: I wished you hadn't busted me out if it's gonna be Canada, I was doing well in the prison art class.

COSTELLO: It was Canada. But I got a call this morning. Orders. They want you to stay in New York.

RUAIRI: That's insane! It's only a matter of time before the FBI haul me up.

COSTELLO stands. With his thumb indicates MICHAEL's room.

COSTELLO: Is this guy serious?

RUAIRI: Yeah. I've been very rigorous with him. He's a big butty of Tom Billy, and his family are Galway people, you know, way back.

COSTELLO: For a RA boy like you, what's the easiest guy to kill?

RUAIRI: A Brit soldier? No. A stickie? No, a tout. Yeah, a tout.

COSTELLO: A tout. Could Michael kill a tout?

RUAIRI: No. He's a fireman. He saves lives. Sorry. I'll tell him it's a no.

COSTELLO: Wait. Do you play chess?

RUAIRI: I've not played since the Kesh.

COSTELLO: What's the most powerful piece on the board?

RUAIRI: The King. No. The Queen?

COSTELLO: The pawns. They don't run around whacking people, but there's a lot of them, and if you hang on to them, they're always there, quietly –

RUAIRI: – ah! he's quiet enough alright!

COSTELLO: – supporting us, the glory boys. I like him.

COSTELLO opens MICHAEL's door. We see MICHAEL sitting passively on his bed drinking coffee.

COSTELLO: I changed my mind.

MICHAEL: OK.

MICHAEL comes out and sits slightly at a tangent to the COSTELLO /RUAIRI conversation. The following is now a performance from COSTELLO.

COSTELLO: Ruairi, history is not made by men who take the easy road.

RUAIRI: Oh fuck. Listen, I'm a foot soldier, you and your big men can have the history books.

COSTELLO: You killed a British soldier in an ambush –

RUAIRI: – I didn't shoot him, I was only the driver –

COSTELLO: – What did you put on your immigration form at JFK?

RUAIRI: I was on a forged passport, so it was hardly me own fucking immigration form now was it. Architect.

COSTELLO: And the box where it asks you 'Have you any previous criminal convictions?' I imagine, since you're sitting here on Manhattan Island six months later you musta checked 'none', 'no criminal convictions'?

RUAIRI: Aye.

COSTELLO: OK. The orders from Dublin are that you turn yourself in –

RUAIRI stands.

RUAIRI: – no fucking way!

COSTELLO: – And invite an American court, to decide whether an Irishman who kills a British soldier is politically motivated, or a criminal. D'yer get it?

MICHAEL: It's brilliant.

RUAIRI: Yeah well you haven't just spent two years in a fucking Brit jail.

MICHAEL: Yeah, but a New York jury gonna find for you man.

COSTELLO: One month after Bloody Sunday. The clever money's on you.

RUAIRI: Aye, well I was a jockey and I've lost count of the number of times the favourite's broke a leg at the first fence and got shot by the veterinary.

COSTELLO: My attorney will represent you. And the mayor will name a street in your honour.

MICHAEL: Hey man! Fifth Avenue becomes O'Drisceoil Way!

RUAIRI: And would they chuck in a visa? I'm serious about the architecture.

COSTELLO: How are you for money?

RUAIRI: I'm down to the bones of me bum.

COSTELLO takes out a roll and gives it to RUAIRI.

RUAIRI: These are orders yeah?

COSTELLO: Yeah. You got coffee here Michael?

MICHAEL: Sure thing.

MICHAEL gets up and goes to the kitchen area and starts making a new pot of coffee for the Bialetti machine leaving RUAIRI and COSTELLO in what is essentially a two hander.

COSTELLO: I didn't know you were a jockey.

RUAIRI: Aye, do you like the horses yourself?

COSTELLO: It's my passion.

RUAIRI: Aye? Cos when I was inside I come up with this idea for fund raising. I've done a bit of research and over here the best horse for me idea would be Captain Pickles. Have you heard of a horse called Captain Pickles?

COSTELLO: Yeah.

RUAIRI: Captain Pickles is retired and worth six million at stud. The boys steal him away, hide him up somewheres and ask for a ransom. The beauty of kidnaping a horse is they're not that bothered about escaping, and –

COSTELLO: – horses can't talk.

RUAIRI: Exactly!

COSTELLO: Except Mr. Ed.

RUAIRI: Hell! That's not a bad idea. A talking horse must be worth a fucking fortune, and you've still got the inherent advantage, even with Mr. Ed, that it can't talk.

COSTELLO: Do you know who owns Captain Pickles?

RUAIRI: It'll be one of them Arabs, which is perfect, cos they don't know the value of money. Have you ever seen Captain Pickles race?

COSTELLO: Yes. Thirty-three times.

RUAIRI: Fucking hell! That's his whole career.

COSTELLO: I've seen all of his races Ruairi.

RUAIRI: Ha! You must be his number one fucking fan!

COSTELLO: I am.

RUAIRI: Do you own any horses yourself Mr. Costello?

COSTELLO: Just the one.

RUAIRI: We'll pick a different horse.

MICHAEL delivers coffees to the table. Mugs, and a carton of milk. All a bit blokey.

COSTELLO: This is the kinda place we need Michael. I guess ya realise that looking after a safe house for us, cannot be separated from becoming one of us?

MICHAEL: Sure.

COSTELLO: We have people every year come through New York. Guys on the run like Ruairi, engineers buying stuff. They kick their heels for a month before we get them into Canada.

RUAIRI: *(Tapping the side of his nose.)* Unless we get orders to send them to Mexico.

MICHAEL: Do we have people in Mexico?

COSTELLO: *(Looking at RUAIRI.)* We have absolutely no connections with Mexico Michael.

COSTELLO takes out a notebook and pen.

COSTELLO: OK. Is there any history of mental illness in your family?

MICHAEL: No.

COSTELLO: You got a girlfriend?

MICHAEL: No.

RUAIRI: He's awful laconic. He likes his little 'nos', and that does for him.

COSTELLO: Are you a homosexual?

MICHAEL: No.

Beat. COSTELLO writes something down. It looks like he's moved on from homosexuality.

COSTELLO: How do you know you're not a homosexual?

MICHAEL: I have feelings for women.

COSTELLO writes something down.

COSTELLO: Are you a communist?

MICHAEL: No.

COSTELLO: Vegetarian?

MICHAEL: No.

COSTELLO writes something down. He then closes the book and puts it and his pen away.

COSTELLO: This will seriously fuck your life. There is hardly a woman out there who would marry into the IRA.

MICHAEL: I understand.

COSTELLO: Do you know the story of Faust and the devil?

MICHAEL: No.

COSTELLO: This guy Faust sells his soul to the devil in exchange for twenty years of glory. What you're doing here, son, is Faust in reverse. Selling your soul for a lifetime of pain.

MICHAEL: I understand…yeah…it will make life more difficult, I guess.

COSTELLO: It will fuck your life. Tell me, how will it fuck your life?

MICHAEL: You know, like, er…finding a woman who would knowingly marry into the IRA.

RUAIRI: – 'cept Elizabeth Ryan herself.

COSTELLO: Ruairi.

RUAIRI: She's single. A lot of the boys have had a crack at her I know that, but none of them got nowhere. She's a lot sharper than that gobshite Danny Morrison and shoulda got the Head of Publicity job in my book. Definitely one of the intellectuals I would say, and possibly the first President of All Ireland Don't you think Mr. Costello? Imagine that, and a woman an'all.

(COSTELLO glares at him.)

I'll shut up now.

COSTELLO: I only have the one child. She's eleven. Every year we take her to the parade. For the first time last night she came to the dinner. We get home, she asks me 'Daddy, what's the money for?'. You're not just fucking up your own life. Those you love, they godda clear choice, they don't love you no more, or they're in deep with you. So tell me again. What will this mean for your life?

MICHAEL: It will fuck my life.

COSTELLO: Well done Michael. Looking good.

They laugh.

COSTELLO: You look at me and you see this coat, this watch, the shoes – outside a new Lincoln Cadillac. They call me the Big Fellah. Bullshit. It's an army. I'm a soldier. I get orders. I fucking jump. I'm a dumbass like every other dumbass. A lot of the time I'm doing shit I don't wanna do.

MICHAEL: I understand.

COSTELLO: Loose talk. There was a guy we had. One time, with a woman, I guess he was tryna screw her, he told her he was a freedom fighter in the IRA.

RUAIRI: Gillespie? I never met him but me brother said he had a helluva tongue on him. Hell! Did he get fucking Mexicoed?!

COSTELLO: Do you need a dump?

RUAIRI: Sorry.

MICHAEL: I think I understand Mexico.

MICHAEL mimes a gun to the head and a shot.

COSTELLO: I guess what happened in Derry got you angry? I celebrated.

MICHAEL: I guess the more we're attacked, the stronger we become.

COSTELLO: Exactly.

RUAIRI: Ah, Jesus. I'll never be a fucking officer.

MICHAEL: I never thought I would see the British Army shooting its own people, and then it hit me, they don't consider us to be *human*, it's like the Confederate view of the negro, and I can't allow that, because, I'm Irish, and I am human. Understand? You godda do something, you can't just watch that shit.

COSTELLO takes out an envelope from his briefcase and gives it to MICHAEL.

COSTELLO: You will attend a weekend upstate. At the end of that period you will be assessed again, and if both parties are happy, you will be sworn in. Now Ruairi has briefed me on your background, and motivation, but is there anything I need to know about you before we start this whole process?

MICHAEL: One thing. My family, my Irish family, my ancestors, if you like, and I guess me now too, er…strictly speaking, what I'm trying to say is – I'm a Protestant.

After a period of silence during which RUAIRI looks at the floor, and rubs his head and COSTELLO seems unmoved, RUAIRI stands and goes to the kitchen, and fiddles clumsily with the coffee pot.

COSTELLO: Ruairi?

RUAIRI: Sorry, look I –

COSTELLO: – Name the greatest Irishman.

RUAIRI: Er… Michael Collins? No? William Butler Yeats. Er… fuck. What was the name of that other fucking play writer fellah?

COSTELLO: Who was the father of Irish Nationalism?

RUAIRI: Oh, I didn't know you were going that far back. Wolfe Tone, o' course.

COSTELLO: Wolfe Tone described British rule over Ireland as a disease. He raised an army in France and sailed to Ireland. The Irish farmers joined his army in battle. Men, women, and children armed with sticks faced the English canon. They were slaughtered. Wolfe Tone was sentenced to death. In his cell he cut his own throat with a pen knife. I've stood on his grave Michael. Bodenstown, County Kildare. And what I sense when I stand there in that tumbledown cemetery is that I am standing on the holiest sod of all Ireland, holier even than the place where Patrick sleeps in Down. Wolfe Tone was a Protestant.

RUAIRI: Beautiful.

COSTELLO: OK. Let's count this fucking money.

They begin sorting money and stuffing wads into the holdall.

End of Scene.

Act Two

SCENE 1

1981. An art gallery. RUAIRI. KARELMA enters.

KARELMA: Ruairi? You remember me.

RUAIRI: I think I do but –

KARELMA: – different outfit.

RUAIRI: Yes, now, no, bollocks. Michael's place. Jesus, Mary and the fucking donkey! Did we?

KARELMA: No. We didn't.

RUAIRI: Bloody Sunday.

KARELMA: Nine years.

RUAIRI: What is this? Black businesswoman of the year awards. I forgotten yer name, so I have!

MICHAEL: Karelma.

RUAIRI: Are yer running for President!?

KARELMA: I'm working in Wall Street, just two blocks, you know –

RUAIRI: – Well fuck me! You got yerself legal then?

KARELMA: Yeah.

RUAIRI: And you won't be rolling no spliffs, or sleeping with the likes of me then?

KARELMA: No.

RUAIRI: Not that you did that afore like.

KARELMA: I've been following your court case –

RUAIRI: – ah, yer a fan now are yer?

KARELMA: It's been running longer than the Mary Tyler Moore show.

RUAIRI: Aye, I hope to win a fucking whatyercallit –

KARELMA: – an Emmi.

RUAIRI: – aye, an Emmi award would be nice before I get slammed up.

KARELMA: I'm so proud of you. And – the other day I met a friend on 'O'Drisceoil corner'.

RUAIRI: They said it was gonna be a whole street.

KARELMA: Having a corner is much better than a street. For going anywhere around 53rd and 3rd people say meet you on O'Drisceoil corner.

RUAIRI: Aye. I'm famous.

KARELMA: Do you like Mondrian then?

RUAIRI: Aye, I do so, and there's always a lot of single women in an art gallery, it's like shooting fish in a barrel. But anywhere that's licenced and don't play Irish music is fine by me.

KARELMA: You don't like Irish music?

RUAIRI: It's the soundtrack of hell.

KARELMA: D'you wanna sit, I've got a minute?

RUAIRI: Sure.

(They sit on a viewing bench.)

But hell, look at yer! You buying and selling the world then?

KARELMA: I'm a journalist. Hey, look I, we do a monthly investment bulletin on Europe, ya know, updated monthly, yeah, and I got the Irish desk, wow! Maybe I could interview you sometime. Cos everyone knows you, and what you have is that smack of truth, yeah? This month I have to do a thousand words on County Wicklow.

RUAIRI: I know fuck all about Wicklow.

KARELMA: No, no, it's about how the Irish think, like, I want to do something on what the Irish feel about the attempted assassination of Ronald Reagan.

RUAIRI: What – cos Reagan thinks he's Irish you mean?

KARELMA: Do Irish Americans think of Reagan as Irish?

RUAIRI: I guess they know he's Irish, but they don't love him like they love the Irish who've done well for themselves over here – like JFK or Billy the Kid.

KARELMA: But do the Irish in Ireland think Reagan is Irish?

RUAIRI: No way. They think he's an eijit someone built for a laugh.

KARELMA: That's real funny man. Look, I can afford a hundred dollars a month. You know, if we could do just one interview a month, maybe an hour.

RUAIRI: I talk bullshit for an hour and then you give me a hundred dollars?

KARELMA: You got it.

RUAIRI: I've been talking bollocks as an amateur for years, I'm not sure I'm ready to step up to professional.

KARELMA: Think about it. I'll need an IRS invoice.

RUAIRI: I'm not an American.

KARELMA: You've not got a visa?

RUAIRI: A visa is exactly what I've not got.

KARELMA: But I thought with the bail bond you got –

RUAIRI: – killing a British soldier –

KARELMA: – which you didn't do man, you were the driver.

RUAIRI: – aye, but you'll remember they dug up me long history of house breaking which even Henry Fonda himself couldn't stretch to calling a political act.

KARELMA: A lawyer friend of mine works for the Donnelly commission. Her whole life is looking at naturalisation cases like yours. D'you wanna meet?

RUAIRI: If she can fix it, yeah.

KARELMA: Here's my card. Give me a call tomorrow.

RUAIRI: Are you an angel? This has been the greatest day of me life so far.

End of Scene.

SCENE 2

September 14th 1981. Music plays – Roxy Music's 'If It Takes All Night' from the album Country Life – on vinyl. The apartment much the same, but with the odd improvement, including a Manchester United scarf. MICHAEL's FDNY coat with logo is thrown on the floor, as are other clothes. MICHAEL and ELIZABETH RYAN sit naked on the sofa. They have recovered from sex, which ended ten minutes or so ago.

ELIZABETH: So I said 'Gerry, I'll show you how to work the overhead projector if you promise to stop looking at my tits.'

MICHAEL: Gerry Adams was looking at your tits?

ELIZABETH: He was growing an Armalite in his pocket.

MICHAEL: They're beautiful tits.

ELIZABETH: You love me for my intelligence Michael.

MICHAEL: I do. I do. Absolutely. Yeah. The tits are a bonus. What did Gerry say?

ELIZABETH: He said – I'm sorry Elizabeth, I thought I could see the outline of a listening device in your bra.

MICHAEL: He said that for real?!

ELIZABETH: No, not for real Michael, as a pathetic joke.

MICHAEL: Oh. Am I dumb?

(She kisses him.)

You're pretty good at some things.

MICHAEL: Did you come?

ELIZABETH: No. When I fake it I don't bother with all that wailing and thrashing around. I just tell a lie with a smile.

MICHAEL: And you think that's why Gerry put the heat on you?

ELIZABETH: Two weeks later I get orders, to honey trap the Brit from the Embassy.

MICHAEL: Sex?

ELIZABETH: I'm not easy. Even if you work for MI6 you buy me dinner first.

MICHAEL: Man, they're real tough orders.

ELIZABETH: I lie back and dream of a United Ireland. Hey, come on, I'm teasing lover. They usually nut the target before the third date.

MICHAEL: Why before the third date?

ELIZABETH: When did Adam and Eve first fuck? On their third date. But this time, very clever Gerry, Belfast 'forget' to nut him. Two years down the line, I've met his mother, we've got a quarter share in a Donegal caravan, and we're saving up for IVF treatment.

MICHAEL: That's your problem. You're too thorough.

ELIZABETH: I'm exaggerating, you know that, don't you Michael.

MICHAEL: Oh OK.

MICHAEL is worried by her frankness. He starts to move off the sofa.

ELIZABETH: Where are you going?

MICHAEL: Ruairi should be back by now and the Big Fellah's got his own keys, and, you know, look at us.

ELIZABETH: Kiss me.

MICHAEL kisses her.

MICHAEL: Oh God I love you.

ELIZABETH: I'm trying not to slip into the love thing with you but with my knickers around my ankles, and my bra round my neck I surely must be losing.

They kiss.

MICHAEL: They might want you to go to Canada.

ELIZABETH: That is why it's important we don't do the love thing.

MICHAEL: Let's get married.

ELIZABETH: Ha! No fucking way. 'Marriage is the institutionalised oppression of women and a capitulation to sameness.'

MICHAEL: What does that mean?

ELIZABETH: After a month we'd be wearing matching anoraks.

They kiss again, a deep sensual kiss.

MICHAEL: I don't understand why it's me.

ELIZABETH: You, yer stuck out, like a beautiful sore thumb. When you came round the corner at the funeral, heading up that bunch of phonies you got the nerve to call a pipe band –

MICHAEL: – the award-winning New York Hibernia Society Police Band.

ELIZABETH: Aye, it was comical, but there was something compelling about you, you I mean, Michael. Some kind of innocence. I might even be here to save yer soul, who knows.

MICHAEL: For me…when you walked out of the Ard Fheis that time, just, you know, you shouted something to the leadership, all those men, I don't remember what you said, but I watched your face, and their faces, and you walked out and they were scared. And I don't know what it was you'd said.

ELIZABETH: 'Welcome to the misogyny club AGM!'

MICHAEL: Yeah, that was it. What's a misogynist? Is that like –

ELIZABETH: – a sexist, anti-women.

MICHAEL: I worked it out.

ELIZABETH: We don't mention 'us' to the Big Fellah. OK.

MICHAEL: Ruairi will have blagged us already, you can put your life on that.

ELIZABETH: Aye, I guess. I doubt the Big Fellah's got any influence over the decision.

MICHAEL: If it's Canada –

ELIZABETH: – don't! We don't know where I've got to go lover. We can't make plans.

ELIZABETH stands and goes through to the bedroom. MICHAEL dresses and continues to talk.

MICHAEL: I'll just walk outa the firehouse. I could do it. I can find work in Toronto.

Re-enter ELIZABETH wearing a dressing gown.

ELIZABETH: You won't. I won't let you. You can visit if it's Canada, but it might be Libya, and I don't care how much you love me I can't see you popping over to Tripoli for a fuck every other weekend.

MICHAEL: We don't have anyone in Libya.

ELIZABETH: After me court martial O'Neill said Libya had become a posting. That's what he said after he'd said I was lucky to be alive.

MICHAEL: Why did he say you were lucky to be alive?

ELIZABETH: The court martial wasn't unanimous.

MICHAEL: But you were told to set the Embassy guy up!

ELIZABETH: I'd been seeing a Brit for two years. That was enough for some of them.

MICHAEL: But it wouldna been two years if Belfast had hit the guy when they shoulda hit the guy.

ELIZABETH: But they didn't.

MICHAEL: Why didn't they?

ELIZABETH: I dunno.

MICHAEL: Did you fall in love with the guy, the Brit?

ELIZABETH: Frig no! I was sick of the fucking oik. The truth is Michael I was a threat to Belfast, they didn't like me, they hate women you see –

MICHAEL: – misogyny!

ELIZABETH: *(Nod to MICHAEL.)* – so they let me go with the Brit for long enough to make it look like a fucking relationship, which made me look like a tout. That's the top and bottom of it. They didn't want a woman in the leadership.

MICHAEL: Why didn't Dublin hit the guy?

ELIZABETH: I was in Belfast. It's tribal.

(There is a buzzer at the door.)

We'll find out now. Canada. Please God!

MICHAEL: Canada.

ELIZABETH: I'm in the shower.

ELIZABETH gives him a final peck, and goes into the bathroom. MICHAELS attends to the intercom.

COSTELLO: *(Distort.)* It's me.

MICHAEL buzzes him in. He gets himself a beer. Hides one of her socks in his pocket. COSTELLO enters, very drunk. He tries the bathroom door which, to his disgust, he finds is locked.

COSTELLO: I need a piss.

MICHAEL: Miss Ryan is in the shower.

COSTELLO: I'll piss in the sink.

MICHAEL: Please, sir, no.

COSTELLO: Have you got a bucket?

MICHAEL: No.

COSTELLO: Ten years ago, you had eighteen fucking buckets. How's it been? With her staying here. Huh?

MICHAEL: Like all the others.

COSTELLO: All the others were guys.

MICHAEL: Nothing sir. I swear. We haven't even…nothing.

COSTELLO: It's not Libya.

MICHAEL: No?

COSTELLO stands underneath the guitar.

COSTELLO: If Frank McArdle ever sees this – he'll kill you. He's very big on traditional Irish music. Frank once killed a guy with a spade for wearing a shirt and tie set, in mustard. Have you got whisky?

MICHAEL: Did you drive here Mr. Costello?

COSTELLO: Tom Billy dropped me. He's outside.

MICHAEL: He can come in. We got food enough. Ruairi's picking up a Chinese to go.

COSTELLO: No. I want him out there.

MICHAEL: It's not Libya, then. Good.

COSTELLO: Why do you care Michael?

Enter ELIZABETH in bathrobe.

ELIZABETH: Mister Costello, good to see you again.

COSTELLO: Yeah. We should do this more often. I'll be in the John.

COSTELLO goes into the bathroom for a piss. He starts pissing with the door open. MICHAEL has to close the door behind him.

ELIZABETH: He's as pissed as a fart. Did he say anything?

MICHAEL: It's not Libya.

ELIZABETH goes into the spare room. MICHAEL tidies up some more. MICHAEL goes to get a drink, sits, feels that something is wrong. He looks out of the window. COSTELLO comes out of the bathroom. Enter ELIZABETH. She is now dressed.

COSTELLO: What do you do two?

ELIZABETH: What do 'we do two'?

COSTELLO: I've been drinking. What do you do two when he's not putting fucking fires out?

ELIZABETH: I've not sat around wasting time Mr. Costello. I wrote that article on the hunger strikers or have you not read it? And I've been waiting for an invitation from you for me to speak to the Hibernia Society about Bobby, and funding for a statue.

COSTELLO: When I came back from Korea, I didn't have Jack shit. I spent my vet's grant on a Chrysler. Then I got another Chrysler. I was living off two Chryslers. It's possible. And a wife. But every day, every day that God sent, a clean shirt. Fucking K Mart shirt – yeah! and twenty dollar suit – yeah! but clean. I'll tell you what I didn't do! I didn't walk around with my hair down to my ass. I didn't cake the walls of my car rental cabin with my own excrement! MY WAR is not a whinge against capitalism. What do they say they want?

ELIZABETH: A democratic socialist republic.

COSTELLO: Yeah, fucking communists!

Enter RUAIRI with Chinese meal. RUAIRI goes straight to sit down at the coffee table.

RUAIRI: I'm starving! I could eat the holy lamb outa God's right hand and fuck the consequences. Are yer alright there Mr. Costello?

COSTELLO: Ruairi! Question!

RUAIRI: Ah fuck! I've just walked in the door!

COSTELLO: Tell this boy here why Frank McArdle killed Bernie Toolis with a spade. It was the mustard shirt and tie set wasn't it!

RUAIRI: It weren't mustard, it was peach.

COSTELLO stands.

COSTELLO: – It was fucking mustard!

RUAIRI stands, mocking him.

RUAIRI: It was fucking peachy, apricoty, salmony thing!

MICHAEL: Did it have a pattern or was it plain?

RUAIRI: Plain, it was completely unrelenting! The odd stripe or check or galloping horse woulda helped us all. The only sense of detail it had was the fucking epaulettes. Also in peach.

COSTELLO: Mustard!

ELIZABETH: Frank didn't kill Bernie cos of that shirt.

COSTELLO: Are you implying that I don't know the history of my nation's struggle?

ELIZABETH: Bernie died cos he accused Frank of raping his brother-in-law in the Maze. The shirt and tie thing was neither here nor there. So, my advice about Frank McArdle is wear what the fuck you like but don't ever suggest that he's a violent rapist.

COSTELLO sits. He's lost the argument and given up.

RUAIRI: *(To COSTELLO.)* You'd do well to write that down.

ELIZABETH: I hate Frank McArdle with a loathing that I cannot describe but if we didn't have him, we'd have to invent him. I'm talking about the role and function of oral history, and myth-making in keeping up the morale of an underequipped people's volunteer army.

(Beat.) And I'm being a bit ironic too.

MICHAEL: We've had a month o' that kind of chat. Do you want to eat with us Mr. Costello?

COSTELLO: I've eaten!

RUAIRI: And yer been on the juice an'all!

COSTELLO stands.

COSTELLO: Who Ruairi!? –

RUAIRI: – Ah fuck.

COSTELLO: – Who is the beating heart of the IRA?

RUAIRI: Every time wid you yer giving me a fresh round in the quiz of life. I'll guess you mean the Catholic, or the Nationalist.

COSTELLO: The farmer!

RUAIRI: I was gonna say the cow farmer but the way yer put it made the question sound more difficult than it was.

COSTELLO: It's not these Belfast hippies.

ELIZABETH: Concur. Belfast has got too much influence now.

COSTELLO: My daughter, she went to Brown University. It took them two months, two fucking months –

RUAIRI: – come on let's eat. Miss Ryan doesn't need to know none of this.

ELIZABETH: It took who two months to do what – to your daughter?

RUAIRI: That's your plate there.

COSTELLO: Narcotics.

RUAIRI: We've all done drugs, it's all part of growing up nowadays and –

COSTELLO: – Now, she's a junkie.

RUAIRI: Na, she's young and having a bit of a laugh.

COSTELLO: My little girl.

RUAIRI: Just a phase.

COSTELLO: And these Belfast long hairs, they wanna nationalise the land! Ha! Hypothetical choice! You can have a united Ireland, BUT yer have to give the family farm to Gerry Adams!

RUAIRI: *(Laughs.)*

COSTELLO: OR! You can keep your land, but three times a day you have to salute the Queen of England! Ruairi! What would happen?!

RUAIRI: There'd be a portrait of Elizabeth the Second on every fucking fridge!

COSTELLO: Thank you! Bobby Sands! Carried my bag. Polite. He will go down in Irish history, but the others. Who gives a fuck about who dies sixth, or seventh?! I bet you none of you can name any single one of the others.

ELIZABETH: Francis Hughes, Raymond McCreesh, Patsy O'Hara, Joe McDonnell, Martin Hurson, Kevin Lynch, Kieran Doherty, Thomas McElwee, and Michael Devine.

RUAIRI: Ha, ha, that's shut you up.

COSTELLO sits.

COSTELLO: *(To ELIZABETH, as if the others know.)* In this town the firemen, the cops, they spend all day busting longhairs, if this goes on they're gonna stop giving money for the war. Cops don't give money to hippies. You know how much money we took the year after Bloody Sunday?

MICHAEL: – six hundred thousand dollars.

COSTELLO: – this year!?

MICHAEL: Less than a hundred thousand.

COSTELLO: We need money to keep this fucking celebrity going with his TV appearances and his attorney's champagne breakfasts. Ha!

(Slaps RUAIRI on the back.)

All around the world Ruairi is known as a martyr.

RUAIRI: Except Downing Street where the phrase they use is 'murdering bastard.'

MICHAEL: You were only the driver.

ELIZABETH: Can you not get Ruairi a visa Mr. Costello. He wants to be an architect.

COSTELLO: He was a certified felon before he was a –

RUAIRI: – Prisoner of Conscience. I got someone from the Donnelly commission working away at the visa. So God Bless America and who wants a crispy duck pancake?!

MICHAEL: Hit me.

ELIZABETH: Did you get my orders today? Do you know where they want me to go?

(Silence.)

Mister Costello? Sir?

COSTELLO: What is that?

MICHAEL: Squid!

COSTELLO: That's my favourite. Ruairi, can I ask you a question?

RUAIRI: For fuck's sake! Question three.

COSTELLO: This green book. Do you know why it's green?

RUAIRI: We're the IRA! We're not gonna have a fucking orange book are we!

COSTELLO: It's green for Islam.

RUAIRI: Yer drunk, and yer've had a tab of acid!

ELIZABETH: He's right. The 'Green Book' is an homage to Qaddafi's terrorist manual.

RUAIRI: An 'homage'? The IRA has been accused of many things lady, but one thing we're not is pretentious.

COSTELLO stands knocking over his chair backwards.

COSTELLO: What am I!? Ruairi!

RUAIRI: A squid lover. Now sit the fuck down!

COSTELLO: Am I a Muslim? Am I a communist!?

RUAIRI: No. I'll tell yer what yer are. Yer the very definition of the American dream. Yer started with fuck all and yer've ended up with too much.

COSTELLO: Am I a communist?

RUAIRI: We've done that one!

MICHAEL: For me, Mister Costello, you're a soldier. And you're an inspiration to me.

COSTELLO: Thank you son. Miss Ryan. What do you see?

ELIZABETH: I see a man usurped. A man who wanted to serve his country, to be remembered as a great Irishman, to do the right thing –

COSTELLO: – to go down in history!

ELIZABETH: But his country looked to someone new. I see a lover, rejected.

Silence.

RUAIRI: Ah fuck. This is me only night off yer know!

COSTELLO: She's right! Go on.

ELIZABETH: Ten years ago you gave us the Armalite Rifle. I stood next to you in the cemetery at Bodenstown.

COSTELLO: The respect!

ELIZABETH: I was nineteen. Shoulder to shoulder with a hero in the rain.

RUAIRI: Ah! Now was it raining?! Well fuck me!

ELIZABETH: Somebody pointed you out. 'That fellah, there, the big fellah, he's the American.'

COSTELLO: The American. That's what they called me!

ELIZABETH: Where did you get those rifles Mr. Costello?

COSTELLO: In America there's two main sources of guns. The Italians.

ELIZABETH: The Mafia?

RUAIRI: Yeah.

ELIZABETH: And what's the second source?

COSTELLO: The shops.

They all laugh. RUAIRI takes a mouthful.

RUAIRI: Fucking hell that's hot. What is that?

MICHAEL: Shredded beef in chilli.

RUAIRI: Give me another beer. Quick!

MICHAEL obliges.

ELIZABETH: But we don't count the rifles we get from Qaddafi. We weigh them in tons.

COSTELLO: And what is Qaddafi buying? Our motherfucking souls! We're all international socialists now!

COSTELLO sits.

RUAIRI: Yer finished now are yer?

ELIZABETH: Mr. Costello. You're staring at me.

RUAIRI: Elizabeth says that the Army Council are keen on me horse napping idea. Taking it very seriously and looking for a big Irish horse.

ELIZABETH: It's a great idea.

COSTELLO goes to the window and gestures to TOM BILLY.

RUAIRI: What yer doing? Who you got out there?

MICHAEL: Tom Billy.

RUAIRI: And what's the fat fuck sitting out there for?

COSTELLO: I feel sick.

RUAIRI: Ah fuck, that's all we need.

MICHAEL stands and helps COSTELLO into the bathroom, where he leaves him. The sound of vomiting. Loud and long.

RUAIRI: *(Pushing his plate away.)* That's done it for me.

MICHAEL starts clearing the food and plates away. The intercom buzzes. MICHAEL goes to it.

TOM BILLY: *(Distort.)* Tom Billy.

MICHAEL buzzes him in.

RUAIRI: Costello must know where yer going or he wouldn't come round.

ELIZABETH: That's why he said he was coming round.

Enter TOM BILLY, silent, serious looking.

TOM BILLY: Where's the Big Fellah?

RUAIRI: He's in there painting the carpet.

COSTELLO comes out of the bathroom. He looks steadier.

COSTELLO: You're here.

TOM BILLY: Yeah. I'm here.

COSTELLO: Miss Ryan! Get your things. We've got orders.

ELIZABETH: I'm not going anywhere.

COSTELLO: Ruairi! Go and get her things.

RUAIRI: Ah fuck, I've just got me feet under the table.

COSTELLO: She's going. She has to go tonight.

TOM BILLY: It's a long drive. We gotta go now.

RUAIRI stands.

ELIZABETH: Where am I going?

COSTELLO: Mexico.

ELIZABETH: Mexico? By car?

MICHAEL: No, not Mexico. Mister Costello –

COSTELLO: Be quiet Michael!

(MICHAEL stands.)

Sit down.

MICHAEL remains standing.

ELIZABETH: What's going on?

COSTELLO: These are orders. Sit down.

TOM BILLY: Sit down Michael.

MICHAEL sits.

ELIZABETH: Where exactly in Mexico am I going?

COSTELLO: Acapulco.

MICHAEL: No. No! NO!

MICHAEL stands, now desperate.

COSTELLO: Michael! Get in your room! I'm telling you – get in your room and shut the door. That's also an order.

TOM BILLY: These are all fucking orders!

ELIZABETH: Michael! What's happening?

COSTELLO: Keep the noise down!

(To MICHAEL.) Get in that room.

(To ELIZABETH.) You, get your coat.

COSTELLO: Michael! Go to your room.

TOM BILLY: Buddy, I think it's best if you go to your fucking room now! This is an operation.

MICHAEL: No!

TOM BILLY goes over to MICHAEL and takes his arm. MICHAEL is crying and moaning.

TOM BILLY: Come on Michael. Now, quit the hollering. Get up!

MICHAEL gets up.

ELIZABETH: Whose orders are these? Is it Army Council?

COSTELLO: Put your coat on lady.

MICHAEL submits and is led to his room by TOM BILLY. TOM BILLY closes the door.

TOM BILLY: Ruairi. Here.

TOM BILLY posts RUAIRI on guard outside MICHAEL's room.

RUAIRI: Ah, fuck.

ELIZABETH: Michael, help me!

MICHAEL opens the door.

COSTELLO: Keep that fucking door closed!

RUAIRI slams the door shut. COSTELLO vomits into the sink.

TOM BILLY: Take it easy sir. If you wanna help lady, put yer coat on.

ELIZABETH: No. I'm not going anywhere. We have no operation in Mexico. I demand to see the orders.

TOM BILLY: You're a tout lady.

COSTELLO: *(To TOM BILLY.)* That's enough.

ELIZABETH: I was exonerated at my court martial. You know that.

TOM BILLY: You know what happens to touts.

ELIZABETH: Michael! They're gonna kill me!

COSTELLO: Ruairi, put some fucking music on!

During the next RUAIRI goes over the record player and sticks the needle on the album which is on the turntable. It's side 1 of Roxy Music's Country Life album. RUAIRI clumsily sticks the needle on the first track 'The Thrill of it All'. He turns the volume up.

ELIZABETH: Michael! Michael!! Help me!

TOM BILLY: Shut the fuck up!

TOM BILLY goes into ELIZABETH's room and comes out with her coat, which he throws at her. She picks it up and throws it back at him. TOM BILLY draws his revolver and points it at her.

ELIZABETH: Come on Michael! You can help me now! Michael! Break that door down!

MICHAEL is barging the door and RUAIRI struggles to keep it closed. ELIZABETH starts to snatch books from the shelves and throw them at TOM BILLY.

COSTELLO: Keep outa this Michael! Get back in there!

MICHAEL eases out of the door, pushing against RUAIRI.

ELIZABETH: Michael! Take the gun off him.

COSTELLO brandishes his gun. MICHAEL backs off. The door is closed again.

COSTELLO: Keep quiet. Keep calm.

(To RUAIRI.) Turn the music up!

(To TOM BILLY.) Knock her out!

TOM BILLY approaches ELIZABETH. She throws books at him.

ELIZABETH: Don't you fucking touch me!

COSTELLO: Knock her out!

ELIZABETH and TOM BILLY wrestle. TOM BILLY eventually has her pinned to the floor where she screams.

ELIZABETH: Michael! Help me! They're gonna kill me!

TOM BILLY: Give me the gun!

TOM BILLY pistol whips her. She lies unconscious. COSTELLO turns the music off.

COSTELLO: Right, let's go. Ruairi, give him a hand.

RUAIRI lets the door go, and goes to help TOM BILLY. MICHAEL comes out and passively watches. TOM BILLY and RUAIRI are now out in the hall.

NEIGHBOUR: *(Off.)* What's all the hollering man!?

TOM BILLY: *(Off.)* NYPD. Cut me some slack man! Just doing my job!

NEIGHBOUR: *(Off.)* OK, OK.

COSTELLO stands in the doorway. MICHAEL doesn't know what to do with himself.

MICHAEL: They gave you orders?

COSTELLO: I got orders.

MICHAEL: Shit man. What she do?

COSTELLO: We got orders.

COSTELLO leaves. MICHAEL goes to the window and looks out. MICHAEL collapses on to his knees in the middle of the room, his head in his hands, weeping. RUAIRI comes back in and closes the door behind him. RUAIRI sits on the sofa. RUAIRI comforts MICHAEL.

MICHAEL: *(Barely articulate.)* Ruairi, what's happened? What have they done?

RUAIRI: I like being in the IRA, but if there's one thing I'd change, it's all the fucking killing.

End of Scene.

INTERVAL.

Act Three

1987. The apartment. Many very significant changes. Polished wood floors. It looks good with modern, new furniture. The guitar is still there on the wall, but in a different place. It now seems symbolic, a combination of an act of defiance and a memorial to ELIZABETH. RUAIRI, dressed in a Hugo Boss suit, sits on the arm of the sofa. He has a can of Bud or similar open. Set downstage left is a tatty, cheap and old suitcase and an old fashioned duffle bag. FRANK MCARDLE sits in the centre of the three piece sofa, looking scary. He is dressed in shirt sleeves.

FRANK: I shot the fucker.

RUAIRI: What?!

FRANK: Through the head. He died instantly.

RUAIRI: Yer shot Shergar!? How could yer shoot a beautiful horse like that?!

FRANK: He was going mad, kicking the fucking fuck out of the fucking horse box.

RUAIRI: Sure, did yer not think of trying him with a carrot first?

FRANK: I thought of that, aye, but it was already dark and all the shops were shut. Is that what you wear for work?

RUAIRI: I been at a clients. It's Hugo Boss. Do you like it Frank?

FRANK: Makes you look like a cunt.

RUAIRI: Aye.

FRANK: You got a good job then now?

RUAIRI: Architect.

FRANK: Fucking hell. Aye, you was always painting in the Kesh.

RUAIRI: I was born on a cow farm but I always knew that was not for me.

FRANK: What's wrong with cow farming?

RUAIRI: Nothing, nothing, no, no, no. We all godda eat, eh?

FRANK: You legal then?

RUAIRI: Aye, been legal for six, seven year now, aye.

(Beat.) So Security thinks that it was one of us here in New York what betrayed that ship?

FRANK: Aye.

RUAIRI: A hundred and fifty tons of arms. Kaw! We coulda won the war in a week.

FRANK: How did you know it was a hundred and fifty tons?

RUAIRI: I read it in *Time Magazine*.

FRANK: I godda have the other fellah here an'all.

RUAIRI: Doyle does his fireman's exams class thingy on a Tuesday, no! wait! it's band practice, aye. They let him play in the police pipe band for some reason and they're all going over to Donegal again to head up the Bobby Sands memorial march, aye.

FRANK: Are they any good?

RUAIRI: No, no. Fucking terrible. They sound like an abattoir with the doors open.

FRANK: Why are they letting them head up the march then?

RUAIRI: The Army Council are dead keen to have American law officers front up an IRA funeral, you know, it'll be on every world leader's telly –

RUAIRI taps the side of his nose knowingly.

FRANK: – aye! that's clever. I need to see the Big Fellah himself.

RUAIRI: I told him to come along later, like yer said, aye, though you don't tell the Big Fellah what to do, understand. It mighta helped if yer'd told us you were coming Frank. And Tom Billy is on a shift, so yers'll have to see him tomorrow.

(Beat.) And how is the lovely Mary?

FRANK: Aye.

RUAIRI: And yer daughter, the eldest, the hairdresser? What's her name?

FRANK: Mary.

RUAIRI: Aye.

FRANK: She married a strong farmer.

RUAIRI: That's a result. How many yer got left at home now?

FRANK: I got three of them married and three left at home.

RUAIRI: Six! Ha! That's a lot of daughters in any culture.

FRANK: Aye.

RUAIRI lights up a cigarette.

FRANK: Did I say you could fucking smoke?

RUAIRI: I'll get rid of the filthy thing.

(RUAIRI puts the cig out and bins it. He gets a beer from the fridge.)

(Beat.) Am I alright with the beer?

FRANK: Aye.

RUAIRI: As a recovering alcoholic are you allowed the odd tin?

FRANK: Am I fuck.

RUAIRI: Do you go to Alcoholics Anonymous back there in Lurgan then?

FRANK: Aye.

RUAIRI: Is it a mixed group?

FRANK: Aye.

RUAIRI: Yer never think of Protestants as having a problem with the drink do yer. How do yer find the process? All that honesty, and publicly facing up to the empty sham of your existence? Has it affected yer fundamentally as a human being?

FRANK: Aye.

RUAIRI: In what way has it changed yer Frank?

FRANK: I've given up the drink.

RUAIRI: No?! Fucking hell! What do you do for fun?

FRANK: I fuck the wife.

RUAIRI: She'll be glad of the week off then.

FRANK: Aye. How do yous know you're not an alcoholic?

RUAIRI: Me? Na!

FRANK: Do you drink at home, alone, of an evening?

RUAIRI: Na, never! I'm always in the pub. So you're here for a week Frank?

FRANK: I might do the sights this time.

RUAIRI: There's a Kandinsky at the Museum of Modern Art? Fantastic! Russian fellah. Maybe a bit abstract for you.

FRANK: I like a good zoo.

RUAIRI: Aye.

FRANK stands and goes to look out the window, and during the next has a look around.

FRANK: Tomorrow night could we go seek out some traditional Irish music?

RUAIRI: Ah, fuck.

FRANK: And I'm not going home until I've walked up and down your street.

RUAIRI: You know that it's not a whole street, don't you? It's like a corner.

FRANK: I don't care. I want to stand on O'Drisceoil corner.

RUAIRI: Aye, well, you might not want to when yer get there.

FRANK: How d'yer mean?

RUAIRI: It's become something of a spot for picking up rent boys.

FRANK: What the fuck's a rent boy?

RUAIRI: Look, I know a good pub for Irish music only two blocks down, will yer be happy with that?

FRANK: I like me music yer see.

(FRANK inspects the guitar on the wall.)

Who the fuck did this? That's a musical instrument that.

RUAIRI: Well it was.

(FRANK sits.)

The Big Fellah's all sore about the whole family thing, and I'd best avoid it as a topic of conversation if I were you.

FRANK: I'm Security, I can ask any questions that take me fancy.

RUAIRI: All I'm saying, for the sake of everyone, if you keep off the subject of his daughter. And the wife.

FRANK: Theresa. She gone?

RUAIRI: Aye.

(Enter MICHAEL in kilt with bagpipes.)

RUAIRI: This is –

FRANK: – did you do that?

MICHAEL: Yes.

(FRANK punches MICHAEL in the stomach. MICHAEL collapses on the floor. FRANK empties his duffle bag on to the sofa, slips the duffle bag over MICHAEL's head, and then manhandles him over to the pouffe.)

RUAIRI: Now come on Frank –

FRANK: *(To RUAIRI.)* – if yer know what's good for yer!

(To MICHAEL.) I got some questions for yer. You're gonna answer those questions and if you don't answer them correctly, I'm gonna punch you like this.

(FRANK punches MICHAEL in the face. MICHAEL groans and collapses on the ground.)

Do you understand?

(MICHAEL groans.)

Fucking say something!

RUAIRI: He's awful laconic, which often comes over as arrogance when in fact it's shyness.

(FRANK goes over to RUAIRI, close up.)

FRANK: I'm working. What am I fucking doing?

RUAIRI: Working.

(FRANK nuts RUAIRI bang on the nose. RUAIRI collapses on to the sofa holding his nose. RUAIRI starts wailing. FRANK hauls RUAIRI into the bathroom and closes the door.)

I'll stay in here Frank, I understand. Agh!

(FRANK goes back over to MICHAEL and manhandles him back on to the pouffe.)

FRANK: OK shy cunt. First question. What's the difference between a canal and a river?

MICHAEL: A canal is man-made.

FRANK: Good. Yer see how easy these questions are? Next question. What was Popeye's favourite food.

MICHAEL: Tinned spinach.

FRANK: Tinned?

MICHAEL: I think it was always tinned.

FRANK: Aye. So. Did I punch yer that time shy cunt?

MICHAEL: No.

FRANK: Do you see how this works shy cunt?

MICHAEL: Yes.

FRANK: OK. Are you a tout for the Brits?

MICHAEL: If I answer truthfully, you're gonna punch me.

FRANK: If you tell the truth, I will not punch you.

MICHAEL: OK. I am not a tout for the Brits.

FRANK punches him viciously. MICHAEL collapses forwards, groaning. FRANK hauls him up.

RUAIRI: *(Off.)* None of us knew about the Eksund. Costello was the only one what knew!

FRANK hauls the prostrate MICHAEL back into a kneeling position on the pouffe.

FRANK: Doyle! Where was that ship loaded?

MICHAEL: Tripoli.

FRANK punches him viciously and MICHAEL yells.

RUAIRI: *(Off.)* What yer punch him for!? That's the right answer!

FRANK takes a battery operated drill off the sofa. It had been wrapped in a towel in the duffle bag. It is fitted with a long drill bit. FRANK gives it a very short spin to check it's working. Then he goes over to the bathroom door. He knocks on the door.

FRANK: *(Quietly.)* Ruairi? Don't open up! Can you hear me?

RUAIRI: *(Off.)* Yes, I'm sorry, I'll shut up.

FRANK: Put your ear against the door.

RUAIRI: Go ahead Frank.

FRANK: Can you hear me?

(FRANK taps on the door gently.)

Can you hear that?

RUAIRI: I can hear that, aye.

FRANK: I want to tell you something. But don't open the door.

RUAIRI: *(Off.)* OK, what is it Frank?

FRANK moves the drill bit to where he thinks RUAIRI's head might be, and drills through the thin quarter panel in one go. RUAIRI screams. During the next RUAIRI's screaming in the bathroom continues. FRANK goes over to MICHAEL and runs the drill near his ear, just so he can hear it. MICHAEL is now whimpering.

FRANK: Is it the Brits you're talking with, or the FBI?

FRANK runs the drill near MICHAEL's ear.

MICHAEL: I'm not talking to anyone about anything.

FRANK places the drill on MICHAEL's knee cap. COSTELLO opens the door with his own keys and enters. He closes the door behind him. COSTELLO slowly pulls out a small handgun from his jacket pocket. He points it at FRANK.

COSTELLO: Did you have a good flight?

FRANK: Cork to fucking Reykjavik. Fucking Reykjavik to fucking Toronto. Toronto to fucking JFK.

COSTELLO: That's the price of fame Frank McArdle. Get that drill outa the way.

(FRANK at first refuses to comply.)

How many men have you killed Frank?

FRANK: Seven.

COSTELLO: Fourteen.

(FRANK complies, dropping the drill to one side.)

Sit on the sofa.

(FRANK complies. COSTELLO pulls the duffle bag off MICHAEL, revealing his beaten face.)

This is no way to treat my people.

FRANK: One of yous is a tout for the Brits.

COSTELLO goes over to the bathroom door. RUAIRI's moans can still be heard.

COSTELLO: You OK Ruairi?!

RUAIRI opens the door. He stands there not wanting to come out. The drill has grazed his shoulder and bloodied his shirt. It looks like he's been making a bit of a fuss. MICHAEL staggers to the bathroom to clean himself up as RUAIRI comes out.

RUAIRI: He tried to fucking kill me. The fucking psycho.

COSTELLO, with gun still out, sits in an armchair a safe distance from FRANK.

COSTELLO: What's the accusation?

FRANK: Someone betrayed that ship from Libya.

COSTELLO: I'm the only one in New York who knew about that shipment.

FRANK: You coulda told one of these two.

COSTELLO: So Security have sent you to insult and torture my people. Find out who it is, and kill them?

FRANK: Aye. How come you knew about the shipment when it was a secret?

COSTELLO: Secret? Bullshit. McGuiness briefed the executive. Has anyone in Ireland considered that it might be McGuinness himself who told the Brits? Or Gerry.

FRANK: The Big Lad? Hell would have to freeze over first.

COSTELLO: What would've happened if those hundred and fifty tons of arms had gotten through. Frank?

FRANK: We'da gone all out against the Brits.

COSTELLO: And every time we have intensified the war they stop voting for Sinn Fein. Am I right? It's not rocket science is it?

FRANK: How are yer gonna accuse them of that?

COSTELLO: I will fly to Dublin, and invite myself to be court martialed.

FRANK: That's a good idea, if you wanna die and be buried in Ireland.

COSTELLO: A court martial will give me a platform to say what needs to be said.

FRANK: I'll have to make a few phone calls.

COSTELLO: Michael! Did I not buy you an eighteen-year-old MacAllan single malt for Thanksgiving?

MICHAEL: You sure did.

COSTELLO: And you're saving it for the right girl?

RUAIRI: I know where he's fucking hiding it!

RUAIRI goes into MICHAEL's bedroom.

COSTELLO: I've heard you've been on the twelve step programme and gotten yourself clean of the drink.

FRANK: Aye.

COSTELLO: I tried that, yeah, I was a friend of Bill W once, but the drink won.

FRANK: 'Keep coming back.'

COSTELLO: Ha! Yeah, 'keep coming back.' Huh! And what the hell was that other one? 'It's cunning' –

FRANK: – It's 'cunning, baffling and powerful.'

COSTELLO: That's it. Your wife must be pleased?

FRANK: She said if I drink again, I'm out. And if I know one thing about meself it's that without her I'm lost.

COSTELLO: I forget her name –

FRANK: – Mary.

COSTELLO: And have you stopped beating her?

FRANK: Long time now. And how's your wife Mr. Costello?

(Beat.) And you got the one girl I think.

COSTELLO: We lost her.

FRANK: That's a bit fucking careless.

COSTELLO: She killed herself. Two months ago now.

FRANK: Slash her wrists? Hung herself? What?

COSTELLO: She'd been a heroin addict for years. Overdose.

FRANK: And she, your only one an'all.

Enter MICHAEL from the bathroom cleaning himself up.

MICHAEL: I would like you, sir, to shoot that fucking animal dead.

COSTELLO: Relax Michael. This is all part of the everyday push and pull of a people's volunteer army. Get some glasses. Four.

FRANK: I'll not be needing a glass.

COSTELLO: Four glasses please Michael.

MICHAEL goes to get glasses. He comes back with four. RUAIRI comes in with the Macallan.

RUAIRI: Ooh, I've been waiting for this day so!

COSTELLO: Do you know this malt Frank? Eighteen-year-old MacAllan, Scotch. My God man, this is, for me, the most beautiful single malt, and I'm gutted that it isn't Irish but hey…what do you do? A hundred and ten dollars a bottle. I bought it for Michael here, my friend and colleague, because I love him.

COSTELLO opens the bottle. He sniffs the bottle. COSTELLO passes it under RUAIRI's nose.

RUAIRI: Will yer give me a shot of that quick!

COSTELLO gives the gun to MICHAEL. He then goes over to FRANK and passes the bottle under his nose. He lets it linger there. There is a hint of struggle.

COSTELLO: Have you never had a slug of this label?

FRANK: No.

COSTELLO: Never had a shot of the best eh? You got well too soon buddy!

They laugh.

FRANK: I can see it's good, but I'm not drinking.

COSTELLO pours a good measure in front of him into what is ostensibly FRANK's glass.

COSTELLO: I bet you gave your life away to two cent brands, grain whiskies, blends. Shit! And now, even though you can see it before you, you can't taste it.

COSTELLO pours for MICHAEL. He drinks.

MICHAEL: Hell!

COSTELLO: Can you taste the money?

MICHAEL stands.

MICHAEL: Ladies and Gentlemen! We've just crossed the border!

They laugh.

COSTELLO: Michael's usually a quiet guy. In ten minutes I'll have his personality on the stage and I'll be selling fucking tickets.

RUAIRI: Me! Me! Me!

COSTELLO serves a drink to RUAIRI. RUAIRI drinks, and slowly savours.

RUAIRI: Christ! That could give a dead man a hard on.

COSTELLO pours for himself. And drinks. He says nothing.

COSTELLO: You don't mind us drinking in front of you?

FRANK: Do what the fuck yer like.

COSTELLO: Do you want a soda?

FRANK: Glass of water.

COSTELLO: Ruairi! A glass of water for this family man farmer.

RUAIRI: Aye, aye.

RUAIRI complies.

COSTELLO: How did you used to drink your whisky Frank?

FRANK: Bit of ice.

COSTELLO: I like a bit of rattle in the glass that's true. Ice for Frank's whisky.

RUAIRI complies. Silence. FRANK stares at the glass. It looks like he might drink but he doesn't. RUAIRI delivers a glass of water to FRANK and puts ice in.

FRANK: I don't want ice in my water.

COSTELLO: I thought maybe you can drink water with ice and maybe you can imagine you're drinking a double on the rocks.

RUAIRI: *(Drinking.)* Beautiful.

COSTELLO: How's the war going Frank?

FRANK: We need Stinger missiles. Can you get us a Stinger? Qaddafi's outa the picture now.

COSTELLO: And your way of persuading me to bust my balls to get you a Stinger is to come over here and humiliate my people?

FRANK: It's not my job to ask for Stingers.

COSTELLO: I guess for that they'll send someone more respectful. You know, I used to read Grainne, off to sleep, kiss her goodnight, when she was a kid, back in the seventies, back when we were busy.

MICHAEL: Packing them Armalites through the night.

COSTELLO: I don't know if you read your children off to sleep Frank?

FRANK: Aye, I do.

COSTELLO: But there's always that moment when you're still reading and they're already asleep, and yer look at them and wonder at their beauty, and their innocence.

FRANK: Aye.

COSTELLO: And I guess before you leave them to the dark, you check they're still breathing. Do you do that Frank?

FRANK: Aye.

COSTELLO: I imagine that that is what every father has always done. Leaving Grainne's room I had to pass a mirror and look at myself, and for me, that was a difficult moment, because that year, after Bloody Sunday, there were five hundred killed in my war, dead by my rifles. And I had to be strong in that moment, like you are now with the drink, so that I didn't slip down into doubt. What has kept me going all these years is a bright, clear, unequivocal shaft of light – a sure knowledge that our war is a just war, with a clear moral purpose.

(COSTELLO walks behind FRANK. He is holding the whisky bottle.)

You see, Frank, unlike you, I'm not mentally ill. I don't do this shit for fun. You've got a fucking nerve coming to my country to abuse and physically assault my people. You're not a soldier. You think soldiering is about violence, don't you? War requires, the first thing it fucking *requires*, is a clear moral purpose!

FRANK: *(Weak.)* I don't know what the fuck you're on about.

COSTELLO: They call me the Big Fellah, over here. I like it. I godda weakness for that kind of shit. But do you know who the real Big Fellah is?

FRANK: No. I don't.

COSTELLO: Gordon Wilson… I mean can you think of a more English name.

FRANK: *(Weak.)* And who the fuck is Gordon Wilson?

COSTELLO: We killed his daughter at Enniskillen…and he is big, and gracious enough not to hate us for it, and said as much on TV. And if he were here now I would hold him in my arms, and I would tell him that I too have lost a daughter, and that I am praying for his girl, the girl my army killed, and I would tell him that he is as good and true an Irishman as any that ever pulled on boots. *(Beat.)* So Frank, tell me, as a member of the IRA council of war, you fucking tell me right now what moral purpose there is in the cold blooded murder of six women on Remembrance Sunday as they stand by the graves of their sons and husbands long dead!?

(COSTELLO pours whisky into his hand and rubs it into FRANK's face and hair.)

Speak or drink.

(FRANK grabs his arm.)

Let go my arm. Shoot him dead Michael.

(FRANK lets the arm go.)

OK. Hold it.

(COSTELLO tilts FRANK's head back and opens his mouth. He then pours the whisky into his open mouth. During the next, FRANK drinks in this way. Then COSTELLO comes round the sofa and sits. FRANK

leans forward and drinks from his glass. COSTELLO tops FRANK's glass up. COSTELLO fills up everyone's drinks. They drink. FRANK drinks, is topped up, drinks again, then sobs. The others drink.)

Keep coming back Frank. Keep coming back.

Fade to black.

SCENE 2

A different art gallery.

KARELMA: Frank McArdle's been over.

RUAIRI: You know?

KARELMA: Sure.

RUAIRI: He's talking to the Big Fellah about gear and that.

KARELMA: OK.

RUAIRI: Stingers.

KARELMA: It's what you need.

RUAIRI: Aye, imagine one Stinger in South Armagh. The Brits'd couldn't move the grunts around so the county would be ours.

KARELMA: Can Costello get Stingers?

RUAIRI: Oh aye. And there's a move to divorce Sinn Fein and start a new army, and Costello's all for that. Which is a shock to me cos I thought he was sick of the whole business with his daughter, and now his wife's walked out on him.

KARELMA: We know.

RUAIRI: Course yer do. His house'll be broadcasting twenty-four hours a day, eh? Do yer listen to us at Michael's?

KARELMA: What do you think?

RUAIRI: I don't care. I wouldn't take a woman back there. I've never been able to give you very much have I, they know I can't keep my mouth shut so they don't tell me nothing. Costello's very low. Never seen him this bad. Except for being very keen to get the Stingers, which is strange.

KARELMA: With Qaddafi out the picture it's a chance to get his war back. Do you know where he would go for his Stingers?

RUAIRI: I do not.

KARELMA: Ruairi, you're being a bit, I dunno, cool with me.

RUAIRI: I don't want paying no more. I got me qualifications, and this new job is a whole lot of money, and I'm moving outa Woodlawn, gonna get me own place downtown.

KARELMA: Are you still gonna talk to me?

RUAIRI: Aye, but I don't want yer owning me no more. I sold yer me soul, and done alright by it, with the visa and the money and that, but I have to work out if I can enjoy the rest of me life, knowing what I done. You *not paying me*, will help with that.

KARELMA: That's an unusual arrangement.

RUAIRI: I still want a free state, and the Brits out, and all the rest of the stuff I've always wanted. I just wished we could do it without anyone ever getting a nosebleed. I'm trapped on the inside with them cos no one leaves the IRA, and I'm tied to you cos I need your protection. One of these nights yer gonna get a desperate phone call from yer old friend Ruairi O'Drisceoil, yer know that don't yer? Yer gonna have to get me out. And to do that yer gonna have to act pretty fucking quick.

KARELMA: Sure.

RUAIRI: A new name?

KARELMA: Yeah.

RUAIRI: Do I get to choose?

KARELMA: No.

RUAIRI: OK. Can you do what you can to avoid 'Humphrey'?

KARELMA: It ain't me that does the choosing.

RUAIRI: And if I got a woman with me?

KARELMA: Congratulations.

RUAIRI: I haven't done the decent thing yet mind. Do you need to know her name?

KARELMA: Sure do.

RUAIRI: Stella Tomaszewski. She's not Irish.

KARELMA: OK. It would help if you're married.

RUAIRI: Understand. Fucking hell don't rush me into stuff.

KARELMA: Sure.

RUAIRI: You know way back, that first St. Patrick's Day, when I kissed you in the pub, and took you home to mine, was you FBI back then?

KARELMA: Sorry, yeah, I was getting paid.

RUAIRI: Not enough obviously, or I woulda got me leg over. OK. Another one. I've been giving you information for six years now, and Tom Billy hasn't even had a knock on the door. Michael. Costello. The bombs keep going off, like I tell yer they will, and it's all as if I'm blabbing away to me barber, and not the FBI.

KARELMA: I've passed on everything you've ever told me. But ya godda understand the Irish got a lot of clout. If it's a firehouse or the Whitehouse – it helps if you're Irish. *(Beat.)* If you make that phone call, where would you wanna go?

RUAIRI: Ireland.

KARELMA: *(Laughs.)*

RUAIRI: Aye, it's fucking hilarious isn't it.

KARELMA: You gonna run an Irish music festival?

RUAIRI: Take the piss, go on. I've got an ache inside for the auld bog, and it's the only place in the world where I don't stick out like a sore thumb.

KARELMA: *(Still amused.)* OK.

RUAIRI: And I might come to terms with what I done. And I don't mean talking to you. When I shot that young lad, the British soldier –

KARELMA: – you shot him? We thought you were the driver.

RUAIRI: I shot him. Me.

(RUAIRI is cracking up.)

Get me back to Ireland. If I can build a grand, proud, useful building, and cast some new fucking shadow on this earth at least I've done something.

End of Scene.

Act Four

1998. The Woodlawn apartment. May. TOM BILLY COYLE, RUAIRI, and
MICHAEL. TOM BILLY COYLE is out of uniform, in casuals. He's put on
weight. They're drinking. It's evening. They're waiting for COSTELLO.
RUAIRI's accent is more and more New York.

RUAIRI: Ah, you're full of shit, Tom Billy! Those pull boxes
are beautiful, iconic, and functional, and a part of New
York. If you don't have a telephone and you're on fire,
you just go out on to the street and tug the handle of a pull
box and you can talk to the emergency services. Brilliant.
Someone who might not have a phone, an example might
be if yer deaf, yer just –

TOM BILLY: – Fuck the deaf! Fuck 'em! Who gives a fuck!
Why should I bust my ass on these streets, risking my
fucking life for a few deaf assholes!

RUAIRI: I see you're finally realising the benefits of that
tolerance training programme.

TOM BILLY: Fuck 'em!

MICHAEL: Ninety percent of those 10 – 75s are bullshit.

TOM BILLY: Bullshit!

MICHAEL: They are.

TOM BILLY: I'm agreeing with you lieutenant! They're all
bullshit! What makes me puke is that we make it easy for
them! We put a fucking pull box on the corner of every
block in – (every fucking project) –

MICHAEL: – every two blocks.

TOM BILLY: – paint the motherfucker red, stick an ice cream
on the top –

MICHAEL: – that's not an icecream Tom Billy, that's meant to
be a torch, a flame.

TOM BILLY: Fuck you lieutenant! Do you think I do not know
that?

MICHAEL: Quit the lieutenant will ya.

TOM BILLY: There it is punk! Lit up in lights, pull the handle and in ten minutes you'll have your own private NYPD, FDNY Barnum and Bailey fucking street circus!

RUAIRI: I sympathise with the deaf. I might be deaf myself one day! Listening to you Tom Billy!

TOM BILLY: Funny guy!

MICHAEL: Get a cell phone.

TOM BILLY: It's nineteen ninety-eight LOSER! If your deaf ass is on fire ring nine one one!

RUAIRI: I know it's difficult for you Tom Billy but if you empathise a little –

TOM BILLY: – 'empathise.' Are you gay?

RUAIRI: *(Shouting.)* IF YER DEAF! – it's not so easy to use a telephone, on account of your inability to hear what the other party is saying.

TOM BILLY: Bullshit!

RUAIRI: That's not bullshit! That's the very definition of deafness, you big lump of fucking muscle!

TOM BILLY: What are you Ruairi? A fucking dumbass architect, a paper chaser –

RUAIRI: – Now you're going to tell me I know nothing about life!

TOM BILLY: Jack shit! Watch out for the paper cuts man!

RUAIRI: I only design buildings, ipso facto – I don't see life in the raw, and consequently end up a fucking LIBERAL! If I were a cop, of course, I would spend all day on the streets flicking bits of dead muggers brains off of me sandwiches and would, over time, accumulate an intelligence born of experience resulting in wise observations like FUCK THE DEAF!

TOM BILLY: *(Stands.)* Fuck you citizen! You fucking wannabe artist!

RUAIRI: Did I abuse you when you were a wannabe comedian?

TOM BILLY: You sure did asshole!

RUAIRI: *(To MICHAEL.)* Do you know what he wants to do with the homeless?

TOM BILLY: Target practice.

RUAIRI: You're sick in the head!

MICHAEL laughs. TOM BILLY mimes a few pistol shots.

TOM BILLY: Where does it say in the constitution of America that it's OK to spend your life sitting on the fucking sidewalk outside Pizza Hut on your fat lazy ass tied to a cross bred mongrel?!

RUAIRI: I'd like you now to slag off the Muslim terrorists. To be here now, awaiting orders for our own little war in the North, and to listen to you riffing away about the barbarism of the towel heads could be wonderfully ironic.

TOM BILLY: Muslims?

RUAIRI: Yes, Muslims, and Tom Billy…don't hold yourself back!

TOM BILLY: Are you serious?! You fucking what? You mental defective. You can't compare what we're doing with what those fucking cavemen want?!

RUAIRI: More, more!

MICHAEL: *(Pretty much to himself.)* What do they want?

TOM BILLY: The fucking guy who tried to blow up the World Trade Center?!

RUAIRI: This is better than television!

MICHAEL: What do they want? I don't get it.

TOM BILLY: Those guys are mentally ill man.

RUAIRI: Are they evil!?

TOM BILLY: Fuck you citizen! He said he wanted to kill two hundred and fifty thousand people!

MICHAEL: Innocent people.

RUAIRI: And we only murder the guilty!

TOM BILLY: He blew that truck up in the basement. He was tryna bring the fucking towers down. Can you imagine that? Can you imagine if he'd brought the towers down!? The fucking World Trade Center! Man! Imagine that!

RUAIRI: *(Laughing.)* You can't see it can yer!

MICHAEL: What is it they want? That's what I don't get.

TOM BILLY: They want the whole fucking world to eat hummus!

(Beat.) (Serious.) They nearly killed me that day.

RUAIRI: Of course it's all about you isn't it Tom Billy?!

TOM BILLY: February 26th nineteen ninety – what was it?

RUAIRI: – ninety-three –

MICHAEL: – how many times have you told us this story!?

TOM BILLY: – that day, I was working that precinct.

RUAIRI: You were the main target Tom Billy!

TOM BILLY: Fuck you!

MICHAEL: The bomb was lunchtime. You were on nights!

TOM BILLY: Yeah, sure, I was on nights.

RUAIRI: But they weren't to know that Michael! How could they know that he was tucked up in bed in Queens with his hand on his knob?! You out fooled them there Tom Billy!

TOM BILLY: Eat shit asshole!

MICHAEL: They gave no warnings man. That's immoral!

TOM BILLY: We give warnings.

RUAIRI: Ah yes! The 'exemplar' terrorist bombing is the way we do it, like Enniskillen!

MICHAEL: Enniskillen was a fuck up.

TOM BILLY: We apologised.

MICHAEL: You can't draw anything from Enniskillen.

TOM BILLY: We should nuke the whole fucking Middle East. Look at the way they treat their women!

MICHAEL: I don't understand what they want.

TOM BILLY: They want the dark ages man. They wanna turn all the fucking lights off.

RUAIRI: But I would guess Tom Billy that you would sympathise with their approach to the thorny issue of the gay community.

MICHAEL laughs.

TOM BILLY: What are you laughing at?

MICHAEL: He's got you there.

RUAIRI: They wanna chuck all the gays off the mountain, and lordy lordy so do you Tom Billy!

TOM BILLY: Some of my best friends are members of the gay community!

(TOM BILLY does a Pinnochio nose. MICHAEL laughs.)

Gay *community*. What the fuck is that? A 'community' is where you can knock on the door and say 'excuse me, can you lend me a bowl of sugar please.' In a faggot community you get a knock on the door and the guy says 'can you lend me a bowl of sugar please, and if you've got a minute spare do you mind nailing my dick to the wardrobe!'

MICHAEL: He's doing old material.

RUAIRI: It wasn't funny then and it isn't funny now.

TOM BILLY: All that federal money to 'AIDS VICTIMS.' Victims? Fuck you! If your idea of a good weekend is fucking fifteen strangers up the ass then sooner or later buddy you're gonna catch a cold!

RUAIRI: Have you ever slept with a man Tom Billy?

MICHAEL laughs.

TOM BILLY: Fuck you!

RUAIRI: I blew a guy once.

Silence. MICHAEL and TOM BILLY stop working.

A telephone engineer from Boulder, Colorado.

MICHAEL: You gave a telephone engineer from Boulder Colorado a blow job?

RUAIRI: Yeah.

TOM BILLY: Why did you do that?

RUAIRI: It felt like the decent thing to do.

MICHAEL: Why?

RUAIRI: Cos he'd just given me one.

TOM BILLY: Wow! I always sympathised with you Ruairi, ya know the way your street started getting a name as the place to go in Midtown East where you could pick up some junky piece of shit faggot, well, I declined to call it what it was and I always referred to it as 53rd and 3rd but now I know you're gay too, I'm gonna go back to calling it O'Drisceoil corner. Faggot!

TOM BILLY and RUAIRI stand aggressively. TOM BILLY throws an empty can at RUAIRI. RUAIRI picks up a can and throws it at TOM BILLY. MICHAEL stands between them.

MICHAEL: Hey guys! Cool it.

TOM BILLY: I'm NYPD ya know. I can have you thrown outa my country. Are you legal yet? Is he legal?

MICHAEL: He's been legal fifteen years Tom Billy. You don't listen.

RUAIRI: Cos you're DEAF!

TOM BILLY sits.

TOM BILLY: Where the fuck is Costello?! Huh? Is he coming? He wants us to do some packing, yeah?

MICHAEL: I do not know.

TOM BILLY: Packing. We're gonna be packing all night.

MICHAEL: He's late, that's all I know.

TOM BILLY: Is it packing? Maybe it's an operation.

RUAIRI: Yeah, big guy, you godda kill a woman.

TOM BILLY: Fuck you man!

RUAIRI: Agh!

TOM BILLY flies across the room and pins RUAIRI to the floor. MICHAEL dives in and separates them. They're all on the floor. TOM BILLY gets one punch in on RUAIRI.

MICHAEL: Guys! Quit! Hell!

TOM BILLY: D'ya hear him. D'ya hear what he said?!

MICHAEL: I heard him. Now cool it guys. Ruairi, cool it.

RUAIRI: You punched me. In the mouth.

TOM BILLY: I had orders. Jerk.

MICHAEL: He had orders. You know he had orders.

RUAIRI: What? To punch me?

MICHAEL: To kill the girl.

RUAIRI: To kill your girl.

MICHAEL punches RUAIRI.

RUAIRI: Agh! You punched me now!

RUAIRI stands and goes to the bathroom, and goes in, closing the door behind him.

TOM BILLY: This might be Aids blood. Jesus.

MICHAEL: Hell, did I punch Ruairi?

TOM BILLY: Yeah.

MICHAEL: Shit.

TOM BILLY: We got a tout ya know. Godda be. One of us. Look at the Stinger operation. Chuck and Francis got four years for that. That whole thing was an FBI set up.

MICHAEL: Costello?

TOM BILLY: It ain't me. That ship an'all. Way back. It ain't me man.

MICHAEL: Ruairi?

TOM BILLY: When did he get his Green Card?

MICHAEL: He's been legal years.

TOM BILLY: I looked on the computer man. He's godda criminal record in Ireland. No way you're gonna get legal with a record like that. Unless you get help.

MICHAEL: What are you saying?

TOM BILLY: It ain't me. That's all I'm saying.

RUAIRI comes out of the bathroom, nursing his mouth.

RUAIRI: *(To TOM BILLY.)* Yer fucking punched me. Yer a violent man.

(To MICHAEL.) And you punched me an'all. And you're not a violent man. He's the nutter.

Enter COSTELLO. He has his own keys. He is carrying two or three big laundry bags packed with folded down cardboard boxes, Teddy Bears in boxes, and boxed up FX401 detonators.

TOM BILLY: *(Looking at the bags.)* Packing. Didn't I tell ya?

COSTELLO: How's it going?

TOM BILLY: Ruairi's telling us about his faggot weekends.

RUAIRI: I blew a guy once Mr. Costello.

COSTELLO: You blew a guy?

RUAIRI: Yeah.

COSTELLO: Why d'yer do that?

RUAIRI: I was having no success with the ladies.

COSTELLO: Did you kiss him on the lips?

RUAIRI: I did not, no.

COSTELLO: That's alright then.

RUAIRI: Thank you.

COSTELLO: Was this before you met your wife?

RUAIRI: Stella.

COSTELLO: Of course, Stella.

RUAIRI: Yeah and she knows about it.

TOM BILLY: Shit man! He's told his wife. Fucking liberals!

RUAIRI hands over a flyer to COSTELLO.

RUAIRI: This is an invitation for my private view –

TOM BILLY: *(Gay stereotype.)* – 'my private view.' Cocksucker!

COSTELLO: You know I wanna buy that one that's a bit like a Mondrian.

RUAIRI: They're all a bit like Mondrian.

TOM BILLY: Fuck, will you cut me some slack here guys!? I'm blue collar, I can't listen to shit like this, I'm gonna chuck.

MICHAEL: Let me get you a drink Mr. Costello.

TOM BILLY: We're celebrating.

RUAIRI: Michael's made lieutenant at last.

TOM BILLY: *(With a giggle.)* Sixth attempt.

COSTELLO: A quitter never wins, and a winner never quits! Lieutenant, wow.

MICHAEL: Ladder 15. Water Street.

COSTELLO: Near the river, near South Street?

MICHAEL: Yeah.

COSTELLO: OK. We must lunch, I'm often in Lower Manhattan.

MICHAEL: I don't get a lunch like that.

COSTELLO: Well done Michael. Good for the pension, huh?

MICHAEL: Hey, don't talk like that.

TOM BILLY: What are we packing?

COSTELLO: FX 401s.

TOM BILLY: Detonators.

RUAIRI: We're gonna blow something?

TOM BILLY: Not you. You've blown enough!

COSTELLO: One big something yeah.

MICHAEL has taken a TEDDY out the box.

MICHAEL: Teddy Bears! Cute!

COSTELLO: We got to get these FX 401s through customs. We stuff each detonator in a Teddy, and let the postman do the rest.

RUAIRI: 'Neither rain, nor snow, nor sleet, nor hail, shall keep the postmen from their appointed rounds.'

MICHAEL: Air mail.

RUAIRI: These addresses can't be Real IRA.

COSTELLO: Sympathisers. They're expecting the Teddys. We only need one to get through. Take out the voice box.

TOM BILLY presses the voice box. The Teddy says 'I love you Mummy!' Or similar.

MICHAEL: Cute.

(TOM BILLY takes out the voice box by opening the velcro/zip back on the Teddy.)

Replace with an FX 401.

(TOM BILLY complies.)

Pack it.

MICHAEL: If customs scan the box they'll think the electrical kit is the Teddy's voice box.

RUAIRI: OK lieutenant, we worked that out.

TOM BILLY: Come on guys! It's us against the Teddys!

TOM BILLY drags the bags on to the coffee table and takes out a pile of Teddy Bears in boxes, and various boxes of switches – branded FX401. The production line is as follows – TOM BILLY pulls out from the back of a Teddy Bear the electronic voice box. He then passes the gutted Teddy Bear along to MICHAEL who sticks one of the FX401 switches in its place. This then goes down the line to be packed and addressed.

MICHAEL: Sit there Mr. Costello.

COSTELLO: *(With a piece of paper in his hand.)* Who wants the addresses?

TOM BILLY/MICHAEL: Ruairi.

TOM BILLY: Women's work. Ha, ha!

RUAIRI: Cos it's real man's work, ripping the guts out of a big hairy-arsed Teddy Bear and way beyond the likes of a nine stone weakling with artistic inclinations.

(MICHAEL places in front of RUAIRI the first Teddy Bear which needs packing. RUAIRI just stares at it.)

What's the target?

TOM BILLY: Pack the fucking Teddy Bear cock sucker!

COSTELLO: Pack the Teddy Bear Ruairi.

RUAIRI: No. I wanna know. What's the target?

TOM BILLY: Pack the Teddy punk!

RUAIRI: Is it a military target?

COSTELLO: It's not military.

RUAIRI: I'm not packing.

TOM BILLY: Pack the fucking Teddy soldier!

RUAIRI: It's not military?!

TOM BILLY: Who – (Gives a fuck.)

COSTELLO: – Tom Billy! Shutup.

(TOM BILLY shuts up and sits down.)

MICHAEL: *(Laughs.)*

TOM BILLY: What are you laughing at?

COSTELLO: It's an operation against those who support the Good Friday Peace Agreement.

TOM BILLY: We're gonna blow up the Pope?

COSTELLO: It's not the Pope.

TOM BILLY: Me and the Pope got a lot in common. He don't like wearing a rubber and neither do I.

RUAIRI: Are we gonna hit Adams?

COSTELLO: It's not Adams.

TOM BILLY: We should be hitting Adams. Shit! I bust my ass for twenty years for Gerry Adams, a fucking lifetime, and when he finally gets a visa, when he finally comes to my town –

RUAIRI: – this ain't *your town.*

TOM BILLY: – this town fucking is my town!

(To COSTELLO.) When he finally comes to my town how come you don't get invited to lunch at the Sheraton huh? How come Adams ain't saying 'thank you' to our Mister Costello, publicly, knowhatimean?

COSTELLO: There was only one seat at the table. It was either me or Clinton.

MICHAEL: I heard they shook hands.

RUAIRI: Of course they shook hands.

TOM BILLY: Shake hands? Fuck you. Gerry Adams got his dick out, and Clinton blew him. Forget Monica whatshername –

Some of them laugh.

MICHAEL: – Lewinsky.

TOM BILLY: Forget Monica Lewinsky, the real scandal is that the President of America flew into my town on Airforce One and blew Gerry Adams at the Sheraton in front of Kissinger –

(MICHAEL is laughing now. RUAIRI giggling.)

– Flynn, and Feeney and –

MICHAEL: – O'Dowd.

They're all laughing now.

TOM BILLY: And Niall O' fucking Dowd, and the scandal is that we, our organisation, him, we were not represented at the function, the blowing event, when it was us that made that event possible.

COSTELLO: So what do you want to do about it Tom Billy?

TOM BILLY: Stormont. The castle. Boof! *(He mimes an explosion.)*

COSTELLO: It's not Stormont.

RUAIRI: If it's not Adams, not military or political, what is it?

COSTELLO: I can't tell you.

RUAIRI: OK. I understand but I'm not touching anything.

(RUAIRI stands, and raises his hands away from the Teddys.)

(To COSTELLO.) After Enniskillen, you said we would only go for the Brits. Military. You, yourself, I heard you say that!

COSTELLO: I have orders from the new people – (I)

RUAIRI: – No! I never believed that about you. That you take orders. You're your own man Mr. Costello. What's the target?

TOM BILLY: He can't fucking tell you, dumbass.

COSTELLO: It's an attack on the peace process. It's a commercial target.

RUAIRI: Commercial?

MICHAEL: What's commercial?

TOM BILLY: A shop. A protestant shop. Marks and Spencer's. No, they're Jewish. We don't want to do that I'm one eighth Jewish.

MICHAEL: You're an eighth Jewish?

TOM BILLY: I'm Brooklyn ain't I. Everyone in Brooklyn's at least one eighth Jewish.

COSTELLO: What do people do when there's peace? They go shopping.

RUAIRI: So we're gonna blow up some women and kids when they're out shopping? I got family all over Ireland. Which town?

TOM BILLY: He can't tell you. Don't tell him sir.

MICHAEL: It ain't gonna be County Cork.

RUAIRI: I got family in the north.

COSTELLO: Omagh.

TOM BILLY: You told him.

RUAIRI: You told me this Real IRA we joined was gonna be an army. I'm out.

TOM BILLY: You're fucking in man.

RUAIRI: I'm out. I said. I'm out.

TOM BILLY: There's in and there's Mexico. OK?

RUAIRI: Yeah, yeah – you threaten me. Go ahead. I'm out.

RUAIRI stands and makes his way to the door. TOM BILLY follows him. And puts himself between RUAIRI and the door.)

COSTELLO: Tom Billy's right Ruairi. There is no out I'm afraid.

RUAIRI: I'm out.

TOM BILLY: Can he go?

MICHAEL: Let him go.

TOM BILLY: Can we let him go? Sir?!

COSTELLO: Let him go.

RUAIRI leaves.

TOM BILLY: We'll get orders. Yeah? On Ruairi.

COSTELLO: Yeah.

MICHAEL: You think?

COSTELLO: Yeah.

MICHAEL: Do they have to know? We don't have to say. Sir?

COSTELLO: We do have to say.

MICHAEL: Shit.

TOM BILLY: Of course we'll get fucking orders.

COSTELLO: We'll wait.

COSTELLO takes over RUAIRI's job, packing, wrapping, addressing etc.

TOM BILLY: We think Ruairi's been informing.

COSTELLO: Yeah?

MICHAEL: The Stingers operation was a set-up.

COSTELLO: And what information did he have about that? None.

TOM BILLY: He got a criminal record in Ireland so how's he get a green card? Huh?

COSTELLO: If Ruairi was a tout we'd all be in the Lincoln Correctional.

TOM BILLY: That ain't how it works Mr. Costello. The FBI, and the Brits, they get someone on the inside, they keep them there. They get the info, they don't bust the unit.

MICHAEL: Why don't they bust the unit?

TOM BILLY: If they bust the unit, then we'd start a new unit, which they wouldn't know anything about.

COSTELLO: Leave it to me, Tom Billy, and pass me that knife will you?

They work.

MICHAEL: We were talking earlier sir. What do these Muslims want? Ya know, if we give in and say 'OK, OK ya got it! You can have what you want.'

TOM BILLY: What the fuck do we give them?

MICHAEL: What do they want?

COSTELLO: Are you religious?

TOM BILLY: Catholic. No. Ya know. I like Christmas.

COSTELLO: They want what all religions want. They wanna punish us all for being human.

(Beat.) Gimme some packing tape.

Fade.

SCENE 2

The art gallery. RUAIRI sits and makes a phone call.

RUAIRI: *(On the phone.)* Karelma? …it's me, …yeah… there's gonna be an operation… we've been shipping detonators…civilian target…Omagh, County Tyrone. …I don't know…I don't know! Fuck! …and you gotta get me out now. Now! Like right now, now… Anywhere you say. But fucking now!

SCENE 3

COSTELLO isolated in a spot, as in Act One Scene One. It is the 1999 St. Patrick's Day Parade dinner. Buzz of laughter, talk, cutlery. COSTELLO in a suit, not Brian Boru, now aged 64, stands, with a smile, gestures with his hand, a blast of the pipes follows, silence.

COSTELLO: Thank you Jerry. Jerry has got a new book out 'Learn to play the pipes in one hour.' Yeah, after just one hour you can be as good Jerry.

(Laughter.)

Can you hear me at the back? One year I said that, someone shouted out 'I can hear, but I'm happy to swap with someone who can't.'

(Laughter.)

St. Patrick's day is a great day for the Irish.

(Cheers.)

It's even better if you're not Irish.

(Laughter.)

If you've spent the day pretending to be Irish you just get up the next morning, brush yourself down, say your apologies, forget the tears and the pain, and go back to being Korean.

(Laughter.)

I would like you to put your hands together for our chef, Wei Chang Lao, for a terrific meal!

(Applause.)

One of the benefits of peace in the north is that a plate of food at this dinner now costs a helluva lot less.

(Laughter.)

My forefathers left Ireland in 1872. Some of the younger contenders for Parade Grand Marshal have started a rumour that I was with them.

(Laughter.)

This year, 1999, I will step aside and give them what they want – I'm resigning after twenty-nine years.

(Applause. Everyone stands.)

I have, in the past, been keen to take your money.

(Laughter.)

Put your cheques away… I have no use for them. Thank God. I know most of you… I've held your babies, I've been there when you buried your dead…hell! How many times have I walked through Queens behind black horses?! We're family, yeah? I'm an intelligent man, though flawed obviously, and I know what you're thinking, sitting there, looking at me, wondering if there'll be any new jokes this year.

(Some laughter.)

– two snails on the freeway, tearing along about eighty-five miles an hour, they overtake this speedcop, one snail on the outside, one on the inside…

(He stops. They wait for the punch line but he doesn't give it. Something weird going on…)

…the Irish built the prisons in this country, and then proceeded to fill them!

(Several laughs.)

That's an old one, one of Ronald Reagan's.

(One laugh.)

I've given you twenty years of jokes, you've had jokes enough.

I got a shock for you tonight. I'm not Irish, you're not Irish. I'm an American. A baby craves the womb. Why? I dunno. Why is it not enough to be merely human? Why was it not enough for me to be born in Burlington New Jersey within a spit of the Tucker's Island light. Get over it. I am a man that's all. If that's not enough, to be an *American,* before you've even started you got a problem. I am sixteen, I come to New York, I meet a girl, the Grand Colleen of the 1952 parade. She is extraordinary. *She* falls in love *with me!?* Most men coulda filled a life loving her.

(Angry with himself now.)

Suddenly I have a business which works, a wife, who loves me, we have a daughter, I'm a father. And that is not enough for me?! Let me try and explain…you know the axis of the earth is slightly outa whack, we're on a tilt, yeah, well I've never been very happy about that. I kinda think someone's gotta fix that, yeah? Understand what I'm saying?

(Silence.)

What I did, and you all know what I did, at one time, was selfish. I so wanted to be The Big Fellah, trying to get history to kiss me, just once, whore that she is.

(Getting increasingly difficult for him.)

I was in the K Mart in Astor Place, ya know Lafayette and Broadway, I was buying insoles, yeah, for my shoes, and this woman, Puerto Rican…we went for a coffee at the Starbucks there…and I was at a low point in my life after Enniskillen, and Theresa and you know…Graunia… they're clever like that, they knew that money wouldna tempted me, so they waited until I was weak, very clever. We, as Americans, should be proud of their professionalism of the FBI. What makes any of us do anything? Huh!? I was a boy once…so many mistakes as a boy, and I thought at some point the mistake making would end…so…yes…I have been working for the FBI for the past twelve years –

(He takes a drink. There is nothing, no murmurs, just silence.)

The worst is to have lived a lie to you guys, my friends who have traveled with me. I thought you would have left by now. That's how I imagined it. I thought you would all walk out on me, leaving me standing here still talking. I rehearsed this speech, I always do. The stuff that looks off the cuff – yeah, well it's written down, mostly, rehearsed, the trick is to make it look not rehearsed.

(Increasingly difficult for him.)

Theresa would listen to me rehearsing. Laugh. Get me to change something. Thank you, thank you all, for being quiet, respectful. Maybe you acknowledge that to do what I am doing before you, my people, to admit publicly to the betrayal of friends is one man taking the hard road and facing up to what he has become. But this is another flaw, they call it 'vanity'. I want you to say – 'that was brave of him', 'he coulda just gone into hiding'; 'the Big Fellah doesn't do things that way.'

TOM BILLY: *(Off.)* You're a dead guy!

(Silence.)

COSTELLO: There was a time when I was confident and could deal with a little heckle.

TOM BILLY: *(Off.)* I said…you're a dead guy!

COSTELLO: *(Taking out a piece of paper.)* I would like to read a verse of a poem. Yeats.

(COSTELLO reads. He needs to read, he doesn't know it by heart.)

COSTELLO: I will arise and go now, and go to Innisfree –

TOM BILLY: *(Off.)* You're a dead guy.

COSTELLO: And a small cabin build there, of clay and wattles made –

TOM BILLY: *(Off.)* You're a dead guy.

COSTELLO: Nine bean rows will I have there, a hive for the honey bee –

TOM BILLY: *(Off.)* You're a dead guy.

COSTELLO: And live alone in the bee-loud glade –

(*Beat.*)

And I shall have some peace there, for peace comes dropping slow.

(*Silence.*)

TOM BILLY: *(Off.)* We're gonna fucking burn you down!

Snap to black.

SCENE 4

The Woodlawn flat. TOM BILLY and MICHAEL just home from the dinner, still dressed in kilts and ceremonials.

MICHAEL: I think we should wait.

TOM BILLY: We don't need no orders. I'm gonna go up Oceanside now. Ya coming with me!

MICHAEL: He won'ta gone back to Long Beach. Not after that.

TOM BILLY: Jesus! I can't believe we let him outa the hall! Someone held me back. Big old guy, face like a fucking map, d'yer see him –

MICHAEL: – I saw him.

TOM BILLY: D'yer know him? I'll fucking waste him an'all.

MICHAEL: I been introduced to all those old timers, I don't remember their names.

TOM BILLY: Give me a clean gun. I ain't gonna use my Glock. What you got? Come on! Fuck!

MICHAEL: What do you want?

TOM BILLY: You got a Smith snub nose?

MICHAEL: Yeah.

TOM BILLY: That'll do nicely! Dig it up then Michael! Come on man! I got a licence! For fuck's sake, what's the matter wid you boy!?

(MICHAEL goes to the door, takes out his keys and locks the door, taking the keys out of the lock. He then finds an electric screwdriver, rolls back a bit of carpet and starts taking up a floorboard.)

It was the Big Fellah all along. Christ! And we were gonna Mexico Ruairi!

MICHAEL: We're still waiting on orders for Ruairi.

TOM BILLY: Fuck it man, he's gone. I coulda sworn it was Ruairi. I miss him. He was funny. Funny bones. You know if Ruairi had been doing my material, you know my material and his funny bones, I coulda made it, you know, as a comedy writer.

MICHAEL: It might have been Ruairi, as well.

TOM BILLY: Two touts in one team?! No way. You gotta come with me, you know the house. I don't want to make a mistake. It wouldn't be right to shoot the neighbours.

MICHAEL: I've only been to the house once, a barbecue.

TOM BILLY: Me, never. He never gave me nothing. Not even an undercooked sausage. You go down Rockaway Boulevard and do a left towards Woodmere. Yeah?

MICHAEL: Yeah. He won't be there.

TOM BILLY: You drive.

MICHAEL: I'm not driving my car.

TOM BILLY: Steal a car. It's easy, I'll show you. And I won't arrest you either, this time. We'll get a Ford, I'm not sitting in a fucking Nissan for an hour with my knees knocking on my chin. If I want my teeth loosened I'll pay a dentist.

(MICHAEL unfolds a cloth and presents TOM BILLY with a Smith and Wesson snub nose.)

Nice. Do you want it back?

MICHAEL: No.

TOM BILLY: OK. Gimme some canon balls.

(MICHAEL hands over a packet of slugs from under the floorboards.)

Why do you hide this stuff? It makes it look like you're doing something wrong.

There is a knock at the door. They freeze.

TOM BILLY: Are you expecting anyone?

MICHAEL: No.

The door handle turns.

TOM BILLY: They're trying to get in.

MICHAEL: I locked it.

TOM BILLY goes to the door listens. The rattle of keys.

TOM BILLY: He's got a fucking key! Who's got keys?

MICHAEL: Ruairi and the Big Fellah.

A key turns in the lock. TOM BILLY backs away from the door as COSTELLO enters and closes the door behind him. He's still in dinner jacket, but without the tie. He's not drunk.

COSTELLO: Good evening.

(Silence.)

My speech went well. I thought. What do you think Michael?

MICHAEL: Good yeah.

TOM BILLY: *(To MICHAEL.)* Shut the fuck up!

COSTELLO: Not as many laughs as usual. But you know… circumstances. I don't want a drink thank you.

TOM BILLY: Lock that door Michael.

MICHAEL does as he's told.

COSTELLO: Still doing as you're told Michael?

MICHAEL: I had it locked.

COSTELLO: Looking at guns?

TOM BILLY: Yeah.

COSTELLO: This should be a job for Michael. You've done enough Tom Billy.

(COSTELLO takes his watch off, and his rings, and puts them on the side.)

This is a good watch, runs a little fast, which means you get there early. In Korea I saw an officer shoot a Gook, stoop down take the watch off the body. I didn't like that. I thought that was unAmerican. I'm serious these are gifts. Whoever. If you want them. Wedding ring. Pawn it. Buy a drink. Buy a round.

(He takes his wedding ring off, puts it on the side.)

Michael?

MICHAEL: I can't. We don't have orders.

COSTELLO: You don't get it do you Michael –

TOM BILLY: – that's what I said, I said –

COSTELLO: – shut up! –

(TOM BILLY shuts up but is not subservient in his body language.)

(To TOM BILLY.) Give him the gun.

(TOM BILLY gives MICHAEL the snub nose.)

MICHAEL: It's not what I do.

COSTELLO: You're in an army. You godda shoot the enemy. You've already killed. Hell, every dollar buys a bullet. How many dollars have you raised? I'll be in here.

COSTELLO goes into the bathroom and closes the door.

TOM BILLY: *(Miming.)* To the head. He'll let you. You can shut your fucking big girl eyes that way.

MICHAEL: I can't do it.

TOM BILLY: You godda. Why's it always me. You think it's easy for me? The fuck. Get in there!

TOM BILLY virtually pushes MICHAEL into the bathroom. MICHAEL goes in. We see COSTELLO sitting on the side of the bath. TOM BILLY closes the door. TOM BILLY sits. Waits. Listens. He doesn't fret, but suddenly he stands, takes his police issue Colt and goes into the bathroom, closing the door behind him. A shot is heard.

End of Scene.

Epilogue

2001. The apartment. Early morning. Sun just coming up. The radio is playing Bruce Springsteen's 'Born to Run'. A new Bialetti bubbles. MICHAEL is cleaning his teeth in the bathroom. Hearing the Bialetti he comes out and turns it off. He is fiftyish now with a belly and a bit of grey. This station is his favourite as it plays his music – rock and punk. The DJ talks over Springsteen and fades it out. MICHAEL goes back into the bathroom and his teeth cleaning.

DJ: The Boss reminding us that 'we were born to run.' 101.7 Apple FM bringing you a New York Rock and Roll sunrise! Who said you can't dance on a Tuesday morning – this is a free country! Manhattan Bridge gridlocked, Brooklyn Bridge moving slow, Holland Tunnel all clear, Lincoln Tunnel all clear. Stay tuned for MTA New York City subway news. It's a beautiful bright day, look at that sky, trust me, it's September 'officially temperate.' Kennedy Airport, La Guardia, and Newark International report – no problems. Don't be a dummy, don't drive, use Airlink, your personal transportation system for all three airports. O456 787878 Now! We got two tickets here for Mark E Smith and The Fall November twenty-fourth at the Knitting Factory, Canal Street – they're yours if you can tell me which New York rock legend was born Jeffry Ross Hyman – born 1951, died this year, 2001. Hey ho, let's go.

The Ramones '53rd and 3rd' plays. Michael comes out from the bathroom. Michael laughs, and sings along. He goes into his bedroom and dresses. Michael comes back dressed in his Lieutenant uniform. He takes a drink of coffee from the pot. He pours some cereal, milk, and eats it. He sits and puts on his shoes. He dresses in his FDNY coat. Time should be taken over the little things here. He sets his ansaphone. He plugs in a new gizzmo, a delayed hot pot cooker, he fiddles with some timer device on the cooker. He leaves.

Slow to black.

The End.

The Troubles – a Chronology

This chronology is necessarily brief. The 3,500 people killed in 'the Troubles' since 1969 cannot be mentioned individually nor can the circumstances be explained in detail. Some incidents mentioned below only warrant inclusion because they are relevant to the play.

1170	The first English invasion of Ireland.
1541	Henry VIII declares himself to be King of Ireland.
1690	Battle of the Boyne fought on Ireland's East Coast between the Catholic King James and the Protestant King William. The latter won, and the battle is commemorated annually by Orange Order marches, or 'walks'.
1798	Wolfe Tone's united Irishmen defeated. Wolfe Tone imprisoned and slits his own throat. He is buried in Bodenstown, Co Kildare which became an annual pilgrimage for Republicans.
1801	United Kingdom created through Act of Union including Ireland.
1916	Easter Rising defeated.
1921-23	Irish civil war. Michael Collins (the Big Fellah) killed. Northern Ireland created.
1939	IRA bombing campaign in England.
1966	Ulster Volunteer Force (UVF) formed in Belfast.
1968	Civil Rights marches in Northern Ireland.
1969	British Army arrive in Northern Ireland. IRA splits. Provisional IRA (PIRA) formed. The Irish Northern Aid Committee (Noraid) is established in the USA, ostensibly to raise money for PIRA prisoners' families. George Harrison begins running Mafia guns to the IRA from his base in New York.
1971	First British soldier shot dead.

1972	Bloody Sunday. British Paratroopers fired on a civil rights march in Derry. 13 died, and a 14th died later as a result of injuries. The Saville Inquiry concluded (in 2010) that all had been unarmed. Bloody Sunday was followed by a swell in support for the Republican cause, and an increase in IRA membership.
	Bombing campaign in England and Northern Ireland.
	PIRA leaders have talks in Libya.
1974	M62 coach bombing. Nine British soldiers and three civilians killed.
	Birmingham pub bombings. Twenty-one civilians killed.
1976	Six Catholic civilians killed by loyalists.
	Kingsmill massacre. Ten protestants killed by Republican faction.
1977	Cellular (small group) structure of IRA introduced.
1978	Martin McGuinness appointed PIRA chief.
1980	Republican prisoners begin a hunger strike in the Maze prison.
1980	Joe Doherty arrested as part of a hit squad that kills SAS officer.
1981	Bobby Sands, a hunger striker, elected to the UK Parliament while in prison. Later that year, he dies, as do a further nine hunger strikers.
	Joe Doherty and seven others escape from the Crumlin Road jail. Doherty travels on to New York where he starts work as a barman.
	Qaddafi showers PIRA with cash.
	Christin ni Elias avoids being assassinated by her own PIRA colleagues following an 'affair' with a British intelligence officer. Escapes to Canada.
1982	Gerry Adams increasingly prominent in Sinn Fein, publicly distancing himself from the IRA. Elected to Northern Ireland Assembly.
1983	Adams elected to Westminster Parliament as an abstaining MP for West Belfast.

Adams becomes president of Sinn Fein.

Harrods bombed. Six people are killed.

The racehorse Shergar is 'kidnapped' by the PIRA. It is believed to have been shot very shortly after its abduction from stables.

1984   Big PIRA arms deal negotiated with Libya.

New York Irish Emerald Society Police Band play in the parade at Bundoran, County Donegal, to commemorate the deaths of 10 republican hunger strikers.

1985   Anglo Irish agreement signed, giving the Irish Government an advisory role in Northern Ireland's government and setting out conditions for the establishment of a devolved government for the region.

The fishing boat 'Casamara' makes two trips bringing arms from Libya.

Boston Police Department flak jackets are found in a PIRA shipment of arms from America on the trawler Valhalla.

1986   The 'Kula' lands 14 tons of arms from Libya.

The 'Villa' lands 105 tons of arms and semtex from Libya.

1987   Inside intelligence leads to the arrest of the trawler 'Eksund' carrying arms from Libya.

PIRA bomb kills eleven on Remembrance Day at Enniskillen cenotaph. Gordon Wilson, father of Marie Wilson, one of the victims, expresses forgiveness to the killers.

1988   Three PIRA operatives killed in Gibraltar.

1990   Gerry Adams working to separate Sinn Fein and PIRA.

PIRA's first use of human bombs i.e. bombs, tied to PIRA prisoners, and driven at troops.

Joe Doherty becomes a cause célèbre in New York and 130 Congressmen back his claim to be a political prisoner. A street corner in New York is named Doherty corner.

1992   Adams loses his West Belfast seat to the SDLP (Social Democratic and Labour Party).

1995	Gerry Adams attends a reception at the White House at the invitation of Bill Clinton.
1996	PIRA bomb London docklands, killing two people. Manchester bombed: 212 people are injured though no one is killed.
1997	Real IRA formed.
1998	Good Friday Agreement reached, Northern Ireland Assembly created.
	Real IRA bomb Omagh town centre, killing 29 people.
1999	Martin McGuinness becomes Minister for Education in the Northern Ireland Assembly.
2001	9/11 attacks on the twin towers of the World Trade Centre in New York.
	George W Bush commits the USA to a war against terrorism.
	John McDonagh, chairman of the New York Irish Freedom Committee says 'we've got a sponsored five mile fun run in October and a dinner dance in January, so we'll wait and see if the take is down.'
2002	Assembly suspended.
2007	Power-sharing Assembly reinstated with Ian Paisley as First Minister and Martin McGuinness as Deputy First Minister.
2010	Department of Justice founded on transfer of powers of justice and policing to the Northern Ireland Executive.
	Real IRA plant car bomb near MI5's Northern Ireland base. No one killed.

THE HERETIC

I'd like to thank the following for their help and support in developing the script. Chris Campbell, Erica Whyman, Sonia Friedman, Jack Bradley, Dominic Cooke, James Fleet, Clive Coleman, Martin Wright, Jeremy Herrin, Lisa Makin, Dr Stewart Bean, Adrian Hood and Jemma Kennedy. And all the cast who have made contributions along the way. Thank you.

Richard Bean

The Heretic was first performed at The Royal Court Jerwood Theatre Downstairs, Sloane Square, London on Friday 4 February 2011 with the following cast:

DR DIANE CASSELL	Juliet Stevenson
PHOEBE	LydiaWilson
BEN SHOTTER	Johnny Flynn
GEOFF TORDOFF	Adrian Hood
PROFESSOR KEVIN MALONEY	James Fleet
CATHERINE TICKELL	LeahWhitaker

Director	Jeremy Herrin
Designer	Peter McKintosh
Lighting Designer	Paul Pyant
Sound Designer	Emma Laxton
Casting Director	Julia Horan
Assistant Director	Sophie Austin
Production Manager	Paul Handley
Stage Manager	Ben Delfont
Deputy Stage Manager	Tilly Stokes
Assistant Stage Manager	Laura Draper
Stage Management Placement	Louis Carver
Costume Supervisor	Iona Kenrick
Fight Director	Kevin McCurdy
Set built by	Scena
Painted by	Charlotte Gainey

The Royal Court Theatre and Stage Management wish to thank the following for their help on this production: Bryn Austin, Department of Earth Sciences at UCL, Dorset Cereal Company, Robin Fisher, Franke UK Ltd, Grove Organic Fruit Company, Ruth Murfitt, Nature Magazine, Jeremy Paxman and the BBC Newsnight team, Rangemaster, Rose Skiera, Keith Stephens at The Royal Holloway University, Chris and Sylvia Stokes, Tyrells Hand Cooked Potato Chips and RobbieWilmot.

The Heretic by Richard Bean was originally commissioned by Sonia Friedman Productions.

'We are dealing with a coupled non-linear chaotic system, and therefore the long-term prediction of future climate states is not possible.'

Intergovernmental Panel on Climate Change
(Third Assessment Report)

'The science is settled.'
Al Gore

Characters

DR. DIANE CASSELL 40s
(Palaeogeophysics and Geodynamics lecturer)

BEN SHOTTER 19
(an Earth Sciences undergraduate)

PHOEBE 21
(Dr. Cassell's daughter)

GEOFF TORDOFF 40s
(Site Services for the University Campus, with a
brief for Security)

PROFESSOR KEVIN MALONEY 50s
(Head of Faculty Earth Sciences)

CATHERINE TICKELL 20s
(Human Resources Officer)

Set

A modern university head of department office. Desk, chair, computer, book shelves, cabinets. A circle of six comfy chairs (dull functional designs, this is not Oxbridge) are set around a coffee table for tutorials. A whiteboard with some climate change algorithms of a difficult, and mathematical nature. The words 'infrared', 'radiation', 'forcing' and 'feedback' feature.

On the wall a series of photos. The first is of a six-year-old girl (Phoebe) standing next to a sapling Betel Nut tree. The second when she is about fourteen and the tree bigger. The photos are taken in the Maldives on the wash limit of the sea.

For Act 4 and 5 the set is Diane's kitchen in the country.

This edition includes changes made during previews,
and is therefore the writer's preferred version.

Act One

SCENE ONE

A September morning, Tuesday of Freshers' Week. DIANE is mounting a photograph of a Betel Nut tree taken on the wash limit on a Maldives beach. She hangs it next to seven other photos of the same tree making a series. PHOEBE stands in front of the first in the series.

PHOEBE: This has just godda be illegal.

DIANE: What?

PHOEBE: Having a photograph of this four-year-old girl on your wall, in a bikini.

DIANE: *(A loud sigh.)*

PHOEBE: Stop sighing mum. You sound like you're in The Archers. Making jam. Or getting raped. From behind. By Jack Woolley.

DIANE: Don't make jokes about Jack Woolley. He's got Alzheimer's.

PHOEBE: Exactly, he thinks you're Peggy.

DIANE: The subject of the photograph is the tree.

PHOEBE: A paedophile would not even notice the tree. *And* I look fat.

DIANE: I know, but you've lost weight since then.

PHOEBE: Bitch. Give me a pen.

DIANE: Get your own pen. There's some about two yards over there.

PHOEBE: Fascist. You're wasted in this job, you could be running Burma.

PHOEBE gets the pen. There is a knock at the door.

DIANE: Come in!

(Enter BEN. His T-shirt bears the slogan FUCK. He carries a cycle seat.)

Hello.

BEN: Yeah.

DIANE: I'm Doctor Cassell. There are no tutorials in Freshers' week. Are you one of mine? PaleoGeophysics?

BEN: Yeah.

DIANE: What's your name?

BEN: Ben Shotter.

DIANE: Can I help?

BEN: Next Tuesday, yeah, we got the trip to the weather station by minibus, yeah, on the Tuesday, yeah, but the modular lecture's in the morning.

DIANE: At eleven o'clock. Yes.

BEN: Which is like course assessed yeah?

PHOEBE: Uurgh. How long's this gonna take?!

BEN: I can't, like, do them both on the same day.

PHOEBE: You haven't got the energy?

DIANE: Phoebe! Please!

BEN: I can't travel by minibus.

DIANE: What have you got against minibuses?

BEN: It depends what kind of minibus it is?

DIANE: I think it's a Toyota.

PHOEBE: Ugh. Is it petrol or diesel?

DIANE: It's going to be one or the other isn't it.

PHOEBE: Muslims and Jews can't eat pork. He can't get on a fossil fuels minibus.

BEN: Yeah.

DIANE: So how are you going to get to the weather station?

BEN: I'm gonna have to like cycle.

DIANE: It's forty miles. There. And forty miles back.

BEN: Yeah, I'll set off like really early.

PHOEBE: He's trying to tell you that he'll miss the modular lecture.

DIANE: Attendance at the modular lecture is worth two credits.

BEN: That's my point.

DIANE: You're going to miss out on two course work credits then, aren't you.

BEN: Harsh man.

PHOEBE: *(To DIANE.)* That's religious discrimination.

(To BEN.) Do you believe in God?

BEN: No.

PHOEBE: I do. Rather controversially I believe that God is an old man with a white beard sitting on a cloud.

BEN: *(To PHOEBE.)* Are you a Fresher?

PHOEBE: Do I look like a Fresher?

BEN: You're not a student?

PHOEBE: No. I'm a farm worker. I drive a tractor.

DIANE: One day a week. In order to consolidate our travel, every Tuesday, I give my daughter a lift into York, in a petrol driven car.

BEN: Why do you have to be in York at all?

DIANE: There's an essential thing we do together on a Tuesday lunchtime.

PHOEBE: Mad club.

DIANE: Family therapy. And we don't mind anybody knowing about it.

PHOEBE: That's how mad we are.

BEN: I've had aversion therapy.

PHOEBE: Did it work?

BEN: No.

PHOEBE: How old are you?

DIANE: Phoebe?!

BEN: Nineteen. I took a year off.

DIANE: What did you do?

BEN: Nothing, like I said, I took a year off.

DIANE: In your green future how would we get fourteen students fifty miles to the North Yorkshire Moors' weather station?

BEN: There should be like an electric car / minibus.

DIANE: OK. This is your first assignment. For next week compare the energy efficiency and emissions of an electric car and a diesel car.

BEN: Electric cars don't have any emissions.

DIANE: Electric cars should be called coal cars. 30% of our electricity still comes from coal. Electricity is not naturally occurring in nature.

BEN: There's eels.

DIANE: Eels?

BEN: Electric eels.

PHOEBE: Yeah, good point.

DIANE: If you want to pursue this argument you'll need to write a letter to Professor Kevin Maloney, Faculty of Earth Sciences.

BEN: Cool. Ta.

DIANE: See you next week.

He studies the photo of PHOEBE as a four year old in a bikini. Then he looks at PHOEBE.

PHOEBE: What?

BEN: Nothing. Laters.

He turns to go. The back of his T-shirt bears the slogan OFF. DIANE closes the door.

PHOEBE: He's really cute.

DIANE: Why is it young women can't resist hopeless romantic visionaries?

PHOEBE: I can and I do. Regularly.

DIANE: That Buddhist monk in the Maldives. He changed your life.

PHOEBE: No he didn't.

DIANE: You'd never had a yeast infection before.

PHOEBE: One area which is not legitimate source material for your pathetic comedy quipping is the medical history of my vagina.

DIANE: Have you joined up then? Are you going to *get active*?

PHOEBE: Yeah. I have. They have a branch in Scarborough.

DIANE: How are you going to get to Scarborough?

PHOEBE: I don't know. Yet. Why do you hate them so much?

DIANE: Because they're bad people.

PHOEBE: They don't sound like bad people. Greeeeen peeeeeeace.

DIANE: Are you joining Greenpeace to save the world or as part of your ongoing project to destroy your mother?

PHOEBE: Can I let you know tomorrow?

DIANE: Come on! I need to eat and you need to eat and throw up, which takes longer.

They exit, the door is closed.

End of Scene.

SCENE TWO

Wednesday of Freshers' Week. GEOFF and DIANE. GEOFF is wearing a cheapish suit with a high vis waistcoat over. He has the trappings of a security guard – boots, name badge, keys, two way radio etc. He has an envelope, and its contents in his hand. DIANE is seated on the edge of her desk.

GEOFF: I can't see that there's owt worth worrying about here.

DIANE: It's a death threat.

GEOFF: Yeah, but –

DIANE: – yeah but?

GEOFF: It's Freshers' Week.

> *(Beat.)* Last night one of the rugby lads got pissed and bit the head off a grey squirrel. Knowhatimean?

DIANE: I do know what you mean. Half a bottle of Pinot Grigio, and I'm out there myself, on my hands and knees, chewing the heads off rodents.

GEOFF: I coulda called the police, but it woulda ruined the lad's career.

DIANE: What's he want to be?

GEOFF: A vet. I'll have a dig around. After I got mesen decommissioned I did a bit of freelance private eyeing.

DIANE: You were in the army were you Geoff?

GEOFF: Marines. Oh aye, I can kill a man with my bare hands.

DIANE: You must give me your card.

> *(GEOFF gives her a card.)*

> First aider too. So you can kill and heal. That's quite a broad vocation.

GEOFF: Have you gone and got yersen you know, whatsaname...with a student?

DIANE: I've never had sex with any of my students.

GEOFF: Can you think of any reason why these radical greens, The Sacred Earth Militia, would want to put a death threat on the windscreen of your four litre, eight cylinder Jaguar XK8?

DIANE: No idea.

GEOFF: You could have that car converted to liquid petroleum gas.

GEOFF gives her a brochure for a garage.

This is an accredited conversion centre. They did all my site services vehicles. Ask for Karl. Opposite The Waggoners Rest in Pocklington. That's your side o' town int'it?

DIANE: Yes.

Enter Professor KEVIN MALONEY.

KEVIN: Sorry I'm late. Ran over a cat. Are you alright Geoff?

GEOFF: Dunno. I never think about it. What about you Professor?

KEVIN: Upset, obviously, about the cat. It's Mrs Nextdoor's.

DIANE: I've had a death threat from the 'Sacred Earth Militia.'

KEVIN: Oh dear. Hell's bells.

(GEOFF hands over the envelope.)

'All heretic's must die.' Ah! Elementary, my dear Watson! Misuse of the possessive apostrophe, incorrectly placed after the C of heretic and before the S.

GEOFF: So what does that tell us?

DIANE: Our suspect is a greengrocer.

GEOFF: It's godda be someone on campus. Staff or student.

DIANE: Geoff has established that I've not had sex with any of my students.

KEVIN: I don't blame you. *(To GEOFF.)* Have you seen them? Kaw!

DIANE: Intimate relations with colleagues is next.

KEVIN: That was twenty years ago. *(To GEOFF.)* Isafjord, Iceland.

DIANE: He put his hands up my jumper.

KEVIN: *(To GEOFF.)* I can explain.

GEOFF: Go on then.

KEVIN: My hands were cold.

GEOFF: I haven't told the Old Bill about the death threat. I like to keep –

DIANE: – I'm sorry Geoff! But I insist that we go to the police.

GEOFF: I'll talk to my mate Dave in Special Branch.

DIANE: You've got direct access to Special Branch?

GEOFF: Yeah. When we had them Muslim nutters on campus Al whatsaname –

KEVIN: – Al Muhajiroun. Arabic Studies' Doctor Mukarjee had three death threats. He'd said there were some grammatical errors in the Koran.

DIANE: Maybe Arabic is Allah's second language.

GEOFF: *(Knowing.)* So what's his first?

DIANE: – Hebrew. I see the problem.

GEOFF: Professor Maloney's parking place is scanned by CCTV. Swap with the Professor we can candid camera the little bugger.

KEVIN: Brilliant! I'll move my car. Where do you want me to park?

DIANE: Between the kitchen bins and the builders' skips.

KEVIN: Excellent.

GEOFF: Give me your keys, I'll move the cars for you now.

DIANE: No, that's alright Geoff, I'll – (pop out.)

GEOFF: – Site Services mission statement is to 'facilitate excellence.' Apparently that's your excellence not mine. I'll get your keys back to you by dinner time, don't panic, dinner time is Yorkshire for lunch time.

DIANE and GEOFF hand over their keys.

KEVIN: Geoff, I got a letter from one of Diane's first year PaleoGs, said he couldn't get on the bus to the weather station, it's against his principles.

GEOFF: What's his name?

DIANE: Ben Shotter.

GEOFF: I'll get Special Branch Dave to check him out.

KEVIN: Can your brother-in-law do an LPG conversion on a Jag?

DIANE: Oh it's your brother-in-law!

KEVIN: Half the price of petrol, and no pollution. They did mine.

DIANE: Kevin, your car is a Toyota Prius.

KEVIN: First one they've ever done. If you got the Jag converted, you get a little LPG sticker. That might put an end to all this.

DIANE: Has Doctor Mukarjee started to wear a burka?

GEOFF: It's worth considering, love, we all have to try and reduce our carbon footprints. You've got children. This is your daughter innit?

DIANE: Yes.

GEOFF: Aye, well then. The future in't ours is it, it's theirs.

(GEOFF is heading for the door when he spots that a desk lamp has been left on.)

Do you want this on?

No one answers, he turns it off and leaves closing the door behind him. KEVIN tries to give DIANE the bound document. She's not interested.

KEVIN: My Draft IPCC chapter.

DIANE: You want me to read it, make some intelligent comments which you can pass off as your own, in order to enhance your international reputation.

KEVIN: Yeah.

DIANE: Kevin, I've had a death threat.

KEVIN: Sorry. Yes, mmm, terrible.

He puts the document down and tries to care.

DIANE: I don't know whether I should tell Phoebe about the death threat. Any stress, like this and –

KEVIN: – I've never properly understood anorexia, is it real, or –

DIANE: – it's the physical expression of self obsession, that's what it is.

KEVIN: Psychosomatic?

DIANE: Laboratory experiments on mice suggest a genetic root, which suits Phoebe because that means it's my fault. I have an alternative theory – they bought a batch of really fucking selfish mice.

KEVIN: Has she got a boyfriend?

DIANE: Sex does not cure anorexia.

KEVIN: You say that, but in 'Cuckoo's Nest' Jack Nicholson fixes up B b b b b billy with a girl, and he is cured of his stammer. How ill can anyone be if they're getting a regular sorting out.

DIANE: Kevin! You're talking about my daughter.

KEVIN: Sorry.

DIANE: Have you ever had a death threat?

KEVIN: Yes. Last year.

DIANE: From whom?

KEVIN: Gordon Brown. 'Kevin' he said, 'you promised me my children would never see a white Christmas. So how come Scotland's cut off and I'm digging them out of a twenty foot snow drift.' I said 'Ah! Not my fault, Prime Minister, I'm your *climate* expert, that snow is *weather.*'

DIANE: Ha! Brilliant!

KEVIN: He called me a wanker.

Beat. KEVIN sighs, looks needy.

DIANE: Are you alright Kevin?

KEVIN: Sabina. Big row, in the car, coming back from Caroline Spelman's fish pie dinner. First she accused me of flirting with Theresa May.

DIANE: Were you?

KEVIN: Obviously. But...Sabina said I was 'tedious'. That's not a good word to use in a marriage about the person you're married to is it – tedious. I stopped the car and said 'only boring people get bored.'

DIANE: Ah, that was the right thing to say.

KEVIN sighs, stands and closely inspects the new photo of the Betel Nut tree.

KEVIN: Do you get bored measuring sea level?

DIANE: In the Maldives?

KEVIN: This tree you planted is still doing well then?

DIANE: Yes.

KEVIN: What –

DIANE: – it's a Betel Nut tree. No saline tolerance. I planted it – you know all this – on the wash limit sixteen years ago, and it's thriving.

KEVIN: So is sea level rising in the Maldives?

DIANE: Technically, no.

KEVIN: No rise and no rising trend?

DIANE: No rising trend.

KEVIN: Mm. Have you written your paper?

DIANE: Yes.

KEVIN: Have you submitted? Which journal? Nature?

DIANE: Yes Nature, no, not yet. What is this?

KEVIN: So Toby's not read it yet?

DIANE: No.

(KEVIN sits.)

You've sat down. You only sit down when you're angry.

KEVIN: We need a new 'business model' for this department.

DIANE: I thought I worked at a university.

KEVIN: After Christmas we're getting a visit from Catalan International Securities. Have you heard of them?

DIANE: Are they Quakers?

KEVIN: One of the biggest insurance and underwriting firms in Europe.

DIANE: Oh yes. They sponsored that mad person who tried to pedalo across the Arctic to show how radical the melt was. He got stuck in pack ice and the dogs had to shoot him and eat him.

KEVIN: Yes that's them. For Catalan, that was a PR disaster. For us, good news. Now they're prepared to pay a very high price to be advised by the best.

DIANE: You and me.

KEVIN: The 'Climate Change Research Unit' would service clients by –

DIANE: – I'm not a sex worker.

KEVIN: Listen! We are the Earth Sciences Faculty of YUIST for teaching, but *virtually* we are a separate budget centre, providing tools to the market.

DIANE: What tools would I be selling?

KEVIN: A computer model of sea level rise.

DIANE: I'd rather sell the fluff from my naval. It'd be more use. After a couple of years they could knit a jumper.

KEVIN: Catalan...how can I explain...there's a Chinese proverb. 'Man must stand for long time, with mouth open, before roast duck fly in.'

DIANE: If I were Catalan I'd go to Hampshire University.

KEVIN: Hampshire is the competition, but they've got all their eggs in one basket, tree ring research. We have me, ice cores, glaciers, you, sea level, Doctor Popodopolos – what does he do?

DIANE: I don't know.

KEVIN: We have intellectual diversity.

DIANE: It would help if Catalan were not aware of the sceptical nature of the sea level expert's views.

KEVIN: And that sea level expert will agree to delay the publication of her latest paper until after the Catalan decision.

DIANE: You're telling me not to publish my research?

KEVIN: I'm telling you to delay the publication of your research.

DIANE: I don't understand. Last year, when we were a designated 'Centre of Excellence' you told me that I needed to publish more research.

Standing excitedly.

KEVIN: I didn't want to be a 'centre of fucking excellence' I was happy being a 'centre of ducking and diving and falling asleep in the afternoons'. But the good old days of being funded from Central Government are dead and fucking buried. And, I now understand that, like everyone, I am only two bad mistakes away from driving a mini cab for a living.

DIANE: OK. I will not submit my paper to Nature until after the Catalan decision.

KEVIN: End of Jan. Goodo.

(He stands.)

I'll go and see Miss Tickle in Human Resources, see what we need to do about this death threat.

DIANE: Miss Tickle? Is she new?

KEVIN: Yes. She ran this 'line manager's course' during the summer. She introduced herself as having worked for Mars for six years. I said 'don't expect us to be impressed because you've worked for a local authority.' Tumbleweed. Disciplinarian, wears a lot of leather. Looks like the kind of woman who might collect Nazi memorabilia.

(KEVIN stands and heads for the door.)

Got the Vice Chancellor at eleven, something about women. Exciting though isn't it. I love September. And Earth Sciences has been ignored for so long, but now, suddenly, the kids think we're cool.

DIANE: Get out Kevin, I might hurl.

KEVIN: It was the Arts forever, wasn't it, until in the sixties Sociology floated to the top like an aerated turd, hung around for a few years, before finally getting sucked down the tube of its own gaping fatuousness. Then in the seventies, the Psychologists took over the asylum. Boy did those tossers fancy themselves. But they could never nail anything properly down. One minute being mentally ill is a crushing personal tragedy, next minute it's a bit of a laugh and you should try to enjoy it. All that Psychology ever achieved was making bullshit respectable, which of course, paved the way for Media Studies. And Christ, how long have those snake oil merchants been top dog? Eh?! Ten years! Ten years of fucking mind-numbing bollocks! So that day, last year, when Media Studies' top witch knocked on my door and begged me to let her first years on to your introductory Earth Sciences modular lecture, that was the moment I knew we'd finally arrived. It's official – we are the kings of the castle. Let's not fuck it up eh!

He closes the door.

End of Scene.

SCENE THREE

Second week of term. DIANE's office on campus. BEN sits diagonally across from DIANE in the easy chairs area. Next to him is a bass guitar case with THE FOUR HORSEMEN stencilled on to it.

DIANE: I can smell garlic.

BEN: That'll be me. I eat a lot of garlic.

DIANE: Is eating garlic a Death Metal ordinance?

BEN: *(Sighing.)* Tut.

DIANE: Your band, The Four Horsemen, they're not a Death Metal band?

BEN: *(Sighing.)* Tut.

DIANE: What other music genres do I know? Grime?

BEN: *(Exasperated.)* Tut. Man, who likes Grime?

DIANE: I don't like grime. I pay a cleaner. Ben, if you want to be a rock star you should be at art college.

BEN: So you're gonna lay on the stress now, yeah?

DIANE: Stress? In Pol Pot's Cambodia, students like you were executed. Why do you think there has never been a single decent Cambodian rock band.

BEN: You're a denier. Right?

DIANE: Holocaust or –

BEN: *(Sighing.)* – Tut. *Anthropogenic global warming.*

DIANE: I'm agnostic on *AGW*, but if you can prove to me there's a God I'll become a nun quicker than you can say 'lesbian convent orgy'.

BEN: That's sexist.

DIANE: No.

BEN: Homophobic.

DIANE: Yes. Semantic specificity is the E chord of science.

BEN: Are you allowed to be homophobic in a government funded educational establishment, in the, like, you know, public sector?

DIANE: I doubt it. Why did you choose Earth Sciences?

BEN: *(Knowing.)* I wanna save the planet innit.

DIANE: The planet doesn't need saving. The planet will be fine. You mean you'd like to save the human race.

BEN: Whatever.

DIANE: I'm a scientist. I'm not a politician.

BEN: You're saying that, like, I can't be a scientist, and an activist?

DIANE: Activism and Empiricism are opposites.

BEN: Do you know a good art college?

DIANE: My job is to make you think like a scientist. You need to be aware of your agenda or leave it at home.

BEN: I don't understand.

DIANE: OK. I would say that the repressed homosexual Baden Powell started the Boy Scout movement on the energy of an unacknowledged agenda.

BEN: If he'd been aware of what he was really after, he'd have set up Gaydar.

DIANE: Yup.

BEN: Or Grindr.

DIANE: What's Grindr?

BEN: It's a gay app utilising like GPS satellite technology that tells you if there's another gay guy within twenty yards of you who's up for sex.

DIANE: You're gay?

BEN: No, but I am passionate about the developments in mobile computing.

DIANE: Let's do some politics disguised as climate science.

(DIANE gives him a whiteboard pen.)

You work for Greenpeace. Illustrate the rise in CO_2 since 1800 on the whiteboard.

BEN: My agenda would be to try and make it look scary.

DIANE: Scare me.

BEN stands at the whiteboard and draws in the x axis writing in the dates.

BEN: So *x* axis is 1800 to 2000. *y* axis is 280 parts per million to 380 parts per million. So the rise in CO_2 since industrialisation is – scary.

BEN draws in a line basically joining the bottom left to the top right in a 45° angle.

DIANE: Excellent. Now you work for Exxon Mobil. Reassure me that driving my car is not a problem.

BEN: I'd want to show a flat line, right along the bottom. Er...I'd change the *y* axis, make the *y* axis percentages, so 0% to 5%, then CO_2 in 1800 is 0.028% rising to 0.038 –

(He draws a flat line across the bottom of the whiteboard.)

– a flat line, across the bottom. Nothing to worry about.

DIANE: And which one is correct?

BEN: They're both correct. That's your point lady.

DIANE: That's terrific Ben. Really. You know for most students I have to draw those graphs.

BEN: Yeah? Why?

DIANE: I admire your passion, your idealism, your cycling. My only fear is that your faith will corrupt your science. So, do you want to go to art college?

BEN: No. I never did. That was your idea.

DIANE: Good. Do you cycle from York to your parents. Brighton isn't it?

BEN: My mother's dead.

DIANE: I'm sorry.

BEN: I killed her.

DIANE: She died in childbirth?

BEN: You get one point lady.

DIANE: But your father's alive?

BEN: I hate him.

DIANE: Why?

BEN: He drives a Volvo.

DIANE: What have you got against CO_2?

BEN: It's the major greenhouse gas –

DIANE: – The major greenhouse gas is water vapour.

BEN: CO_2 destroyed Venus.

DIANE: Venus has two hundred and thirty thousand times as much CO_2.

BEN: Look, if we double CO_2, we double temperatures, that's bare bait man, and that is the end of the world. Common sense innit.

DIANE: If common sense trumped science my mother would be running a nuclear power station. The relationship between CO_2 and temperature is not linear, it's logarithmic. Think of an example, from everyday life, where doubling a variable does not double the effect.

BEN: Now?

DIANE: Yes right now, time's running out, apparently.

Silence. He thinks hard.

BEN: If you're depressed, yeah, and you buy a dog, that might make you + 3 happier. If *double* the number of dogs, that wouldn't *double* your happiness, cos the second dog, because it knows it is *'the second dog'* would develop psychological problems and start pooing on your head, and that, and you would consider having it put down, which makes you feel guilty, so you start self-harming, and drinking, secretly, which means you neglect the dogs, and in the end the RSPCA break the door down, take both dogs off you, and you're back to where you started.

Depressed, on your own, only it's worse this time cos you got no front door.

DIANE: For next time, you are Archimedes, observe the world, find an example, not dogs, of a variable which when doubled doesn't have a doubling effect.

BEN: *Homework?*

DIANE: Yup.

BEN stands. Makes to leave.

BEN: Is Phoebe in today?

DIANE: She only comes into York on a Tuesday.

BEN: I couldn't find any Phoebe Cassells on Facebook.

DIANE: She uses her father's surname.

BEN: What's her father's name?

Silence.

DIANE: Gallagher.

BEN: Safe. Cool. I like you.

He leaves. She shuts the door behind him.

End of Scene.

Act Two

Mid term. KEVIN, GEOFF and DIANE. It's colder now, and GEOFF is wearing a high vis coat. KEVIN is also wearing a winter coat. KEVIN is reading a second death threat.

KEVIN: *(Reading.)* 'The earth's future is more important than one human life.'

Ah! This time, correct use of the apostrophe!

GEOFF: So what – probably a different perpetrator?

DIANE: Or it could be the same person who's been on a course.

KEVIN: Was it on the windscreen again?

DIANE: It was in the car.

KEVIN: They broke into the car?

GEOFF: They smashed the windscreen.

KEVIN: Hell's bells.

GEOFF: Special Branch Dave has found out some stuff on The Sacred Earth Militia. They're are a pacifist environmentalist militia that seem to have morphed out of the Animal Rights Movement.

DIANE: A *pacifist militia.* What do you call that?

KEVIN: What? When two words in a phrase contradict.

DIANE: It's on the tip of my tongue.

GEOFF: Oxymoron.

DIANE: That's it!

KEVIN: Thank you Geoff.

GEOFF: Just doing my job. Facilitating excellence.

DIANE: Doesn't make any sense, 'pacifist militia.'

GEOFF: Led Zeppelin didn't make sense, but they did quite well.

DIANE: Did we catch him on video?

GEOFF: The kid's wearing a hoodie, and a balaclava, and army surplus fatigues.

KEVIN: Can't see his face?

GEOFF: No. But. Listen. Dave has run a check on Benjamin Orlando Shotter. He's a loner. Yeah. Lives on a canal boat. Alone. He's a loner who lives alone. Born in Brighton. And whadyerknow, The Sacred Earth Militia started in Brighton.

DIANE: You know, Special Branch haven't even spoken to me. I've had no advice, no offers of protection, I've not been interviewed –

GEOFF: – Yeah but –

DIANE: – Yeah but what?

KEVIN: Diane! Please!

GEOFF: You've got to be security cleared first.

DIANE: I don't need fucking security clearance, I'm the one being threatened!

KEVIN: Sorry Geoff.

GEOFF: I've worked hard on this. I wish I hadn't bothered.

GEOFF turns to go, he's in a sulk.

KEVIN: Geoff!

GEOFF: *(At the door.)* Tata.

As he goes he turns the lamp off again, and gives an imperious glare to DIANE. He's gone.

DIANE: There's your bloody IPCC report. I've used highlighter to identify statements that I consider to be politics.

KEVIN: *(Looking at it.)* It's all pink!

DIANE: Exactly.

KEVIN: '2.7 billion people could see greater water stress with global warming?' Why is that pink?

DIANE: You're cherry-picking bad news. Why not tell us how many billions will have their water problems solved by climate change. Like most things to do with humans wet and warm is good.

KEVIN: Unless you're an Inuit.

DIANE: And that's just a typo. The Himalayan glaciers will not have all melted by 2035, surely, I think you mean 2350.

KEVIN: OK. Thank you.

KEVIN makes to go.

DIANE: I'm scared Kevin.

KEVIN: About what?

DIANE: The fucking death threat!

KEVIN sits reluctantly, dutifully.

KEVIN: Alright. Good friend of mine, the UK archivist for The Grateful Dead, he works in research genetics – vivisection, hamsters. He uses hamsters because they breed like rabbits. He's had death threats. They painted his house red, and his car red, which was stupid actually because it was a red car. His wife couldn't handle it, she left him, but he was going to leave her anyway, not that she knew anything about that, but I did, because he'd told me, so he ended up saving himself about a hundred grand, and kept the house, which he certainly wasn't expecting –

DIANE: – what's your point?

KEVIN: They never actually tried to kill him. Did you say anything contentious in your modular lecture? What was the subject?

DIANE: Paleoclimate proxy temperature reconstructions.

KEVIN: The Hockey Stick?

DIANE: It got a mention.

KEVIN: Yes, and, what did you say?

DIANE: I said that in the Roman Warming they grew grapes north of Hadrian's wall, and in the Medieval Warming the Vikings colonised Greenland and grew corn. You know, all the stuff about natural climate cycles that you taught me. Before The Hockey Stick came along.

KEVIN: Doctor Popodopolos sat in on the lecture, at the back –

DIANE: – why?

KEVIN: He said that at one point instead of saying 'climate change' you said 'climate change, the artist formerly known as global warming.'

DIANE: Doctor Popodopolos is an idiot.

KEVIN: Yes, I know.

DIANE: He's got a cuddly toy polar bear on his desk.

KEVIN: Did you communicate your scepticism of The Hockey Stick to the students?

DIANE: You're sceptical of The Hockey Stick!

KEVIN: Privately, yes, we all are, but every good thing that's happened in Paleo in the last ten years is because of The Hockey Stick.

DIANE: That's like getting in the society columns for murdering the Queen.

KEVIN: You can't go global warming sceptic on me! This is the faculty of Earth Sciences not the editorial office of the Spectator! All the evidence from the computer models suggests –

DIANE: Computer models are not evidence, they're just another hypothesis, or have you turned science on its head?! Computer modelling is what brought the global economy down. Computer modelling convinced you, thirty years ago that millions would die in a new ice age. I have your book. 'Snowball Planet.' Actually, you've never signed it.

She stands and looks on her bookshelves.

KEVIN: OK, unfortunately for me millions didn't die. We had one Commodore 64 between ten of us. I had twenty minutes on it every day when James Lovelock went for his mid-morning shit. That was then, and this is now, and now the vast majority of climate scientists have no doubt –

DIANE: – the vast majority of people on earth believe in God, and they're all wrong.

KEVIN: The 'overwhelming consensus' of serious –

DIANE: – there was once an overwhelming consensus that the earth was the centre of the universe. Galileo –

KEVIN: – Oh you're Galileo now are you!

DIANE: – Galileo didn't agree, got death threats, and no support from his peers.

KEVIN: OK. I'm shocked. I want you to put your hand up any time –

DIANE: – put my hand up?

KEVIN: Yeah. Put your hand up whenever you hear me make a statement that you do not believe to be true. One. Carbon dioxide is a greenhouse gas. (Beat.) You agree. Thank God for that.

DIANE: You can't treat me like this Kevin.

KEVIN: Two. Greenhouse gases trap infrared radiation. (Beat.) Good. Going well. Three. Since the beginning of the industrial revolution we have increased the concentration of carbon dioxide in the atmosphere by thirty percent. *(Beat.)* Fine. Where are we?

DIANE: Four.

KEVIN: Four. Melting ice will reduce the earth's albedo so less of the sun's rays will be reflected back into space. As the oceans warm, they will expand, causing sea level rise. *(Beat.)*

DIANE: Five.

KEVIN: When the permafrost melts methane will be released.

DIANE: A much more potent greenhouse gas than CO_2.

KEVIN: Meaning what?

DIANE: Nothing, I was gilding your lilly.

KEVIN: Yeah, well, it doesn't need it.

DIANE: I do one thing! One thing! I measure sea level!

KEVIN: In the Maldives!

DIANE: And it's not rising!

KEVIN: It is everywhere else! What's so special about the frigging Maldives!

DIANE: I've cracked it Kevin. For seventeen years I've been looking out to sea wondering why I can't record a sea level rise. I've been looking in the wrong place. The land is rising with the sea.

KEVIN: Isostasy?

DIANE: Oh you haven't forgotten. No, not isostasy. Low lying islands seem to be growing organically with sea level rise.

KEVIN: Coral?

DIANE: No! New sand, and sediment deposits are secured by ammophila grasses which protect them from wind and wave erosion. It's all in here.

(She gives him a copy of the Journal Energy and Environment. KEVIN sits.)

You've sat down.

KEVIN: You little fucker. I told you not to publish.

DIANE: You told me not to send it to Toby, at Nature.

KEVIN: I meant don't send it to anyone. This rag is a sceptic's platform.

DIANE: It's a peer reviewed scientific journal.

KEVIN: Catalan will have a spotty youth reading everything published on sea level. You've handed Catalan on a plate to those cowboys at Hampshire University.

KEVIN stands and closes the office door.

DIANE: The man who introduced the open door policy has closed the door.

KEVIN: I'm going to have to give you a verbal warning, yes –

DIANE: – A what?

KEVIN: An informal verbal warning as part of the disciplinary procedure. Yes. For doing something I told you not to do, as your line manager.

DIANE: What's a line manager? We're not making Mars bars.

KEVIN: I'll get you a written copy of this verbal warning as soon as I can.

DIANE: So it's not a verbal warning it's a written warning?

KEVIN: I think I've got to do you a letter which will act as a record of the verbal warning.

DIANE: But that'll make it a written warning.

KEVIN: Oh hell's bells! I don't know. Just hang on.

(He picks up the phone and dials a three digit internal number.)

(On the phone.) Miss Tickell? ...it's me…Professor Maloney…yes, I've had to issue Doctor Cassell with a verbal warning…OK, well I'm sorry, I forgot…

(To DIANE.) You've got the right to a union rep with you apparently. Do you want one?

DIANE: Fuck off.

KEVIN: *(On the phone.)* I don't think she wants one. Do I need to give her a written record of the verbal warming, warning?…no, OK, I just make a note for myself in my own records…and that can be in writing can it? …of course. Thank you.

(He puts the phone down.)

Right! You can't have it in writing, that would make it a written warning. The verbal warning is in verbal only.

DIANE: But I want it in writing!

KEVIN: A written warning is stage two.

DIANE: Let's go straight to stage two then!

KEVIN: But stage two is really serious!

DIANE: And stage one is just a bit of a laugh?!

KEVIN: Look! You've had the verbal, and that's all you're fucking getting!

DIANE: I want a written warning! It can't be more serious than a death threat.

She begins to cry. KEVIN is marooned.

KEVIN: Oh hell's bells D.

DIANE: Don't call me D! And I'm not crying.

KEVIN: Look –

DIANE: – *(To herself.)* Oh God, stop it! Stop it! I never cry. Never, ever.

KEVIN: No, no, it's er…it's good to cry.

DIANE: No it's not. It's so weak. Stop it woman! Stop it. I promised myself I would not ever cry about this fucking death threat!

A knock at the door. DIANE is still crying.

KEVIN: Shit. There's someone at the door.

DIANE: Let them in.

KEVIN: But you're still crying.

DIANE: *(Crying.)* I'm not crying! I don't know what this is. Let them in. I'll stop if it's a stranger.

KEVIN opens the door, slightly reluctantly. DIANE is still crying. PHOEBE comes in.

KEVIN: Ah! Phoebe, hello.

PHOEBE: – is she crying?

DIANE: No!

PHOEBE: What have you said to my mum?

DIANE: – he's given me a verbal warning.

PHOEBE: Why have you given her a verbal warning? My mum's brilliant! I'll give you a verbal warning – fuck off!

(KEVIN starts to back out. He's gone. PHOEBE puts an arm round DIANE. She's still crying.)

You had a death threat, didn't cry once, you get a verbal warning and you go all Gwyneth Paltrow on me. What does this verbal warning say, where is it? I want to read it.

DIANE: It's verbal. It's not written down.

PHOEBE: This place is weird.

(Knock at the door. PHOEBE goes to the door.)

Who is it?

BEN: *(Off.)* Ben Shotter. First year PaleoGeophysics.

PHOEBE: It's the cute boy mum! Can we let him in. Please!

(DIANE nods. PHOEBE opens the door.)

Hi Ben.

BEN: Oh. Yeah. It's you. Safe.

DIANE: What is it Ben?

BEN: Got a tutorial.

PHOEBE: She's been crying.

DIANE: Urgh! Sit down.

PHOEBE: Sit down Ben.

(BEN sits on one of the tutorial chairs.)

BEN: *(To PHOEBE.)* I sent you a friend request on Facebook. Archimedes.

PHOEBE: Oh that was you was it.

BEN: Yeah, that oil painting of Archimedes is like my Facebook icon, yeah?

PHOEBE: Oh. I thought that was what you looked like.

(Beat.) How did you find me on Facebook?

BEN: Chill, man, I did a search, alright, on your name.

PHOEBE: You don't know my name. It's not the same as hers.

DIANE: Observe the world, find a variable which when doubled does not have a doubling effect.

BEN: Yeah. So I went out the other day, yeah, on a bike ride, and I observed the real world yeah and I've got this idea, kinda like an hypothesis.

PHOEBE: Like a young attractive Archimedes on a bike might have.

BEN: Yeah!

DIANE: Phoebe! This is work. I'll be ten minutes.

PHOEBE: I understand what's going on. She's fucking with your head. Three years of her and you'll be working for Exxon Mobil. Be strong Archimedes.

PHOEBE leaves.

BEN: I was cycling past this chicken farm, yeah, and there was this like fence made of wire mesh, and then beyond that a second fence made of like the same gauge wire –

DIANE: – the same size holes?

BEN: Yeah! Pointless! If a chicken is small enough to get through the first fence, it's gonna get through the second fence an'all, innit.

Beat.

DIANE: And from this observation you have formed an hypothesis about the relationship between CO_2 and temperature?

BEN: Yeah. I've called it the thermal chicken theory. The first bit of CO_2 –

DIANE: – 'the first bit?'

BEN: The first 280 parts per million CO_2 is the first fence. Shit, I should've started with the chickens. The sun, yeah, fires thermal chickens at the earth. The chickens bounce and start heading back into space but get trapped by the first fence –

DIANE: – the pre-industrial carbon dioxide.

BEN: – yeah, that first fence traps all of the thermal chickens in the wavelength band 14 to 16.5 microns. The second fence –

DIANE: – the next 100 parts per million anthropogenic CO_2?

BEN: – yeah, has nothing to do, all the work's been done.

DIANE: This is a saturation theory of CO_2. You're challenging the accepted logarithmic relationship between CO_2 and temperature. You're saying that anthropogenic CO_2 does not cause warming. A sceptic's fantasy.

BEN: Look, I just saw these two stupid fences round a chicken farm.

DIANE: It's a bit mad, but OK. How are you going to test it?

BEN: Dunno. Fun innit. Science. Yeah.

DIANE: I think so, yes. You have an hypothesis, now you need an experimental design.

BEN: I'd need a scale model of the earth, with a cryoshroud –

DIANE: – write it down. Next week. How's the coal cars assignment?

BEN: You only gave me that to piss me off. To attack my belief system.

DIANE: I'm trying to teach the importance of scepticism.

BEN: The shield of science, and the sword of scepticism.

DIANE: OK we'll do move on. This paper is a proxy temperature reconstruction using tree ring data. Kieron McKay, University of Hampshire. We're going to peer review it.

BEN: It's in Nature, it's already been peer reviewed.

DIANE: Yeah, by his best friend.

BEN: But if this guy's been all the way to China –

DIANE: – I know Kieron McKay, he wouldn't stray five hundred yards from a subsidised canteen. Our job is to try and replicate his results. That is how science moves forward. But Kieron McKay is destroying the thing I hold most dear, that process. He's refused to release his data. I've taken out a Freedom of Information request.

BEN: This don't sound like science. You have an agenda man!

DIANE: Of which I'm aware.

BEN: I'm up for it.

He stands, makes to leave.

DIANE: I heard you moved off campus.

BEN: Had to yeah, they turned the heating on.

DIANE: How's the new place?

BEN: It's a boat on the River Oose. But British Waterways are pressuring me, yeah. I don't have a license. I'm stressed man, I don't know what to do.

DIANE: You could get a license.

BEN: Yeah, that's a good idea.

DIANE: What is it, a barge?

BEN: A narrow boat.

DIANE: Great. What's it like?

BEN: Alright. Bit narrow.

He closes the door.

End of Scene.

SCENE TWO

The Newsnight studio.

PAXMAN: Mark Urban from Stonehenge. The President of the Maldives recently held a cabinet meeting under water.

(Photo of President Nasheed and cabinet in wet suits under water.)

Rising sea level, he claims, is a threat to his islands. So, are we in the West to blame, and should we be made to pay? We're joined now by Ahmed Waheed, the Maldives High

Commissioner to London, and Doctor Diane Cassell from the Earth Sciences Faculty of YUIST. High Commissioner, if this is a publicity stunt, what's the message?

WAHEED: We are the lowest lying nation on earth. Our President is saying 'Western industry, Western pollution, your lifestyles' –

DIANE: – like flying to the Maldives for a holiday –

PAXMAN: – hang on!

WAHEED: – you in the West are slowly killing us.

PAXMAN: Doctor Cassell, you don't buy this do you?

DIANE: I've been measuring Maldives sea level for sixteen years, it's not rising. The President can tell his people to relax and enjoy their island paradise.

PAXMAN: High Commissioner, I'm presuming you have scientific evidence to support your fears?

WAHEED: Greenpeace, the World Wildlife Fund, environment NGOs, they all say –

DIANE: – they're not scientists, they're advocacy groups –

WAHEED: – the IPCC –

DIANE: – a UN committee with a political agenda –

PAXMAN: – Doctor Cassell, please. High Commissioner –

WAHEED: The IPCC is reporting an annual sea level rise of 2.3 millimetres.

PAXMAN: 2.3 millimetres? I've got kidney stones bigger than that.

WAHEED: We have not one island higher than two metres above sea level.

PAXMAN: This is the point isn't it, even these tiny annual rises are the death knell to low lying nations.

DIANE: The IPCC is a political body and should be ignored.

PAXMAN: But presumably this 2.3 millimetre rise was measured and observed by one of your colleagues.

DIANE: The researcher has used a single tide gauge in Hong Kong harbour, a port built on shale sediment which is prone to compaction.

PAXMAN: You're saying he's not measuring sea level rise, he's measuring how much the pier he's nailed his tide gauge to is sinking?

DIANE: You'd make a good climate scientist Jeremy. You have a laser eye for the truth and a natural grumpy scepticism.

PAXMAN: Thank you, I think. And thirty years in the BBC means I know a bit about chaos. Are you conning us High Commissioner?

WAHEED: All the global warming deniers live in the West. We did not cause the problem, you did, so the bill must land on your mat.

PAXMAN: Doctor Cassell, are you a global warming *denier*?

DIANE: There is no evidence that CO_2 is the cause of twentieth century warming.

PAXMAN: You're pretty much alone in this belief aren't you.

DIANE: It's not a belief. I'm a scientist, I don't 'believe' in anything.

PAXMAN: Is it your assessment then that the IPCC are being alarmist?

DIANE: The real global warming disaster is that a small cohort of hippies who went into climate science because they could get paid for spending all day on the beach smoking joints have suddenly become the most powerful people in the world.

PAXMAN: *(Laughing.)* With that trenchant assessment of your colleagues, we'll have to leave it there. Like mankind, we've run out of time, or maybe not. Thank you both.

(To different camera.) Sea levels may be rising, but bee levels are falling. The global population of bees –

To black.

End of Scene.

Act Three

SCENE ONE

December. Heavy snow is falling. BEN has just come in and is standing, very well wrapped up in jumpers and scarves. His clothes are matted with snow.

BEN: I've heard, that the other lecturers have stopped talking to you.

DIANE: I'm about as welcome in this building as Abu Hamza at a hook-a-duck stall.

BEN: That's racist. No. Disablist. Semantic specificity.

DIANE: You're learning.

He shuts the door.

BEN: Been thinking about killing myself.

DIANE: This is in my diary as a tutorial to discuss clouds. Have you seen the student counsellor?

BEN: I can't. She drives an Alfa Romeo. I thought you might have been trained in, like, I dunno, active listening skills?

He sits.

DIANE: *(Picks up his essay.)* Your essay doesn't adequately –

BEN: – You don't want to talk about my suicide attempt?

DIANE: No. I was hoping for an acknowledgment of the complexity of climate dynamics. Einstein said 'before I die I hope someone will explain quantum physics to me, after I die, I hope God will explain turbulence'.

BEN: Einstein was a wanker. He cheated on his wife.

DIANE: Did you know his wife?

BEN: No.

DIANE: Don't judge him then.

BEN: That's what fascinates me about climate man. That kind of endless infinity dynamism which almost by definition cannot be modelled, or written about cogently, cos it's what it is, it is like totally random man, it is…ha! It's too difficult, there's just too many fucking factors man, it's unpredictable, beyond prediction, it's massive, massive, it's a beast, I mean, if you could do it, you couldn't do it, you'd get it wrong, it's proper harsh, like endless turbulence, it's infinity, it's chaos.

DIANE: That's what I was looking for in the essay. Climate is stochastic.

BEN: What does stochastic mean?

DIANE: 'Like totally random man.'

BEN: Don't take the piss out of someone who is suicidal. Ridicule can have no part in student centred learning.

BEN stands and from his pocket he takes a Stanley knife – the retracting blade type.

DIANE: What's that Ben?

BEN: It's a Stanley knife. Six ninety nine, B & Q.

DIANE: What are you going to do with it?

BEN: Hobby stuff?

He rolls his sleeve up to reveal his left wrist.

DIANE: Do you always slash your wrists in front of people?

BEN: What it is yeah, I get these waves of happiness man, standing in a queue, anywhere, this wave of joy just hits me. And it's a shock, and it pisses me off, cos I'm not happy, so it's an invasion really, yeah? I feel this pressure, the future, like weighing down on me, and I'm stressed again, and that's alright, it's shit, yeah, but that's what I'm used to, feel comfortable with that. Do you get them? Like funny waves of happiness. Inexplicable.

DIANE: Yes.

BEN: Why is it that everything that humans touch turns to shit?

DIANE: Beavers don't hate themselves because they gnaw down trees.

BEN: I've joined Vehement. You can join online. D'ya know them?

DIANE: No.

BEN: Stands for Voluntary Human Extinction Movement. We believe that the biosphere, earth, would be better off without humans. We're working towards removing human life from earth by non-reproduction. Yeah.

DIANE: I'll join. I can't do Tuesdays.

BEN: Taking the piss again. I don't eat you know. All food has to travel, so I don't eat, except locally grown vegetables. And if I do eat I fart, that's methane, methane is a greenhouse gas. That's why I eat garlic. There's compounds in garlic, yeah, that kill off the methane. And when I breathe, yeah, I breathe in like half a percent of carbon dioxide, and when I breathe out, yeah, cos I've consumed oxygen from the air five percent of my emissions –

DIANE: – your *emissions?*

BEN: – yeah, my out breath is like a massive five percent carbon dioxide.

DIANE: To get your carbon footprint down to nothing, you'd have to kill yourself, and not be cremated.

BEN: Yeah.

DIANE: This aggression towards yourself, do you ever turn that on others. Car drivers for example?

BEN: The perfect death for me would be to blow myself up on Top Gear.

DIANE: Have you ever physically attacked anyone?

BEN: Yeah, when I was eighteen. My dad. I caught him watching porn. I hit him on the head with one of them orange casserole dishes.

DIANE: Le Creuset?

BEN: Yeah.

DIANE: They're really heavy.

BEN: And it was hot.

DIANE: It must've hurt him.

BEN: Put it this way, he stopped wanking.

DIANE: It's perfectly normal for a boy to hate his dad. You should start to see your life as a –

BEN: – 'should' – that's didactic. My therapist never uses the 'should' word.

DIANE: Have you had a lot of therapy?

BEN: Yeah.

DIANE: How am I doing?

BEN: You're crap. You haven't even worked out that I hate myself cos I killed my mother in childbirth.

DIANE: I thought that was so obvious it wasn't worth saying. Every man and woman that has ever been born on this earth has eaten, and kept themselves warm.

BEN: Something terrible has happened. Bust this. My dad has gone green. Like bare mad green. He's scrapped the Volvo, bought solar panels, started cycling. And my brain is like totally fing!

DIANE: You're suffering from what psychologists call cognitive dissonance. That doesn't help does it?

BEN: No.

DIANE: If you like Gary Glitter, and hate child porn, and then one day it's in the news that Gary is into child porn, you will suffer cognitive dissonance. To regain balance you must decide that you no longer like Gary Glitter.

BEN: Or…you could get into child porn.

DIANE: Yes! That would give you balance. This is an opportunity for you to love your dad.

BEN: I hate the bastard.

DIANE: OK. But you have to find balance somehow.

BEN: I think I could hate like unquestioning greens, who don't know anything about Earth Sciences but who just buy stuff 'cause they're gullible or do stuff 'cause they're credulous, or just 'cause they think it's cool.

DIANE: People like your dad. So that's achieving balance by carrying on hating your dad?

BEN: Yeah.

DIANE: OK then. Can we do some work now? Kieron McKay has rejected my Freedom of Information Request.

BEN: Hampshire University?

DIANE: Yes. There's something dodgy going on. And that excites me and should excite you, since it's your assignment.

BEN: Is that your best shot? To get my mind off this?

DIANE: I'm not a therapist. I'm a fossil basher. You're lucky I'm not using a hammer.

(BEN runs the knife along the skin. A little blood shows.)

Ben! Please, just, please don't do that.

(Beat.) Phoebe asked after you. I think she likes you.

BEN: Can I come for Christmas?

DIANE: No.

BEN: What do you do at Christmas?

DIANE: My brother drives my mother over for Christmas dinner. On Boxing day my mother makes a turkey bolognese Irish lasagne hot pot thing. We eat it, Phoebe throws it up, and my brother takes my mother home. Phoebe and I go for a walk over the hills to this Medieval abandoned village. The ruins of a church, manor house, you know, it's fun.

BEN: Can I come for the walk?

DIANE: Are you going to be alone on the boat?

BEN: Yeah.

DIANE: I'll ask Phoebe.

BEN: No way man! Don't tell her!

DIANE: You like Phoebe?

BEN: She's mint, yeah.

DIANE: Just turn up then. After lunch.

BEN: I know, with an essay!? No. That's crap.

DIANE: It's a village off the A166, on the way to Bridlington. Fimber.

BEN: *(Writing.)* Fimber? I'll Google Earth it.

DIANE: Go a mile through the village, pond on your left. Manor Barns.

BEN: Cool! Er…Merry Christmas.

DIANE: Keep warm. Burn something you're allowed to burn.

BEN is gone. The door is left open. DIANE is thoughtful. KEVIN sticks his head round.

KEVIN: Are you…?

DIANE: Yes.

KEVIN: I didn't think you'd make it in.

DIANE: I had a morning of tutorials.

KEVIN: You don't still do tutorials do you?

DIANE: Yes.

KEVIN: They're not cost effective. The radio said the Wolds were white over.

DIANE: They are. How did you get in?

KEVIN: Mrs. Nextdoor gave me a lift in her 4x4.

DIANE: She's forgiven you for running over her cat?

KEVIN: Yes. Fascinating woman. She used to be in the IRA. Yeah. Properly worked for them as a quartermaster.

DIANE: What does she do now?

KEVIN: She's the skiwear buyer at Millets. Did you drive?

DIANE: Phoebe was brilliant. She put her boots on, and walked out into the blizzard. Ten minutes later she pulled up the drive on a tractor, hitched a rope to the Jag, and towed me down to the main road, which was gritted. She crushed my favourite rose in the operation.

KEVIN: Shame.

DIANE: It was a wild white rose, a cutting I took from a hedge.

KEVIN: I'm sorry.

DIANE: Don't be sorry Kevin. It was a plant.

(KEVIN sits down.)

Oh dear. You've sat down.

KEVIN: Miss Tickell from Human Resources will be joining us in a minute.

DIANE: Frau Tickell?

KEVIN: I've arranged for Doctor Popodopolos to take over all your teaching for the rest of the term.

DIANE: Fuck off.

KEVIN: I'm the Professor here! I'm unfuckoffable.

DIANE: I've had sex with you. In a tent. I can tell you to fuck off whenever I like!

KEVIN: Hell's bells! What made you think that you could be fucking interviewed on fucking Paxo, representing my fucking Earth Sciences Faculty of York University Institute of Science and fucking Technology and not ask for permission from either me, or the Vice fucking Chancellor?!

DIANE: Because the fucking BBC needed a fucking sea level expert. It was either me or Doctor Popofuckingdopolos.

There is a knock at the door. DIANE opens the door to MISS TICKELL.

I know you. You're one of the human resources of Human Resources.

TICKELL: Catherine Tickell.

DIANE: Guten morgen. What's going on Kevin?

KEVIN: We're going to have to suspend you.

TICKELL: You have the right to be accompanied by a union official or colleague.

DIANE: Alright. I'll go and find my union official. Ein Augenblick, bitte!

DIANE exits, closing the door. TICKELL and KEVIN sit.

TICKELL: Why is she speaking German?

KEVIN: I don't know. Insane! She home educated her daughter, six years. That's not normal is it. No one's good enough to teach her precious Phoebe. Poor kid. Made her an anorexic.

TICKELL: I've got a tip for these sort of situations, say as little as possible, think before you speak, bite your tongue, count to ten.

KEVIN: I want her out of my building.

TICKELL: When do Catalan visit?

KEVIN: January.

TICKELL: Who's the union rep in Earth Sciences?

KEVIN: Doctor Popodopolos.

TICKELL: Oh Christ.

Re-enter DIANE carrying Doc Pop's cuddly toy polar bear. DIANE sits behind her desk and plonks the polar bear on the desk, holding it, moving it so it seems to look around the room taking in the scene.

DIANE: This is my shop steward, Maureen. Kevin. Say hello to Maureen.

KEVIN: Nice to meet you Maureen.

DIANE: *(As Maureen.)* Hellooo!

Miss Tickle?

TICKELL: Tickell.

DIANE: Sorry. Say hello to Maureen.

TICKELL is biting her tongue and counting to ten.

TICKELL: Hello.

DIANE: Maureen.

TICKELL: Hello Maureen.

DIANE: *(As Maureen.)* Hellooo!

Lovely! Now, how can I help?

KEVIN: I'm sorry Diane –

TICKELL: – No. We are progressing from your verbal warning to stage three, suspension, on the grounds of mental capacity.

DIANE: Surely, 'mental incapacity'? Or 'lack of' mental capacity?

TICKELL: In employment law it's called mental capacity.

DIANE: I bet you're good fun at parties.

TICKELL: It is outside your contractual terms to give a media interview as an employee of the university without prior clearance from your line manager, and the Vice Chancellor. Additionally, the sceptical position you have taken on climate change damages the image of Professor Maloney's Climate Change Research Unit, which threatens its ability to raise industry funding in the market place. Consequently we require that you go for an assessment of your mental capacity to fulfil your contract.

DIANE: You're sacking me because you think I'm mad?

TICKELL: This is not dismissal, this is suspension on the grounds of mental capacity pending medical assessment. Do you have any questions?

DIANE: I do, yes. Only one. What happened to the beautiful boy I fell in love with in a tent on the banks of Isafjord?

Silence.

TICKELL: If you're making an unlawful sexual harrassment accusation against –

KEVIN: – it's alright.

DIANE: He began his seduction by teaching me how to gut a cod. Stick your thumb and index finger in the fish's eyes, the eyes will pop out, but, hell's bells, don't cry for me Argentina, the fish is dead. Find the gateway of bones below the gills and run the knife quickly south dragging the guts out with your trailing thumb. Wash the fish in the fjord, triple wrap in foil and place in the embers. Whilst it's cooking, create a map sized Rizla, spread evenly with tobacco from two broken cigarettes, and dress with the crumblings from a lump of Lebanese. Lick the Rizla along its length, and look the girl in the eye. She will blush. Tell her your heroes. Robert Johnson – King of the Delta Blues singers, Charles II, Henry Miller, Rosa Parks – why Rosa Parks and not Martin Luther King? Because her motivation was pure, not political. She was on a bus, tired, and she wanted to sit down. Your enemies were hilarious. Mother Teresa of Calcutta – pure evil?! Gandhi – a cretin!? The clergy of all religions. On science, brilliant, but frightened. The enlightenment project would never be secure because of the ubiquitous human need to be crushed under the wheels of the supernatural. And then a hand found its way under my jumper and cupped my left breast. I welcomed it. I was in love. That was a tutorial, Kevin. Not cost effective obviously, but inspirational. What happened to you? *(Beat.)* I've finished. You can sack me now.

TICKELL: You will get a letter outlining your rights and your responsibilities. We require you to leave the campus immediately.

DIANE: Can I confer with my colleague?

TICKELL: Er…yes.

DIANE whispers into the polar bear's ear. The polar bear whispers back into DIANE's ear.

DIANE: Maureen says that in the twenty-seven years she's worked in industrial relations she's never met a bigger pair of cunts.

To black.

Interval.

Act Four

Boxing Day afternoon. Not yet dark. DIANE's kitchen in the country. Main entrance door up stage centre, which is a stable door design ie: top half opens independently. Open stairs. The back wall has a big picture window, the old barn entrance, through which we see that although it is not snowing now, snow has fallen and drifted. PHOEBE and DIANE sit at the table staring at a Scrabble board. A laptop is plugged in and set beside PHOEBE.

PHOEBE: Why did you invite that fucking insane racist Mrs. Boston over for Christmas dinner yesterday?

DIANE: Mrs Boston is my mother.

PHOEBE: I need alcohol.

DIANE: We have contracted with Maeve not to drink until it's dark.

PHOEBE: Uurgh! I bet Boxing Day on a London sink estate isn't this boring.

DIANE: What would you be doing Phoebe?

PHOEBE: I'd deal some skunk; stick fireworks through a paedophile's letter box; organise a dog fight in a lock up; watch some porn; buy a gun; get drunk; superglue a tortoise to the railway lines; bomb some amphetamine; go home and have sex with my step dad. Yes! What a fucking brilliant Christmas! But no, I'm middle class, so I play Scrabble.

PHOEBE lays four tiles to make LIONPERM. DIANE frowns.

DIANE: Lionperm?

PHOEBE: Ya.

DIANE: What's a lionperm?

PHOEBE: A hair do. Makes you look a bit like a lion.

DIANE: I challenge.

PHOEBE opens the dictionary as if to look for lionperm.

PHOEBE: Lingerie. Lion. Lioness. *Lionperm.* A hairstyle originating in South Shields remarkable for the mane-like ridge of hair matted with blood and excrement. Triple word. Thirty-nine.

DIANE: Take your tiles back.

PHOEBE: No! I refuse to conform to the rules of this quasi-educational, fascist mind fuck, wank fest.

DIANE: The snow on the tops is drifting.

PHOEBE: Why have we not gone on our walk to Wharram Percy?!

DIANE: It's getting dark. It's dangerous. We might die.

PHOEBE: I want to die. I wish your mother had aborted you. And I wish you'd aborted me. I'm never gonna have kids.

DIANE: We can't recycle the dead.

PHOEBE: This planet cannot sustain an ever growing population.

DIANE: We can walk to Len's. Give him his presents, pick up half a dozen eggs.

PHOEBE: Len's is twenty yards?! That's not a Boxing Day walk. Alright! Anything to get out of here.

PHOEBE puts her coat and wellies on. Picks up Len's present – a wrapped bottle of whisky.

DIANE: If Len says come in for a cup of tea, I'm not going in, he's filthy.

PHOEBE: Eighty-six-year-old Yorkshire farmers who live on their own don't floss.

DIANE puts her coat and wellies on. She picks up a present, a small wrapped block.

DIANE: What did you get him?

PHOEBE: Whisky. You?

DIANE: Soap.

PHOEBE: Fascist! I hate you.

DIANE: The reasons why we hate each other are many and complex.

PHOEBE: No! I'm an active member of Greenpeace and you're a gas guzzling planet rapist.

(They leave. DIANE makes a point of locking the door.)

(Off.) Why are you locking the door?!

DIANE: *(Off.)* Because I'm mad!

We see them walk off in the direction of the road. Silence. Then the land line phone rings and rings, then off. Someone in ski mask and fatigues approaches the house, looks in the window. He unlocks the door with keys and enters. He closes the door behind him. He locks the door. He has a cursory look around. He takes off his ski mask. It is GEOFF. He is cold. He seeks out warmth. He goes in the fridge, finds something to eat, eats it. He takes all the knives from a knife block, wraps them in a tea towel and puts them inside his jacket. He is distracted by the Scrabble board, takes one look, looks away moves on, stops himself, looks back at it again. Picks up the dictionary, starts to check LIONPERM. The sound of PHOEBE's voice in the garden.

PHOEBE: *(Off.)* That's what farmers smell like!

DIANE: *(Off.)* I'm not disputing that.

Unlocking the door.

GEOFF: Oh shit!

GEOFF crouches and runs for the stairs. He disappears upstairs as DIANE is unlocking the door. DIANE and PHOEBE come in. DIANE is carrying a box of eggs.

PHOEBE: Why can't we go on our proper walk? You're punishing me for last night.

DIANE: I will punish you for last night when I can think of something appropriately elegant.

PHOEBE: You deserved to be punched.

DIANE: You have contracted with Maeve to stop punching me.

PHOEBE: No! I have contracted to *try* to stop punching you. Semantic specificity. You – *try* to drop this wooden spoon.

She gives DIANE a wooden spoon. DIANE lifts it up and drops it.

PHOEBE: I didn't ask you to drop it, I asked you to *try* and drop it.

DIANE: You hurt me. I'm your mother.

PHOEBE: When I punch you it is me *trying* to stop punching you. This is how you *try* to drop a spoon.

PHOEBE holds the wooden spoon up and tries to drop it, holding on to it all the while. She becomes distressed with the effort, breathing hard, crying.

DIANE: Ok, I get it! Stop it!

PHOEBE throws the spoon away. She is now distraught. DIANE comforts her. Sound of a car pulling into the drive. A mobile phone rings. DIANE answers.

DIANE: *(On phone.)* What do you want? …we're having a traditional Christmas, almost Dickensian in its various extremes of suffering…you're outside? I don't know.

(DIANE switches the phone off.)

Kevin.

PHOEBE opens only the top half of the stable style door, revealing KEVIN with a hastily wrapped climbing rose in a pot.

PHOEBE: Fuck off!

KEVIN: Merry Christmas!

(PHOEBE closes the door. DIANE approaches the door, opens it.)

This is for you.

(He hands in the climbing rose. DIANE takes it and puts it on the table. It looks pathetic.)

It's a climbing rose. Rambling Rector. It's won awards.

DIANE: Not this one surely?

KEVIN: No, you know, the breed. Best climbing rose.

DIANE: What are the judges looking for? Speed?

KEVIN: It's from that garden centre just this side of Flamborough Head.

DIANE: You went to Flamborough Head on your own? On Boxing Day?

KEVIN: Sabina's been having an affair. She's left me.

DIANE: At Christmas?

PHOEBE: I'm in an episode of EastEnders!

DIANE opens the door and lets KEVIN in. Closes the door after him.

KEVIN: Thank you.

PHOEBE: *(To DIANE.)* Have you had sex with him?

DIANE: Once.

PHOEBE: Why only once? Is he rubbish?

KEVIN: She means *once* as in once upon a time.

PHOEBE: Would you like a glass of red wine?

KEVIN: Thank you, but I'm driving, so I can only have the one.

DIANE: And would you like that one now?

KEVIN: Yes please.

PHOEBE: Large or small?

KEVIN: Large.

PHOEBE gets herself a glass of red. And pours one for KEVIN.

DIANE: Very clever.

PHOEBE: *(Drinking.)* It's genetic.

KEVIN: You've seen the papers, obviously.

DIANE: I told you about that typo.

KEVIN: They're calling it *Typogate.*

DIANE: Why didn't you get it proofed properly?

PHOEBE: Transparency!

DIANE: Kevin is like a rash across all the papers. They're all going crazy about a typo, which I spotted three months ago, in his IPCC chapter which says that the Himalayan glaciers will all have melted by 2035.

KEVIN: *(To PHOEBE.)* 2035 is about three hundred years wrong.

DIANE: I knew you weren't listening to me, I –

KEVIN: – It wasn't a typo.

(KEVIN sits.)

I knew it wasn't a typo. I put it in deliberately. I got the date from a WWF document.

DIANE: Oh my God! Oh fuck! You put some made-up stuff from an activist in the IPCC report. When this gets out they're gonna crucify you. What were you doing?

KEVIN: The people in the foothills, I've been there, they're really beautiful people, when you get used to them, they depend on the melt waters. They need action now, not in three hundred years' time.

PHOEBE: I don't think you've done anything wrong.

DIANE: Oh he has, and he knows he has!

KEVIN: You don't have to talk to politicians. I do, it's impossible, they're all so –

DIANE: – thick?

PHOEBE: Liars yes, but thick?

DIANE: If Frankenstein went into the House of Commons, chopped them all up, he wouldn't be able to build one single decent scientist.

KEVIN takes a drink, empties his glass.

PHOEBE: Your glass is empty. And you can only have one because you're driving.

KEVIN: I'll be alright, it's an automatic.

PHOEBE pours him another glass.

PHOEBE: Have you been reading her column in the Telegraph?

KEVIN: Yes. Very provocative. Your tree, in the Maldives; sea levels not rising; Al Gore buys beach house.

DIANE: They've offered me a regular column.

PHOEBE: Can you tell her that writing for the Daily Telegraph is not a victimless crime.

DIANE: They want a hard scientist to go head to head with George Monbiot.

PHOEBE: Fight! Fight! Fight! Fight! Fight! Fight! Fight! Fight! Fight! Fight!

DIANE: Why have you come here Kevin?

PHOEBE: It's obvious. He was going to throw himself off Flamborough Head because of this Himalayan thing, because his wife has left him, and because Christmas is always a bit shit.

KEVIN: I thought that looking at the ocean might give me some perspective, which it did. Which is why I bought you a rose. I'm not suicidal.

He finishes his second glass.

PHOEBE: Maybe, but you're definitely an alcoholic.

(There is a knock at the door.)

I knew you were expecting someone!

(BEN appears at the window.)

Shit! It's that cute student. Mum! And I look like a yak!

PHOEBE puts a hat on. DIANE opens the door. He has cycled. His left wrist is bandaged.

DIANE: Hello Ben!

BEN: Have you got Wi-Fi?

DIANE: Yes! Come in! You cycled? In this. You know Professor Maloney, Kevin.

KEVIN: Whappen?!

BEN: What?

KEVIN: Hi.

BEN: Hi.

BEN: *(To PHOEBE, keen.)* Hi.

PHOEBE: *(Dismissive.)* Hi.

DIANE: Sit here Ben. Get warm. Would you like a drink?

BEN: Couple of cans of lager please.

PHOEBE: What's wrong with your wrist?

BEN: Er…I play bass in a band, and it catches on the bridge.

PHOEBE: Why do you play in a band?

BEN: 'cause, like, it's a good way of getting your shit out.

PHOEBE: But where does that shit go? Into other people's ears.

DIANE: It must be cold on your narrow boat?

BEN: No, I've got a log burning stove.

PHOEBE: *(Amazed.)* You burn wood?!

BEN: Burning logs is carbon neutral.

PHOEBE: Fantastic! We should be burning logs mum!?

DIANE: OK, go and chop some then.

PHOEBE: We could get some delivered.

BEN: No.

PHOEBE: No, of course not! Oh! It's so difficult isn't it!

BEN: I'm moored at King's Staithe, a lot of driftwood comes down.

PHOEBE: I know King's Staithe. There's about eight boats, all bright colours with geraniums, and then on the end there's this sinister-looking black boat, lying low in the water with old newspapers for curtains. Which one's yours?

DIANE gives him two lagers. He opens one immediately and swigs.

BEN: *(To DIANE.)* D'ya get my email?

PHOEBE: She's not been online for two days.

DIANE: Christ was born in a stable, not live on webcam.

BEN: OK. Bust this. We hacked the Hampshire mainframe man! I've got the Chinese data.

KEVIN: Hampshire University?

BEN: Believe!

DIANE: You said 'we' hacked?

BEN: My mate Fran, he's the hacker, he's autistic, like Rain Man. He was my best mate in prison.

DIANE: You've been in prison? Why don't I know that?

BEN: Data Protection innit. GBH on my dad.

DIANE: And why was Fran in prison?

BEN: Hacking.

DIANE: Prison's not working is it.

PHOEBE: Was it an open prison?

BEN: No. It was one of those prisons where they, like, lock you up, yeah?

PHOEBE: Did you get anally raped?

BEN: In prison, they rape you, like, spiritually. You wake up, and, like, your Blu-Tack will be gone, yeah? Like, all your Blu-Tack. Just gone, yeah? And the next morning, yeah, it's back again.

KEVIN: What's going on Diane?

DIANE: This is illegal Ben, you've broken the law.

BEN: *(To KEVIN.)* Kieron McKay refused Dr Cassell's Freedom of Information request for the Chinese tree ring data, so I couldn't like, you know, further my education, so I got my mate to hack the mainframe.

KEVIN: Is there any chance of a sandwich?

DIANE: Sausage roll?

KEVIN: Fantastic!

> *KEVIN swigs at the red wine. DIANE opens the fridge, finds the sausage rolls.*

Do you remember those sausage rolls we bought in Reykjavik?

DIANE: Don't start Kevin!

DIANE puts the sausage rolls in either the microwave or the Aga.

BEN: You know your mum's a brilliant teacher.

PHOEBE: I found her a bit didactic. I didn't go to school. I was home taught.

BEN: But…ain't that…I mean…socially…er…I mean getting taught on your own…er…don't you like kind of miss out on …fuck I dunno, er…

PHOEBE: – social skills?

BEN: Yeah. Where can I boot my lappie?

DIANE: There's power points, here, under the lip, I'll get my laptop.

DIANE heads to her office, stage left, to get her laptop. BEN stands, and roots around in his pannier for his laptop.

KEVIN: *(To BEN.)* Do you believe that we're warmer now than we've ever been.

BEN: Ever been, or in the Holocene?

KEVIN: Christ! You can tell he's one of yours. Of course, in the Holocene.

BEN: I'm a scientist yeah. I can't allow myself to 'believe' in anything.

KEVIN: Good for you. I *believe* we're warmer now than we've ever been, and getting warmer, and the cause of that is us.

DIANE arrives with her ancient looking laptop and puts it down alongside BEN's.

DIANE: *(To BEN.)* Have you told anyone else about this?

BEN: No. It's me and Fran. We're tight.

PHOEBE stands.

PHOEBE: I'm going to ring Daz, in the pub, see if he'll sell me some K.

KEVIN: What's K?

DIANE: Ketamine. It's a horse tranquiliser. It's very popular round here.

KEVIN: What kind of a trip is it?

PHOEBE: In a K hole you get a separation of mind and body.

KEVIN: Can you get me some?

PHOEBE: *(To DIANE.)* Why is what you're doing now, more important than talking to me?

DIANE: Ben came here, today, because he wanted to show me this data.

PHOEBE: No! This is obviously just an elaborate ruse to see me! Isn't it, Ben?

BEN: Yeah. But let me do this first, alright? Have you got a laptop?

PHOEBE: I'm twenty-one-years-old. What do you think?

DIANE: That's hers.

BEN: *(To DIANE.)* I've pasted a link in the email I sent you. Can you forward it to Phoebe. I don't know her email.

PHOEBE moves her laptop and places it down between DIANE's and BEN's thereby separating them with her presence. KEVIN has removed himself from the table and is investigating the sausage roll situation.

DIANE: Your link has taken me to a Slovenian pizza takeaway site.

BEN: Yeah, it's a dead site. Double click on the Florentina.

KEVIN: I'll have a deep pan meat feast please.

PHOEBE: What are we doing?

BEN: You know that graph Al Gore has where temperature is steady forever then it, like, suddenly takes off in the twentieth century?

PHOEBE: The Hockey Stick?

BEN: Yeah.

KEVIN: In that film of his, Al Gore, he's got the y axis upside down.

DIANE: I told you that two years ago.

KEVIN: You work your guts out, a lifetime, then some smarmy tit in a suit comes along, gets his y axis upside down and picks up a Nobel Peace Prize.

DIANE: He's got fat hasn't he, Al Gore.

BEN: Got rich man.

PHOEBE: I like him. For every mouthful of food Al Gore eats he gives two mouthfuls to a starving child in Africa.

DIANE: The poor kid must be huge by now.

PHOEBE: He cares about the future! Because his son died.

KEVIN: No! The kid was hit by a car but he didn't die.

PHOEBE: His child didn't die?

DIANE: Have you gone off him now?

PHOEBE: A bit.

BEN: Harsh man! You can't think less of him, 'cause his child *didn't* die.

DIANE: He's also the world's first carbon trading billionaire.

PHOEBE: So he's a carbon trading billionaire, whose child didn't die?

DIANE: Yes.

PHOEBE: What a cunt.

DIANE: This isn't just Chinese Pines, there's ten years' of private emails here.

KEVIN: Kieron McKay's private emails?!

DIANE: Merry Christmas Kevin.

KEVIN looks over their shoulders, whilst opening a bottle.

PHOEBE: What am I looking for?

BEN: OK, 'cause we've only got the instrument record, that's like thermometers yeah, from about like the nineteenth century, in Paleo we have to kinda like guess, temperatures from what we call proxy data. Proxies are like lake sediments, ice cores, tree rings.

PHOEBE: I'm the daughter of a climate scientist, I know what a paleoclimate proxy temperature reconstruction is you dick.

DIANE: She only abuses those she loves.

PHOEBE: 'The Proxy Lovers.' That would be a good name for a band.

KEVIN: I was in a band once. The Moscow Jam Lovers.

BEN: Cool name.

KEVIN: Yeah, we were all communists who liked jam.

BEN: I've brought my guitar. Feel free.

KEVIN: Ta.

PHOEBE: What's the name of your band Ben?

BEN: The Four Horsemen.

PHOEBE: How many in the band?

BEN: Seven.

PHOEBE: Have you considered sacking three of them?

DIANE: Why should his band willingly subject itself to the hegemony of language? What kind of rock band is that?

PHOEBE: Because then it'd be a crap band with a congruous name, instead of a crap band with an incongruous name. In anyone's book, that's progress.

BEN: It doesn't matter now anyway.

PHOEBE: Because you've split up?

BEN: Yeah.

PHOEBE: What a waste of thirty seconds that was.

KEVIN has picked up the guitar, taken it out of its case. KEVIN strums and – .

KEVIN: *(Singing.)* I'd better drink a bit more first.

DIANE: Ben, Google Chinese White Pines, Phoebe go on Wikipedia and search for Songhua river valley China. I want latitude, climate etc.

KEVIN: Been there. The river freezes every winter, melts every spring, floods the plains, hundreds drown and they all act surprised.

DIANE: Thank you. Professor.

KEVIN: Yeah! They didn't give me an OBE for my apple crumble.

KEVIN stands and looks over DIANE's shoulder.

BEN: Chinese White Pines can be susceptible to Cronartium Ribicola.

DIANE: Thanks.

PHOEBE: 'The Songhua river valley freezes from November to March.'

BEN: Yo!

High fives with BEN.

KEVIN: I've still got it. The passion. Yeah.

DIANE: I can't find Kieron McKay's twentieth century trees. I've got every cohort from eleventh century right through to nineteenth but there's no twentieth century records.

BEN: I think he's given them, like really obscure labelling.

DIANE: He's hidden them. Why's he hidden them?

KEVIN: In case someone hacked the mainframe?

PHOEBE: *(To BEN.)* Do you want the second of your two beers now Ben?

BEN: I can get it.

PHOEBE: No, you're working.

KEVIN: Step aside. I'm world class.

PHOEBE: Use mine.

KEVIN: You sure?

PHOEBE: I can share with Ben.

KEVIN: How's he tagged them?

DIANE: C14 is the fourteenth century cohort; C15 is fifteenth.

KEVIN: But no C20?

KEVIN squeezes in taking over PHOEBE's computer.

BEN: Zero. None. Nandos.

PHOEBE: Do you like Nandos?

BEN: I'm vegetarian.

PHOEBE: I'm anorexic.

BEN: Cool.

PHOEBE: I judge all restaurants by their toilet facilities.

Finger in throat.

BEN: I thought that was bulimia.

PHOEBE: Bulimia's gorge purge, I starve purge.

KEVIN: Voila! I have a cohort of eight trees dated 1952.

DIANE: How's he labelled it?

KEVIN: TT52.

BEN: I got a TT04. It's a cohort of five trees alive in 2004.

KEVIN: TT04 is the last of his files.

BEN: That's it man. There's like no more trees.

DIANE: His twentieth-century sample is five trees, and eight trees.

KEVIN: *n* equals thirteen!?

PHOEBE: Is that unlucky?

BEN: It's not statistically significant. *n* equals thirteen describes the sample size. You knew that, sorry.

PHOEBE: So what's going on then mum?

DIANE: Whatever's going on, it's not science.

PHOEBE: Yes! But why are you so excited!?

DIANE: Because this effectively destroys The Hockey Stick, and The Hockey Stick is the single most important icon of the IPCC.

KEVIN: If you right click, you get the individual tree ring graphs.

DIANE: I'm in the 2004 file. Ben do 1952.

BEN: OK! I'm in.

DIANE: What are you getting? Any sharp temperature rises?

BEN: The first two trees are flat.

DIANE: I've looked at three trees. Their graphs are flat.

BEN: Flat as roadkill.

PHOEBE: That's funny Ben. You can be quite amusing can't you?

BEN: Yeah.

DIANE: There's nothing going on! I'm up to number seven. Flat as a pancake.

PHOEBE: Flat as roadkill mum!

DIANE: How the hell do you get a Hockey Stick from this cohort?!

BEN: I'm one hundred percent roadkill.

DIANE: Woah! Look at that! Oh, ho, ho, ho!

They all look at DIANE's screen.

KEVIN: What tree is that?

DIANE: Number eight.

PHOEBE: – sexy Kate!

DIANE: – Is she late!

PHOEBE: – Harry Tate!

BEN: Bingo rhymes freestyle, man, I dig!

PHOEBE: Bingo is cutting edge in the countryside.

KEVIN: A perfect Hockey Stick.

BEN: One tree.

DIANE: Do you see, Phoebe? After 1950, this tree, just takes off.

PHOEBE: Why?

BEN: Kieron McKay would say it's temperature rise.

KEVIN: Mmm.

PHOEBE: Yeah, I think he's right.

DIANE: I think Sexy Kate is a young tree in 1890 surrounded by mature trees, struggling for water, growing in the shade, in 1950 there's a storm, the old trees fall down, because they're weakened by –

BEN: – Cronartium Ribicola –

DIANE: – the dead trees fertilise the ground, and sexy Kate feels the sun for the first time, and has her fifteen minutes of fame.

BEN: That is like the single most important tree in the world man!

DIANE: One tree! I don't believe it!

KEVIN: Your tree in the Maldives is one tree.

KEVIN: Yes, ha ha! Yes! Good point.

BEN: Is this dangerous? Like globally, economically. If I post this on the net.

KEVIN: The carbon markets are not going to respond to one bit of bodged science coming out of Hampshire.

BEN: But the world economy is already dodgy dodgy.

PHOEBE: I like it when you say words twice.

DIANE: I can imagine carbon trading collapsing.

PHOEBE: Banks close their doors, seal up their ATMs. Riots. Street fighting.

BEN: Anarchy in the UK.

PHOEBE: Chavs invade the countryside and pull crops up with their bare hands, and discover the dignity of labour.

BEN: Farmers fire at the urban working class from motorway bridges.

PHOEBE: Babylon is burning, ruined, wrecked.

BEN: Disease, war, and famine.

PHOEBE: No one can survive. Except one man. Mum?

DIANE: Mel Gibson. Mel is an astronaut returning from Venus with gas.

PHOEBE: Mel Gibson is the last man standing. Humanity is on the brink of extinction. Ben?

BEN: Mel can't find a woman but befriends a wolf called Dennis.

PHOEBE: Dennis and Mel spend twenty years wandering about in a cinematic mist looking for a human female. Mum?

DIANE: One day Mel sees a beautiful girl –

PHOEBE: – a beautiful nude girl bathing naked in a river with no clothes on. Who would that be Ben?

BEN: Gemma Arterton.

PHOEBE: I am so disappointed. Mel and Gemma must make a baby, but, plot twist, Mel's character is gay.

DIANE: Fortunately, Gemma understands the principles of aversion therapy so she draws pictures of boys in the sand, gets Mel to look at them whilst she thrashes him with a stick until he becomes heterosexual.

PHOEBE: Brilliant! Mel and Gemma make love!

PHOEBE kisses BEN. It's a proper kiss. Outside it is now dark.

KEVIN: Bloody hell.

DIANE: I've seen hard-core porn that was easier to watch.

PHOEBE: Would you like to walk around a medieval plague village in the dark, with me, Ben? Now?

DIANE: No! It's too late for Wharram Percy. It's dark, and the snow is drifting.

KEVIN: What is this Wharram Percy? A kind of lost village?

DIANE: How does one lose a village?

PHOEBE: The Black Death wiped them out.

DIANE: No! Every Boxing Day Phoebe and I walk around Wharram Percy. *Every year* I explain to her that in the sixteenth century there was a change of land use, the landlord switched to grazing sheep, so everyone left to look for work somewhere else.

KEVIN: How prosaic.

DIANE: Yes. But this generation –

PHOEBE: – it's not my generation that has fucked the planet.

DIANE: This generation, are disaster junkies. Armageddon in three acts.

PHOEBE: Fuck off.

DIANE: It's as if their every last twitching synapse has been transplanted from the stolen corpse of a Hollywood screenwriter. Why be content with 'a change of land use' when you can have the drama of 'wiped out by the Black Death.' Every day they wake up craving a narrative fix. When they see a photograph of a polar bear, hitching a lift on a passing ice flow, they cannot see a wild animal at ease in its natural habitat. What they see is the last five minutes of Titanic! That one ton carnivor's contented yawn becomes Leonardo di Caprio's hopeless scream as he drifts inexorably away from that posh girl who's normally in a corset.

BEN: Kate Winslet.

KEVIN is clicking on the computer now.

KEVIN: This is a text file right?

BEN: Yeah.

KEVIN: I want to see what McKay told Toby at Nature about *n* equals thirteen.

PHOEBE: So, are you a sceptic now Professor?

KEVIN: No!

DIANE: He can see a way of bringing down Hampshire University.

KEVIN: Correct.

BEN: Would it be alright, if I like played a song?

DIANE: Sure.

BEN: This is a song I wrote for you.

PHOEBE/DIANE: Me? / For me?

BEN: Whatever.

PHOEBE: Give me a drink.

DIANE pours PHOEBE a glass of wine, and herself.

KEVIN: *(Re: something on screen.)* No! Ha!

DIANE: I'll put some pizzas in. Pizzas!?

KEVIN/BEN: Yeah / Great.

PHOEBE: This is going to be really weird. I mean…shouldn't this be in private?

During the next DIANE gets pizzas from the fridge. BEN sings and plays.

BEN: *(Adagio.) I met her first in the fall*
she looked past me at the wall
my lobster skin and lobster hair
were not what she had in mind
at all
met her once again in town
we're both a week older now
and I felt like an ocean inside
but spoke to her confidently
do you remember me?

(Spoken.) She said – no, I don't, go away.

(Allegro.) but it's early days,
and things might change

and love might wax
and love might wane
and the sun might shine
and the rain might rain
on us some time one day

(Adagio.) in the spring I saw her again
through the window of a train
and destiny took the controls
and waved my arms joyously
I'm here, hello, yes it's me!

(Spoken.) nothing

(Allegro.) but it's early days,
and things might change
and love might wax
and love might wane
and the sun might shine
and the rain might rain
on us some time one day

KEVIN and DIANE applaud and cheer. PHOEBE has her hand over her mouth.

KEVIN/DIANE: Brilliant mate. / It's lovely!

BEN: *(To PHOEBE.)* Did you like it?

PHOEBE: Some bits were alright. *(To BEN.)* Do you like badgers?

DIANE: No, you're not going outside! It's dark now.

PHOEBE: It's dark!? I'm not a child! Ben, do you like badgers?

BEN: Badgers? Dunno. I haven't like properly thought it through.

PHOEBE puts her coat and hat on and picks up a bottle of wine.

DIANE: *(To BEN.)* We have a shed, with a telescope. You can watch the stars or you can watch the badgers.

PHOEBE: Shagging.

KEVIN: You won't see any badgers shagging in winter.

DIANE: In winter, 'badger watching' means drinking, and smoking dope.

KEVIN: I could do with a joint. I've had a difficult last ten years. I'll give you some money.

PHOEBE: Do I look like a dealer?

DIANE: We need to find Ben a coat. Will this be a problem? It's mine?

BEN: Cool.

He puts the coat on. BEN slips the woolly hat on and pulls it down.

PHOEBE: Oh God, I can't watch, it's so Freudian.

KEVIN manages to give PHOEBE a fiver, which she takes. They exit.

DIANE: Get out!

KEVIN: *(Re: the screen.)* What!? I don't believe it.

DIANE: I only let you in today Kevin because I'm frightened.

(She goes to her office and comes back with a Christmas card, in an envelope.)

I got a Christmas card. There's no stamp. They know where I live! One of them came here to my home!

She hands it to him. He reads it.

KEVIN: 'Continue your column in the Torygraph and you will get a visit from Father Christmas. The Sacred Earth Militia.'

KEVIN: Have you told the police?

DIANE: They wanted to come and look at security. So I had to say no. This is the kind of thing that can flip Phoebe.

KEVIN: Is the front door locked?

DIANE: And bolted, it's never used.

KEVIN: Bolt that door too. The kids'll have to knock.

DIANE: Do you think they're OK in the hide?

KEVIN: What would The Sacred Earth Militia do with the kids? Kill them? My sister, London, drives a big fuck off 4x4, she gets mad green stickers on her windscreen all the time. But there's this grungy converted ambulance camper van, ancient, three litre diesel, filthy –

DIANE: – never gets a sticker.

KEVIN: Never. What's that about?

DIANE: All religions are shot through with inconsistencies.

KEVIN: It's not a religion!

DIANE: It's the perfect religion for the narcissistic age. It provides a clear definition of sin. Drive to work – sinful. Cycle – righteous. Fly to Crete – sinful. Go camping in the New Forest – righteous.

KEVIN: In the rain.

DIANE: Martyrdom! Why drink the blood of Christ, when you can score a regular epiphany recycling The London Review of Books.

KEVIN: You just like driving Jaguars!

DIANE: Cars are liberating, democratic, and feminist. And the day when Greenpeace has succeeded in pricing the poor off the roads will not be a good day for the planet, it will be a good day for totalitarianism.

KEVIN: What do these buggers want? To go back to nature?

DIANE: Nature is hell. Nature is hunger, cold, dying in childbirth. I want electricity, a car, central heating, and I don't want to have to eat my own pigs, I want to eat someone else's pigs.

KEVIN: You could eat my pigs D?

DIANE: Stop trying to get in my knickers!

KEVIN: God put me on earth to try and get into your knickers.

DIANE: You're an atheist.

KEVIN: I am, yes, but He isn't.

DIANE: You're reading their private emails.

KEVIN: Yes I am, and it's the best fun I've had since Jamaica entered a bobsleigh team in the 1988 Winter Olympics.

DIANE: *(Looking over shoulder.)* Kieron McKay has a spare ticket to a Rolling Stones gig at Wembley. Forty quid. Cheapskate.

KEVIN: What have I always said D? About tree rings?

DIANE: Don't call me D.

KEVIN: They're lousy proxies. Look.

(Reading.) 'I've binned the tree ring data, and pasted in the instrument record from 1960 to bury the downturn.'

Do these tree ring guys make a habit of pasting in the instrument record on the end of a proxy series?

DIANE: You're not seriously telling me that you did not know that *Professor*?

KEVIN: No! Fucking no! They can't do that! That's like a vegetarian getting his blood sugar up with a bacon sandwich. Why don't I know this!?

DIANE: I'm more interested in what he means by the downturn.

KEVIN: There seems to have been a sudden collapse in the correlation between tree ring and temperature from about 1960 onwards.

DIANE: They're admitting that tree rings have become lousy proxies

KEVIN: Admitting to each other, yeah, but not telling us. I've always said tree rings are lousy proxies.

DIANE: Without knowing anything about dendrochronology.

KEVIN: Ignorance has never stopped me having an opinion.

DIANE: So you've got exactly what you want, Kevin. Hampshire University is all tree rings.

KEVIN: Yes! Catalan won't want to hang their jacket on a shaky nail! This is brilliant news for us Diane!

DIANE: Us? There is no us Kevin. You sacked me because I'm mad.

KEVIN: You're mad, I'm mad. Who cares! Today, looking at the sea, I thought of King Cnut, and his – what's that word, sounds like you should eat it with pitta bread and olives?

Diane: Hummus?

Kevin: No, not hummus, but it's like hummus. Oh! Where's Geoff when you need him!?

DIANE: Hubris?

KEVIN: Hubris. Yes. Are we all Cnuts? Am I a Cnut?

DIANE: How are you spelling it?

KEVIN: C.N.U.T.

DIANE: In that order?

KEVIN: Yeah.

DIANE: Cnut wasn't trying to stop the sea coming in. He knew he couldn't. He was demonstrating his impotence in the face of nature to his court who believed he could control the elements.

KEVIN: I didn't know that.

DIANE: You didn't know that, because Cnut commanding the waves is a better story. Media crap wasn't invented in the last ten years.

KEVIN: You're such a good teacher. I'd like you to come back to work with me.

DIANE: *(DIANE throws something at him.)* Fuck off!

KEVIN: And swear at me.

(DIANE throws something at him.)

And throw things at me.

DIANE: You're offering me my job back?

KEVIN: Yes. That is what I'm doing right now.

DIANE: Because the argument is the science?

KEVIN: Exactly.

DIANE: And you'll need me if you win the Catalan contract when this gets out about McKay.

KEVIN: We'll be busy, yes.

DIANE: You can't go public with this. Hacking is a criminal offence.

KEVIN: What can we do?

DIANE: Wikileaks.

Banging on the door. The door is bolted. DIANE jumps, frightened.

PHOEBE: *(Off.)* Mum!

KEVIN: Come back and teach D. Please.

DIANE opens the door, lets her in.

PHOEBE: Why have you bolted the door?

DIANE: What is it?

PHOEBE: Ben said I can live with him on his barge! Is that alright?

DIANE: Has he got a license?

PHOEBE: You don't need a license to live with a woman.

KEVIN: No, but a training course would help.

DIANE: I want to see the state of the boat first.

PHOEBE: Fascist!

DIANE: I'm your mother! This is a reasonable request. Tell Ben to come in for his pizza.

PHOEBE: Ben doesn't want to eat.

DIANE: Oh!

PHOEBE: But I'm…I might have a bit.

KEVIN: B b b b b b –

DIANE: – shutup Kevin.

PHOEBE: Why is he doing an impression of Billy from One Flew Over the Cuckoo's Nest?

DIANE: Just tell Ben I need to talk to him about the joys of living with a purging anorexic. And close that door!

PHOEBE: Don't you dare fuck this up for me.

PHOEBE turns to go. She looks at KEVIN.

KEVIN: I paid for a joint.

PHOEBE: I don't deliver. I'm not Ocado.

She turns and is gone. Door closed. KEVIN stands, intent on going out to the hide to get a joint.

KEVIN: Can I smoke in here? I think they want to be alone.

DIANE: I don't fucking care any more.

KEVIN: I lived on a wreck of a boat once and – (it didn't have.)

DIANE: – get out!

KEVIN leaves. The door is closed. DIANE, stressed, tries to compose herself. Looks for a knife. The knife block is empty. She checks the drawers, the sink. She is confused, now scared, as she thinks about it. She looks around the room, opens the walk in cupboard, looks in, closes it. She stands with both hands rooted on the table, she looks down, breathes. Her mobile phone rings.

DIANE: *(On the phone, speaking loudly.)* Youssef! …yes, I can hear you, can you hear me?…yes, Phoebe is here and we're having a lovely Christmas… there's a lot of snow… what?…OK…a group of environmentalists?…

(She sits. Enter BEN. He listens.)

…this must be costing you an arm and a leg, can we do this by email?… great, OK, send me the JPEGs, …thanks Youssef, see you in the summer. Goodbye.

(Off the phone.) Some 'group of environmentalists' has dug up my tree. In the Maldives.

BEN: They dug a tree up? Environmentalists? We're out of paraffin.

DIANE: In the cupboard, in the hall.

BEN goes in and comes out with the paraffin.

Phoebe is a bully. And it's not a rational decision to choose to live with an anorexic.

BEN: I don't want it to be a rational decision.

DIANE: It's not a silly thing about slimming! If she has a bad couple of months, she might die. She came close last year.

BEN: What, she nearly, like, actually died?

DIANE: Every organ in the body needs fuel in order to function. And I would rather have her alive than everyone in Bangladesh, or Tuvalu, or Suffolk. And every glacier in the world, and every coral reef, and every single last bloody polar bear can die, drown, melt, go impossibly acidic and fall to pieces and I honestly wouldn't care, as long as I've still got her.

BEN: Has she ever lived away from home?

DIANE: We tried university. She was seventeen. It was my fault. She stayed a week. She was appalled at the lack of intellectual rigour of the lecturers.

BEN: Which university?

DIANE: Oxford.

BEN: I just think she's slammin', and I was going to ask her out.

DIANE: Listen! She may have started menstruating again. Can you try very hard please, not to get her pregnant.

BEN: I guess with her not eating, getting pregnant could be –

DIANE: – no, no, she has threatened to kill herself. Bringing children into the world is irresponsible, apparently. Do you need condoms?

BEN: I've got enough for today.

DIANE: Get some more.

(She gives him a twenty pound note, thinks, then gives him another.)

Food, calories, minimum 800 –

PHOEBE appears at the door. Top half open.

PHOEBE: What are you talking about?

BEN: Pizza toppings.

PHOEBE: She's a control freak. You think she's being open, and generous, but she's really only drawing you in so she can tie strings around your arms and legs and neck. Strings she can pull. In the future.

BEN: I'll get the stove working.

BEN picks up the paraffin and is gone. Door closed. PHOEBE bolts it from the inside.

PHOEBE: I don't need my mother to pimp for me. OK?

DIANE: I prefer the word facilitation.

PHOEBE: And stop trying to change him. That first time, in your office, I fell in love with him that day.

DIANE: You fell in love with the idea of him.

PHOEBE: It's a start!

DIANE: Oh why don't you go and stare at the fucking stars, go on, you're a young person, go and be overwhelmed by your own insignificance!

PHOEBE: I will because there are phenomena in this universe that can't be pushed around a petri dish. Your scepticism is nothing more than a catastrophic failure of the imagination.

DIANE: He doesn't believe.

PHOEBE: Stop trying to make him like you. Stop teaching him! Stop evangelising your lousy religion!

DIANE: He chose a science course!

PHOEBE: Empiricism is a fucking ism like any other fucking ism!

PHOEBE punches DIANE.

DIANE: No! Phoebe, please! Don't start that!

PHOEBE picks up a bottle, and attacks DIANE. DIANE protects herself by curling up and covering her face with her arms and hands. She's done this many times before. PHOEBE lays in to her.

DIANE: Phoebe, you'll hurt me!

PHOEBE: Stop teaching him crap!

Another blow.

DIANE: Agh! Stop it!

(PHOEBE lays in with punches as well as the bottle.)

PHOEBE: Stop teaching, teaching, fucking teaching!

DIANE: Agh! You're hurting me Phoebe!

(PHOEBE is breathing hard. She takes her time. Silence.)

PHOEBE: Mum! I've got that pain, across my shoulders.

DIANE: You've got yourself excited. Just slow down.

(PHOEBE puts the bottle down.)

Sit down. Breathe.

PHOEBE: My shoulders mum! Agh! My shoulders! Aggggh!

DIANE: Just keep breathing, I'm getting your nitro.

PHOEBE: Oh my God! Ohhh!

KEVIN tries the door. It's locked. He knocks. Then looks through the window. DIANE lets him in, and goes for her phone. KEVIN enters, joint in hand.

KEVIN: If we'd had skunk when we were kids, really, we would not have got a lot done. Now, what this party needs is some Lynyrd Skynrd.

PHOEBE: Agggghhh! Mum!

KEVIN: What's this now?

DIANE: We're trying to stay calm.

KEVIN: Why?

DIANE: We are both working hard to ward off a heart attack.

KEVIN: A heart attack! Bloody hell, what do you want me to do?

DIANE: *(To KEVIN.)* Get the first aid kit down. There!

(On the phone.) Hello. Ambulance please, thank you… my daughter is having a heart attack…she's 21, she's anorexic…I'm sorry you will have to trust me I have seen these symptoms twice in the last year…

(KEVIN finds the first aid kit. DIANE takes it off him.)

I'm about to give her three shots of sublingual nitroglycerine…yes! I've done it before…yes, we are prepared, yes, but I am not a medic, we still need an ambulance please! …a helicopter will be fine.

(DIANE takes the first aid box and gives the phone to KEVIN.)

Tell them the postcode. They can land near the pond.

During the next DIANE adminsters the nitrostat to PHOEBE and KEVIN takes the phone.

PHOEBE: Agggh! Mum!

DIANE: Just breathe baby, don't do anything else.

KEVIN: Hello…yes, you can land next to the pond, the address here is …

(DIANE points to some bills on the wall. KEVIN reads them.)

Manor Barns…Fimber…post code YO25 5BG. OK… Is there anyone here with paramedic training? …no…is there anyone here who has carried out what? …say it again?

DIANE: Cardiopulmonary Resuscitation. No!

DIANE shakes her head.

KEVIN: Yeah?…er, no…

DIANE: Fuck! This is the real thing.

KEVIN: The helicopter is on its way…do we have a defibrilator?

DIANE: No.

KEVIN: No…can you talk me through CPR?…No, OK…yes, she has had the nitrosat…good, that's handy, the helicopter was in the sky already.

DIANE: Come on Phoebs! Don't do this to me! You can't do this! I'm not gonna let you get away with this! Breathe! One more spray!

(PHOEBE is not responding.)

She's not breathing. Come on girl! I want you to breathe baby! For Christ's sake, breathe! Breathe girl! Breathe!

There is a thump on the floorboards above. KEVIN instinctively looks upwards. There are heavy footsteps towards the stairs.

KEVIN: Jesus! What the fuck is that! Is Ben upstairs?

DIANE: Someone's in the house! I told you. Come on Phoebe! Kevin! NO! She's stopped breathing.

KEVIN: Oh Christ.

(GEOFF appears quickly, arms raised as if to say 'don't worry I can explain.')

Geoff?! What –

GEOFF: – I can explain.

DIANE: You're The Sacred Earth Militia?

GEOFF: Aye, I am, that's me, but I was 42 Commando. In the Falklands. I was our section medic.

DIANE: You can do CPR?

GEOFF: Yeah. And she's had her nitro, yeah? Sublingual?

DIANE: You know?

GEOFF: You can hear every word upstairs.

(GEOFF approaches PHOEBE and physically throws an obstacle out of his way so that can sit with one knee by PHOEBE's head and one knee by her chest. He does a skillful head tilt chin lift.)

Head tilt, chin lift. Look, listen, feel.

KEVIN: How long have you been up there? Listening?

DIANE: Shutup Kevin.

GEOFF: Couple of hours. I were gonna kidnap her.

KEVIN: With The Sacred Earth Militia?

GEOFF: I'm The Sacred Earth Militia. Me. On me tod. Sorry, alright.

DIANE: I don't care!

GEOFF: Now I know what I'm doing alright, but CPR ain't like what you see on Casualty. I don't want you getting your hopes up, it ain't exactly got the statistics behind it. But I was 42 Commando, so give me a chance.

(GEOFF bends his head down to PHOEBE's to listen for breathing. He looks for a rising and falling chest. And he feels for air. He doesn't find any evidence of breathing. GEOFF places his mouth on PHOEBE's and administers two short breaths, looking for evidence of a rising chest. He then checks for a pulse with two fingers, not the thumb, on the carotoid artery [neck].)

One, two, three, four, five, six, seven, eight, nine, ten.

DIANE: Come on babe! Breathe! You can, you can!

GEOFF does not find a pulse and so begins CPR. He gets in position and counts as he does 30 compressions in 23 seconds.

GEOFF: One, two, three, four, five, six, seven, eight, nine, ten, come on love! You can do it! eleven, twelve, thirteen – *(Continuing during next up to 23.)*

Enter BEN as GEOFF continues. He closes the door behind him.

BEN: Like, who's he? What's happened?

GEOFF: Twenty, twenty-one, twenty-two, twenty-three.

(On 23 GEOFF delivers two in breaths to PHOEBE. GEOFF frowns, and starts a second course of CPR, counting as he goes.)

One, two, three, four, five, six, seven, eight, nine, ten.

The sound of the helicopter kicks in, very loud as it gets low to land, lights beam across the stage.

DIANE: Come on Phoebs! You can do it!

As the sound intensifies from the helicopter landing, the lights fade. Music for the scene change is a full band version of BEN's song, properly doom laden.

End of Act Four.

Act Five

August the same year. Afternoon. Sunshine, birdsong. The door is open. A car arrives, engine off, doors open, doors closed. Enter KEVIN, dressed in a black suit, white shirt, and black tie. He could be dressed for a funeral. The door is open, with summer sun streaming on to the kitchen floor. KEVIN pushes the door, and walks in without knocking. He looks around. He sits. He looks at his watch. At one point he puts his head in his hands, as if stressed, tense. Enter DIANE. She is wearing a bright, summer frock, and wedding hat. She looks bright and happy.

KEVIN: You look gorgeous D.

DIANE: Thank you. You look dressed for a funeral.

KEVIN: You said you would have a button hole for me.

DIANE: I do. I'm talking about the tie. It's terrible.

> *They kiss, it's a welcoming kiss. DIANE pins a wedding button hole flower on his jacket.*

KEVIN: My father said never trust a man in a tie.

DIANE: Take it off then.

> *KEVIN takes the tie off.*

KEVIN: Thanks.

> *(Enter PHOEBE via the stairs door. PHOEBE is about eight months pregnant and wearing a full white wedding dress.)*

You look fantastic.

PHOEBE: Thank you Professor Kevin. You look like shit.

KEVIN: *(To DIANE.)* Is shit good?

DIANE: No.

PHOEBE: Mum's in a mood.

KEVIN: Is she? Why?

DIANE: She wouldn't let me invite my mother.

PHOEBE: Every girl has the right not to have the British National Party at her wedding. Anyway, she wouldn't have come even if she had been invited.

DIANE: She would. It's a white wedding.

Enter BEN from upstairs. He's dressed in a black kilt, with black socks, black Doc Martens and a black tuxedo. It's all charity shop but he looks fantastic.

BEN: Alright! I'm nervous.

KEVIN: I didn't know you were Scottish.

BEN: I'm not. This is all Help the Aged had left.

DIANE: You know it's unlucky for a groom to see the wedding dress before the church?

PHOEBE: Is it unlucky for the bride to have sex on the morning of her wedding?

DIANE: Yes it is, if it's with someone other than the groom.

PHOEBE: *(To BEN.)* Have you written a speech lover?

BEN: I've written a new song.

PHOEBE: *(To DIANE.)* Oh isn't he beautiful mum. My intended.

DIANE: Yes, I chose well.

PHOEBE: Bitch.

KEVIN: Right! It's me and the bride in the Jag, with the top down. You're driving the Prius, and Ben is on his bike. Shall I take the guitar for you?

BEN: Na, I'm cool. I better set off now. See you down there.

(BEN kisses PHOEBE.)

DIANE: That's also unlucky.

BEN leaves. PHOEBE follows him out.

KEVIN: Are you ready?

DIANE: No. I'll never be ready.

DIANE shuffles some notes on the table.

KEVIN: What's this? Your speech.

DIANE: Yes. I'm worried it might be a bit pompous.

KEVIN: Would you like me to peer review it?

DIANE: Please.

> *KEVIN shuts the door.*

KEVIN: Go on then!

DIANE: Friends. What a beautiful day. What a really very beautiful day. Wharram Percy is my favourite place. Phoebe and I come here every Boxing Day. We walk around this abandoned village and we try and imagine life in Medieval times. No electricity, no central heating, no cars, sharing the house with a cow. That's easier.

KEVIN: *(Laughs.)* No, no. You don't need to say 'that's easier.'

DIANE: Thank you Kevin. You're a kind man.

KEVIN: It's not kindness Diane. I'm nuts about you.

DIANE: This year has not been easy. It has been *my* annus horribilis.

KEVIN: No. Don't say that. People start thinking about horrible arses.

DIANE: Do they?

KEVIN: I think normal people do, yes. Nobody had the guts to tell the Queen.

DIANE: This last year has not been easy. Pause. Ironic laughter. In the middle of my personal hell something happened. Ben and Phoebe fell in love. They fell in love as many young people do gazing at the stars in wonder whilst out of their heads on skunk. But this year, I've changed my opinion of the stars, I've decided that the stars are rubbish.

KEVIN: Oh!? I like it!

DIANE: The stars are dead, burning rocks. Barren, lifeless. Stars don't consider your feelings, they never write, they never phone, they forget your birthday. The stars know nothing of love. Stars are self-obsessed, look at me, look at me, look at me. Stars are thick. Which star came up with the idea of using the energy stored in a lump of fossilized swamp to power the internet? Which star invented air travel, the internal combustion engine? Which star split the atom? The stars are God's mistakes. We are the miracle. Life. Human intelligence. Human innovation, creativity, invention. That is why every night the stars gaze down on us in awe.

(She is crying.)

It's too pompous for a wedding isn't it?

KEVIN: Yes. But it's true, and it's beautiful.

DIANE: And it's all about me, again. It's always about me!

KEVIN: Yes. It's all about you.

He comforts her. They hold each other. They don't kiss.

DIANE: I never cry. Never.

She exits, he follows.

Fade to black.

The End.

OTHER RICHARD BEAN TITLES

England People Very Nice
9781840029000

One Man, Two Guvnors
9781849430296

One Man, Two Guvnors
(Broadway Edition)
9781849433846

Smack Family Robinson
9781840023732

Mr England
9781840021707

Harvest
9781840025941

The God Botherers
9781840024159

The Big Fellah
9781840027754

Pub Quiz is Life
9781840029598

The English Game
9781840028539

The Heretic
9781849431200

The Hypochondriac
9781840026177

House of Games
9781849430081

London Assurance
9781840029994

Bean: Plays One
The Mentalists, Under the Whaleback and *The God Botherers*

9781840025699

Bean: Plays Two
Toast, Mr England, Smack Family Robinson and *Honeymoon Suite*
9781840026627

Bean: Plays Three
Harvest, In the Club, The English Game and *Up on Roof*
9781840029130

WWW.OBERONBOOKS.COM

Follow us on www.twitter.com/@oberonbooks
& www.facebook.com/oberonbook